ENCYCLOPAEDIA OF INDIAN GOVERNMENT: PROGRAMMES AND POLICIES

ENCYCLOPAEDIA OF INDIAN GOVERNMENT: PROGRAMMES AND POLICIES

ENCYCLOPAEDIA
OF
INDIAN GOVERNMENT:
PROGRAMMES AND POLICIES

Vol. 6

Transport and Communication

Edited by

Satish Tiwari

ANMOL PUBLICATIONS PVT. LTD.

NEW DELHI - 110 002 (INDIA)

ANMOL PUBLICATIONS PVT. LTD.
4374/4B, Ansari Road, Daryaganj
New Delhi - 110 002

Encyclopaedia of Indian Government: Programmes and Policies

First Edition, 2000

ISBN 81-261-0515-1 (Set)

PRINTED IN INDIA

Published by J.L. Kumar for Anmol Publications Pvt. Ltd., New Delhi - 110 002 and Printed at Mehra Offset Press, Delhi.

Contents

Preface

Encyclopaedia of Indian Government: Programmes and Policies contains authoritative information on about fifty departmental policies and their future developmental programmes.

Organised to be completed in 40 volumes, this gigantic work covers Agriculture; Atomic Energy; Chemicals and Fertilizers; Coal; Commerce; Communication; Culture; Defence; Education; Environment and Forests; External Affairs; Finance; Food & Consumer Affairs; Food Processing Industries; Health and Family Welfare; Home Affairs and Internal Security; Human Resources; Industry; Information and Broadcasting; Labour; Law, Justice and Company Affairs; Non-conventional Energy Sources; Ocean Development; Parliamentary Affairs; Personnel, Public Grievances and Pensions; Petroleum and Natural Gas; Planning and Programme Implementation; Planning and Statistics; Posts and Telegraphs; Power; Rural Development; Science and Technology; Social Justice and Empowerment; Space; States Affairs; Steel; Steel and Mines; Sugar and Edible Oils; Surface Transport; Textiles; Tourism; Urban Development; Water Resources; Women and Child development etc.

Based on the information derived from authoritative sources, this work contains authentic facts and figures. I am deeply beholden to all the scholars whose writings are cited or substantially made use of in the present work. I am also thankful to Anmol Publications Pvt. Ltd. for undertaking publication of this encyclopaedia. I am solely responsible for shortcomings in presentation of matter.

Encyclopaedic in nature, this will prove a dependable reference work for scholars and academics besides those appearing for different competitive examinations.

—**Satish Tiwari**

1

Introduction

For the Shipping Sector, in the 9th Plan, an outlay of Rs. 5906 crores has been tentatively approved. During the first two years of the Plan i.e. the year 1997-98 and 1998-99, an outlay of Rs. 910.19 crores and Rs. 1177.61 crores respectively has been provided for the ongoing and new schemes.

It has been proposed to achieve a net growth in tonnage of 2 million GRT taking the total tonnage to 9 million GRT at the end of the 9th Plan by acquiring 3.7 million GRT (2 million on additional account and 1.7 million on replacement account) at an investment of Rs. 15000 crores during the 9th Plan period.

During the year, this Ministry has accepted 15 out of 26 recommendations accepted by the Empowered Committee constituted to examine the Report of the National Shipping Policy Committee. Necessary action on such recommendations has also been initiated.

Transchart (Chartering)

In general, the freight market has been weak and in a very bad shape throughout the year for dry bulk trades. Freight indices for handymax and large bulkers have dropped 20/34 per cent respectively since last December. The general view seems to be that the low levels will continue well in to the New Year 1999. The BFI (Baltic Freight Index) at the end of 1998 is at 752 points corresponding to its level of 1231 points at the end of 1997. This reflects the shipping market for dry bulk sector.

The tanker market when compared to the bulk cargo market though remained steady during the year in contrast to last year, showed weakness during the year.

During the year under review, Chartering Wing arranged shipment of approx. 218.82 lakh tonnes of Government cargoes (from January, 1998 to December, 1998). Out of this, 59.84% was carried by Indian bottoms. The major items under dry/liquid cargoes for which shipping arrangements were finalised during the year included 74 lakh tonnes of coking coal, 97.21 lakh tonnes of Petroleum product, 21.82 lakh tonnes of Fertilizers/ Fertilizers raw materials and 14.69 lakh tonnes of wheat. As a result of negotiations with member lines of IPBC Conference, rebate of tariff has been increased from present level of 15 and 17.5% to 22.5% for break bulk general liner cargoes and 35% in respect of full container load (FCL). This is going to save a substantial amount in outgo of freight by importing PSUs.

Transchart successfully arranged charter of specialized vessel for XVIIIth Antarctica Expedition, an ambitious programme of Deptt. of Ocean Development.

Concerted efforts were made to provide shipping coverage at competitive freight rates as per the requirements of the indenting Departments.

Inland water transport

Activities related to development, management and regulation of Inland Water Transport (IWT) are being carried out by the Inland Waterways Authority of India

(IWAI).

During the year, various developmental works have been executed for providing the necessary infrastructure for navigation and shipping in the three National Waterways. Many new initiatives have been taken to accelerate the pace of development of IWT in the country.

- National Waterways (NWs) viz; the Ganga (NW-1), Brahmaputra (NW-2) and West Coast Canal (NW-3) were maintained with improved navigational facilities.
- "M.V. Rajagopalachari" of IWAI continued promotional sailings in NW-1 (The Ganga) carrying various commodities between Allahabad and Calcutta.
- Movement of POL by HPCL between Kochi and Edapallikotta through NW-3 continued successfully during the year.
- Schemes for acquisition of two numbers hydraulic surface dredgers for NW-1 & NW-2 and two numbers new survey launches for NW-2 & NW-3 were sanctioned and construction commenced.
- Schemes for procurement of four numbers pontoons for providing floating terminal at Karagola & Ballia in NW-1 and Sadiya & Saikhowa in NW-2 were sanctioned and construction of pontoons commenced.
- Implementation of the schemes for providing 24 hrs. navigation facility on NW-1 & NW-2 has been commenced by placing orders for supply of lights and buoys.

Floating terminals at Haldia, Calcutta, 2.3.8
Karagola, Bhagalpur, Monghyr in river Ganga (NW-1) and at Dhubri, Jogighopa, Pandu, Tezpur, Naemati in river Brahmaputra (NW-2) were maintained.

Work of construction of permanent terminal at Gaighat, Patna on NW-1 has been taken up through CPWD on deposit work basis. Action was initiated for setting up of another permanent terminal at G.R. Jetty, Calcutta on NW-1 for taking over land from Calcutta Port Trust. For permanent terminal at Pandu on NW-2, preliminary design and estimates are under preparation through CPWD. For NW-3, a scheme for construction of 11 Nos. permanent terminals was prepared and is under consideration.

Environmental clearance for proposed development of East Coast Canal in NW-3 was obtained from Ministry of Environment & Forest in February, 1998. Capital Dredging in this waterway has commenced after floating "Global Tender" for a total quantity of 21.2 lakh cu.mtrs. Land acquisition also commenced for widening of narrow stretches and construction of terminals.

Techno-economic Feasibility Studies on the waterway stretches of Visakhapatnam-Polavaram canal system, extension of NW-3 from Kovalam to Kolachal, assessment of IWT tourism potential on NW-2, study on improvement of safety of life on river boats and a transport economic study for all the three National Waterways have been taken up in addition to ongoing studies and environmental impact assessment studies on identified waterways.

Scheme for installation of computer based Automatic Hydrographic Survey System at IWAI Head Office, Noida and at field offices on NW-1 (Patna), NW-2 (Guwahati) & NW-3 (Kochi) has been sanctioned and is under implementation.

For NICNET connectivity among the offices of IWAI, procurement of computer hardware and software was completed at Noida, Calcutta, Patna, Bhagalpur, Guwahati & Kochi.

..he Major Port Trust Act, 1963 ..t Laws (Amendment) Act, 1997 (15 of 1997) was amended by ..or an independent Tariff Authority for Major Ports for fixing and revising the port tariff. An independent authority for the above purpose has been set up on 10.4.1997 with headquarters at New Delhi. The Authority consists of a Chairman Shri S. Sathyam and two part time members, Shri Rakesh Mohan and Shri J.V.Shetty.

Road development

During the year 1998-99, it is expected that 300 kms. of National Highways will be widened from single lane to double, 40 kms. will be widened to four lane, 700 kms. of National Highways would be strengthened and 60 bridges are likely to be completed.Till December, 1998, 280 kms. has been widened from single lane to double, 10 kms. widened to four lane, 270 kms. of National Highways strengthened and 48 bridges have been completed (achievement is based on ongoing works completed after 31.3.98). Remaining works are at different stages of progress.

New policy initiatives

National Highways have been accorded the top most priority by the Government. Recently, the Hon'ble Prime Minister has announced six-laning of the North-South corridor connecting Kashmir to Kanyakumari and East-West corridor connecting Silchar to Saurashtra, in an aggregate length of 7000 kms. In this regard, a Task Force has been set up, which is headed by Dy. Chairman, Planning Commission and has Minister and Secretary (SFT) as Members, to monitor the project. The Task Force has finalised the alignment of these corridors and the Ministry proposes to commence construction works on atleast 20 locations out of which, work at one location at Bangalore has already commenced with the foundation stone for this project laid by the Hon'ble Prime Minister on 2nd January, 1999. The implementation of this programme has been handed over to the National Highways Authority of India.

National Highways Authority of India (NHAI) has already been entrusted with development of Golden Quadrilateral linking four main metros viz. Delhi, Calcutta, Chennai and Mumbai, which aggregates to a length of 5800 kms. NHAI has commissioned feasibility studies along these corridors, and projects will be identified after these studies are completed.

The Ministry has also embarked upon a strategy to plan and implement Expressways for rapid, unhindered and safe movement of fast moving vehicles leaving National Highways for normal traffic, The Ministry 2.5.8 proposes to establish National Expressways Authority of India on the lines of National Highways Authority of India. The National Expressway Authority of India will be solely responsible to plan, design, develop and maintain the expressways in the country. A preliminary study for the construction of expressways has already been conducted by the Ministry. It is now proposed to conduct feasibility study followed by detailed project reports on a few of the expressways planned. In view of the severe resource constraints, it may be difficult to finance the construction of these expressways from general budgetary support. Efforts will be made to have the expressways implemented with private sector participation under Build Operate and Transfer (BOT) Scheme.

The Ministry of Surface Transport recently conducted an International Congress on Express Highways Development in India. The Congress was held at Vigyan Bhawan from 14 to 17 December, 1998. The foreign delegate participation was encouraging.

The Task Force has been coordinating all these development needs. It has been decided to integrate the North-South and East-West corridor with the existing plan for the Golden Quadrilateral. It has been decided to develop some of these stretches as expressways.

To encourage private sector participation, in continuation of facilitating measures already taken, on December 28. 1998, a Model Concession Agreement has been released for major projects (costing more than Rs. 100 crore) to be undertaken under BOT Scheme. Further, foreign direct investment (FDI) up to 100 per cent have been allowed in the road sector (with total foreign equity up to Rs. 1500 crores) to attract foreign investors.

Besides speed and mobility of traffic on Highways, safety of users is another important aspect. An International Seminar on Highway Safety on 6th & 7th November, 1998 was held at Vigyan Bhawan, New Delhi, to disseminate knowledge on safety aspects/devices/methods etc.

World bank second national highway project

A loan Agreement was signed in June 1992 with World Bank for Second National Highway Project (LN. 3470/OR 2365-IN) comprising four laning of National Highway sections in the State of Haryana, Punjab, Maharastra, Orissa, Madhya Pradesh and West Bengal. The total amount of the loan and credit is US $306 million. This project also includes reconstruction of damaged bridges on State Roads in Orissa. Works on all the six National Highway sub-project are in progress. The sub-project for reconstruction of damaged bridges in Orissa is also in progress.

Asian development bank - first road project loan

Loan Agreement No. 918-IND was signed in December, 1998 with the Asian Development Bank (ADB) for a loan amount of US $ 198 million (revised to US $ 177 million), and is effective since April 1989 for financing road projects both in the Central and State Sectors covering the States of Andhra Pradesh, Haryana, Karnataka, Tamil Nadu and Uttar Pradesh. All the sub-projects under the loan have been completed. Loan has been closed with effect from 31st March, 1998.

Asian development bank - second road project loan

Loan Agreement No. 1041-IND was signed in May 1991 with Asian Development bank for loan assistance of US $ 250 million for financing Second road project in Central and State sectors covering the States of Kerala, Karnataka, Rajasthan, Andhra Pradesh, Orissa, Uttar Pradesh and West Bengal. The loan is effective from July, 1991. The National Highway projects in Rajasthan and Karnataka and the State road projects in Andhra Pradesh and Orissa have been commissioned. The remaining works are in progress and are likely to be completed by the present loan closing date i.e. 31st December, 1999.

Asian development bank - third project loan

Loan Agreement No.1274-IND was signed with Asian Development Bank in March, 1995 for a loan assistance of US $ 245 million for improvement of National Highways in the states of Andhra Pradesh , Bihar, Haryana, Rajasthan and West Bengal. The loan is effective from May, 1995. The National Highway Authority of India is the executing agency for these works. These stretches of NH have been transferred from state PWDs to NHAI who is responsible for maintenance also. The works on all NH sub-projects are in progress.

Overseas economic co-operation fund (OECF), Japan, national highway loans

Five loans have been approved for various National Highways and the position is as under :

OECF-I (IDP-81)

(i) A Loan Agreement No. IDP. 81 for Japanese Yen 4855 million was signed in January, 1992 for four laning of Agra-Mathura Section of NH-2 in Uttar Pradesh. The work is in progress.

(ii) A Loan Agreement No. IDP. 91 for Japanese Yen 10037 was signed in January, 1994 for the project of construction of a bridge over river Yamuna at Naini on NH-27 in Uttar Pradesh. The detailed design for the project has been completed. The tenders for the work have been received and the work is likely to be awarded by NHAI during the current year.

OECF (IDP-92)

iii) A Loan Agreement No. IDP 92 for Japanese Yen 11360 million was signed in Jan., 1994 for four-laning of Chilakaluripet-Vijayawada section of NH-5 in Andhra Pradesh. The tenders for the project have been received and the work is likely to be awarded by NHAI during the current year.

OECF (IDP - 100)

iv) A Loan Agreement No. IDP. 100 for Japanese Yen 5836 million was signed in February, 1995 for the project of four-laning of Jagaat-Chandikhol section of NH-5 in Orissa. The tenders for the project have been received and the work is likely to be awarded by NHAI during the current year.

OECF (IDP - 101)

v) A Loan Agreement No. IDP. 101 for Japanese Yen 4827 million was signed in February, 1995 for four laning of Ghaziabad-Hapur section including construction of Hapur bypass on NH-24 in Uttar Pradesh. The tenders have been received and the work is likely to be awarded by NHAI during the current year.

Grant-in-aid from government of Japan

The Government of Japan has also provided grant-in-aid of Japanese Yen 2830 million (approximately Rs. 88 crores) for construction of second Nizamuddin Bridge across river Yamuna on NH-24 in Delhi. The work has been completed.

Borders roads development board

Border Road Organisation has a formidable reputation ot fulfilling the annual targets laid down every year. This year was no different and the BRDB completed all tasks alloted for completion during the year.

FIP Symposium

Lt. General R.J. Mordecai, AVSM, Director General Boarder Roads and Shri B.K. Basu, SC, Chief Engineer Project Pushpak attended the 13th FIP Symposium and Exhibition from 23rd to 29th May, 1998 at Amsterdam (Netherland).

International congress on road maintenance and uses

Lt. General R.J. Mordecai, AVSM, Director General Border Roads and Shri B.L. Tikoo, DDG (D&S) attended the 4th Congress on Road Maintenance and Uses, organised by Directorate of Roads, Ministry of Public Works, Transport and Housing, France, in Grenoble, France from 29th September to 1st October, 1998.

88 personnel of the Border Road Organisation were conferred honours and awards in recognition of their services to the nation.

The Organisation has undertaken successfully many tasks allotted to it by the Government and we are looking forward to a greater participation in. nation building, being a vibrant and leading construction organisation in the country.

Road transport

This Ministry is concerned with the formulation of broad policies relating to road transport besides making arrangements for movement of vehicular traffic with the neighbouring countries.

The 28th Transport Development Council meeting was held on 10th October, 1998. Ministry is contemplating to enter into bilateral agreement regarding regulation of movement of vehicular traffic with neighbouring countries like Bhutan, Bangladesh, Nepal and Pakistan.

This Ministry has initiated a dialogue with Government of Pakistan for entering into an agreement for Delhi-Lahore bus service and vice-versa. It is also contemplated to make certain amendments regarding Road Safety, Pollution etc. in the Motor Vehicles Act, 1988 and Central Motor Vehicles Rules, 1989.

In order to curb the menace of vehicular pollution, this Ministry has taken several steps in this direction. There are 71 State Road Transport Undertakings having a fleet of nearly 1,05,201 vehicles providing passenger transport in various parts of the country.

This Ministry in consultation with Planning Commission is actively considering revival of the scheme for granting capital contribution to SRTCs. 10th Road Safety Week, with the theme of 'Safe Transportation of School Going Children' was observed from 4th to 10th January, 1999 throughout the country.

Refresher training to heavy motor vehicle drivers in the unorganised sector was arranged through the Automobile Association of Upper India, New Delhi (AAUI) and Krishna District Lorry Owners Association, Vijaywada, Andhra Pradesh. Amendment in Road Transport Corporations (RTC) Act, 1950, is underway and a proposal in this regard is to be sent to Cabinet very soon.

2

Transport and Communication

Existing transport system of the country comprises several modes of transport including rail, road, coastal shipping, air transport, etc. Transport has recorded a substantial growth over the years both in spread of network and in output of the system.

The railways in india provide the principal mode of transportation for freight and passengers. It brings people from the farthest corners of the country and makes possible the conduct of business, sightseeing, pilgrimage and education. Indian Railways have been a great integrating force during the last hundred years.

It has bound the economic life of the country and helped in accelerating the development of industry and agriculture. From a very modest beginning in 1853, when the first train steamed off from Bombay to Thane, a distance of 34 km, Indian Railways have grown into a vast network of 7,050 stations spread over a route length of 62,462 km with a fleet of 7,202 locomotives, 34,088 passenger service vehicles, 5,955 other coaching vehicles and 3,12,405 wagons as on 31 March 1994.

The growth of Indian Railways in the 141 years of its existence is thus phenomenal. It has played a vital role in the economic, industrial and social development of our country. The network runs multigauge operations extending over 62,462 route kilometre. The gauge-wise route and track lengths of the system as on 31 March 1994 were as under:

Table : Respective Gauge Length

Gauge	*Route km*	*Running track km*	*Total track km*
Broad Gauge (1,676 mm)	37,824	53,560	76,295
Metre Gauge (1,000 mm)	20,653	21,643	28,156
Narrow Gauge (762 mm and 610 mm)	3985	3,985	4,469
Total	62,462	79,188	1,08,920

About 18 per cent of the route kilometre, 27 per cent of running track kilometre and 26 per cent of total track kilometre is electrified. The network is divided into nine zones and further sub-divided into divisions. Divisions are the basic operating units. The nine zones, their respective headquarters and the route kilometre for each as on 31 March 1994 are given below:

Table : Track Length Covered

Railways	*Headquarters*	*Route Kilometre*
Central	Bombay	7,158
Eastern	Calcutta	4,303
Northern	New Dehi	10,993
North Eastern	Gorakhpur	5,144
Northeast Frontier	Maligoan (Guwahati)	3,728
Southern	Madras	7,021
South Central	Secunderabad	7,227
South Eastern	Calcutta	7,161
Western	Bombay	9,727
Total		62,462

Cooperation between public and railway administration is secured through various committees including Zonal Railway Users's Consultative Committees and Divisional Railway Users' Consultative Committees. The rolling stock fleet of Indian Railways in service as on 31 March 1994 comprised 911 steam, 4,174 diesel and 2,117 electric locomotives. Currently, the railways are in the process of inducting new designs of fuel-efficient locomotives of higher horse power, high sped coaches and modern bogies for freight traffic. Modern signalling like panel inter-locking, route relay inter-locking, centralised traffic control, automatic signalling and multiaspect colour light signalling, are being progressively introduced to increase the throughput. Indian Railways have made impressive progress in indigenous production of rolling stock and a variety of other equipment over the years and is now self-sufficient in most of the items.

The main objective of railways planning has been to develop the transport infrastructure to carry the projected quantum of traffic and meet the developmental needs of the economy. since the inception of the planned era in 1950-51, Indian Railways have implemented seven Five Year Plans, apart from annual plans in some years. During seven Plans, emphasis was laid on a comprehensive programme of system modernisation. With capacity being stretched to the full, investment in cost-effective technological changes became inescapable in order to meet ever-increasing demand for rail transport. Along with the major thrust directed towards rehabilitation of assest, technological changes and upgradation of standards were initiated in important areas of track, locomotives, passenger coaches, wagon bogie designs, signalling and telecommunication. for long-term requirements, the railways have also prepared a 'corporate plan' covering 15 years period, 1985-2000. It

Table: Progress of Railways Traffic and inputs

Year	Route Length (Kilometre)			Running track	Passenger originating	Goods originating	Number of locomotives			Number of Coaching vehicles	Numuber of wagons
	Electrified	Non-Electrified	Total	(Km.)	(lakh)	(lakh tonne)	Steam	Diesel	Electric		
1950-51	388	53,208	53,596	59,315	12,840	930	8,120	17	72	19,628	2,05,596
1960-61	748	55,499	56,247	63,602	15,940	1,562	10,312	181	131	28,439	3,07,907
1970-71	3,706	56,081	59,790	71,669	24,311	19,65	9,387	1,169	602	35,145	3,83,990
1980-81	5,345	55,895	61,240	75,860	36,125	2,200	7,469	2,403	1,036	38,333	4,00,946
1985-86	6,517	55,319	61,836	77,153	34,335	2,864	5,571	3,046	1,302	38,277	3,59,617
1986-87	7,275	54,538	61,813	77,254	35,937	3,073	4,950	3,182	1,366	37,988	3,54,041
1987-88	8,157	53,819	61,976	77,671	37,921	3,185	4,427	3,298	1,433	37,746	3,46,844
1988-89	8,880	53,105	61,985	77,845	35,003	3,295	3,826	3,454	1,533	37,867	3,45,821
1989-90	9,100	53,111	62,211	78,320	36,531	3,343	3,336	3,610	1,644	37,953	3,49,661
1990-91	9,968	52,399	62,367	78,607	38,576	3,414	2,915	3,759	1,743	38,511	3,46,102
1991-92	10,653	51,805	62,458	78,969	40,486	3,600	2,492	3,905	1,871	39,350	3,46,394
1992-93	11,064	51,422	62,486	79,200	37,494	3,709	1,725	4,069	2,012	39,924	3,37,562
1993-94	11,260	51,202	62,462	79,188	37,080	3,775	911	4,174	2,117	40,043	3,12,405

seeks to provide 370-400 billion net tonne km freight traffic, 310-330 billion non-suburban passenger kilometre and 105-110 billion suburban passenger kilometre by the turn of the century. Progress of railway traffic and inputs is shown in table.

There are five undertakings under the administrative control of the Ministry of Railways viz., (i) Rail India Technical and Economic Services Limited (RITES); (ii) Indian Railway Construction Company Limited (IRCON); (iii) Indian Railway Finance Corporation Limited (IRFC); (iv) Container Corporation of India Limited (CONCOR); and (v) Konkan Railway Corporation Limited (KRC). Centre for Railway Information System (CRIS) was set up as a registered society to design and implement various railway computerisation projects.

The Research, Design and Standards Organisation (RDSO) at Lucknow is the R&D wing of Indian Railways. It functions as a consultant to the Indian Railways in technical matters. It also provides consultacy to other organisations connected with railway manufacture and design.

A substantial part of defence stores needed by the Services is now being developed and produced within the country. The responsibility for this has been entrusted to the Department of Defence Production and Supplies in the Ministry of Defence. The Department directs and coordinates production of material and equipment required by the Armed Forces.

At present, 39 ordnance factories spread all over India operate a wide-range of technologies and product mix. Some of the important products are field guns, anti-aircraft guns, mortars, various small arms and ammunition for weapons and guns, rockets, projectiles, pyro-technics, bombs, grenades, mines, demolition charges, depth charges, infantry combat vehicles, battle tanks, self-propelled guns, transport trucks and petrol vehicles, high-altitude and combat clothing, optical and fire control instruments, engineering equipment, supply dropping equipmet including parachutes, rubberised items, various knitted and woven items like blankets, web equipment and a wide range of general stores are produced by them. Production of 5.56 mm (indigenously designed) weapon system has started in ordnance factories. These factories are also producing bombs required by Air Force. Besides, liquid fuel required for successful flight trials of Prithvi and Agni missiles, igniters and copper liners for the warheads were also supplied in the development of Prithvi missile. The production of Ajeya tank (T-72), Sarath (BMP-II), infantry combat vehicle are carried out at Heavy Vehicle Factory, Avadi and Ordnance Factory, Medak, respectively. A sophisticated opto-electronic production unit has been set up at Dehra Dun to produce the opto-electronic fire control and night vision devices required for Ajeya Tank (T-72-MI and Sarath* infantry combat vehicle is planned from 1994-95. To utilise the sparable capacities, after meeting the services requirements, linear and lateral shift in customer product profiles has been taken up as a major thrust area of operations.

As a part of diversification efforts, Vehicles Factory, Jabalpur (VFJ) has taken up modification and upgradation of Jonga. The vehicle, conforming to military standards, is not only sturdy but also has a very high pick up, high fuel efficiency of 16 km per litre (under test conditions) and a maximum speed of 120 kmph with gradient climbing capability of one in three. It has been decided to launch Jonga in the civil open market. VFJ has a captive capacity to manufacture 20,000 Jonga per annum. Out of this, 10,000 vehicles are to be released in the civil market and remaining 10,000 are reserved for the Army and exports. The release to the civil market would be done without effecting any erosion in the Army requirements.

There are eight public sector undertakings (PSUs) under the Department of Defence Production and Suppliers. These are: Hindustan Aeronautics Limited (HAL), Bharat Electronics Limited (BEL), Bharat Earth Movers* rail coaches, track laying equipments, heavy duty trucks, trailers, diesel engines etc. BEML is a leader in earth-moving industry with over 70 per cent market share. Its equipments and systems are productively deployed in India and over 30 other countries across the globe.

Mazagon Dock Limited (MDL) is the country's leading shipbuilding yard and can build warships up to 6,000 DWT displacement and merchant ships up to 27,000 DWT. It has units at Bombay, Nhava and Mangalore and headquarters at Bombay. At present, its major activities include construction of sub-marines, missile-boats and destroyers etc., for the Indian Navy and off-shore supply vessels and well-head platforms etc., for the Oil and Natural Gas Commission (ONGC). The company also provides diving services as well as services for coating/ laying sub-sea pipes.

Garden Reach Shipbuilders and Engineers Limited (GRSE) is a multi-unit shipyard-cum-general engineering company. It has six units in and around Calcutta and a Diesel Engine Plant at Ranchi (Bihar). Its corporate office is at Calcutta. It has three distinct divisions, namely, ship, engineering and engine divisions. It is presently engaged in the construction of war ships and auxiliary vessels of various types for the Navy and the Coast Guard and to undertake repair of vessels of these two organisations. Other products of the company include a variety of high technology ship-borne equipments, portable Bailey type steel bridges, marines sewage treatment plant, dock-machinery items, turbine pumps for the agricultural sector, diesel engines, etc.

The activities of Goa Shipyards Limited (GSL) located at Vasco-da-Gama, primarily comprise construction and repair-reit of ships/vessels. It has undertaken construction/refit of variety of vessels for the Indian Navy and the Coast Guard as well as for the non-defence sector. It is currently building advanced off-shore patrol vessels of in-house design.

Bharat Dynamics Limited (BDL), established in 1970, is primarily engaged in the manufacture of guided missiles and allied equipments. It has units at Hyderabad and Bhanur (Medak district). Its corporate office is at Hyderabad. It is also the prime production agency for manufacture of four new missile systems, namely, Prithvi, Trishul, Akash and Nag, being developed indigenously. Its activities which had earlier been diversified into a number of Naval projects now proposes to take up manufacture of small arms required for para-military forces of the country.

Mishra Dhatu Nigam Limited (MIDHANI) located at Hyderabad was incorporated in 1973. MIDHANI's product range includes super alloys, maraging steels, heat resistance alloys, controlled expansion alloys, tungsten, molybednum etc., in variety of mill forms.

Surface Transport

Looking back it is noticed that a lot has been done in the post-Independence era for the development of surface transport, the linchpin of the cuntry's prosperity, however much more still needs to be done in this vital sector. Surface transport is a key comment of the infrastructure of sustained economic growth. A well-knit and co-ordinated system facilitates its better utilisation necessary for sharpening the country's competitive edge. Through eight five-year plans progress in developiong the system of transport by land and sea has designed it to operate at peak efficiency. Admittedly, much more needs to be done to attain this goal for a country of continental size like India.

But looking back at the last 50 years one finds the achievements to be in no way in a small measure. With a network of two million kilometres India has now the third largest road network in the world. Similarly, the shipping fleet has increased manifold to attain a strength of 480 ships with a gross registered tonnage of 7.02 million. The post-independence period has seen the country grow as a ship-building nation with four major and three medium size shipyards in the public sector. The total capacity of Indian major ports numbering 11 is estimated at 174 million tonnes in 1995-96.

The growth of the national economy during this period has of course made a quantum leap imperative in all these areas. Since the ushering in the economic reforms there has been a reorientation of shipping policy, liberalisation in acquisition of ships, record handling of cargo and containers by major ports, incentives and facilities to encurage private sector participation in modernisation and development of ports and national highways and mass rapid transit systems.

All these are within the charge of the Ministry of Surface transport which is responsible for the formulation and implementation of related policies and programmes. Easy and speedy movement of commodities for domestic consumption and exports has direct co-relation to its efficient functioning. A measure of the magnitude of the first plan and at present in respect of freight carried by the roads. In 1950-51 roads carried nearly six billion tonne kilometers (btk) of freight and 23 billion passenger kilometers (bpk) of passenger traffic. The current level of estimated freight and passenger traffic are 650 btk and 1500 bpk respectively. Roads have emerged as the preferred mode of transport and the situation in likely to continue for years to come.

Another aspect of the network is that national highways built up to 34,068 km, much of it in the last fifty years carries nearly 40 per cent of the total road traffic. If this is an indicator of the high growth in road transport, it also suggests the colossal nature of the needs of the future as the national highways constitute less than two per cent of the road network. Since the First Plan, the problems of growth in demand for road transport have been addressed to. These cover improvements in the area of road design, construction, maintenance and materials, quantum change in the quality of rural roads, modernisation of construction equipment and transport vehicles, traffic transport management, traffic regulation, multimodel transport, choking urban roads and solutions to the problems of urban transport. Still, 46 years later, on the threshold of the Ninth Plan it has been noticed that development of roads and road transport has still to keep pace with the demands of economic growth.

With the set objective of the removal of those dificiencies, reforms have been initiated and more are contemplated. The Economic Survey for 1995-96 lists among the measures already taken: declaration of the road sector as an industry to facilitate borrowing on easy terms and to permit floatation of bonds; relaxation of MRTP provisions to enable large firms to enter the highway sector; amendment of the national highways Act to enable the levy of a fee on national highways, bridges and tunnels and lowering of customs duties on construction equipment and streamlining of the related procedures. The contemplated reforms are: private sector participation including foreign investors in the development of stretches of national highways and construction of expressways on BOT basis for a period of thirty years, the traffic will be normally regulated by entrepreneurs but to ensure free and uninterrupted flow of traffic, sales tax and barriers will not be established on the expressways and the checks by the authorities will be conducted at the entry and exit points only; the land acquisition and removal of utilities to be done by the government. These reforms underpin the need for expansion of the road network which since the beginning of national planning is up 500 per cent from 0.4 million kilometres. Road transport has increased by 60 to 65 times. It is estimated that road traffic now accounts for 80 per cent of passenger traffic and 60 per cent of good traffic. By 2000 AD, just four years away, passenger and goods traffic will go up to 87 and 65 per cent respectively.

The number of vehicles has gone up to 27.5 million, an increase of 90 times in the past 50 years. Cars sporting all famed international brand manufactured under Indian licence threaten to clog the roads.

National highways constitute the primary network of the road system. A recent study by the Asian Development Bank has noted that the country needs the construction of another 10,000 km of the national expressway network. Obviously, capacity has to go up; payment has to be sufficient; riding quality should be better and bridges should be strengthened, there should be more rail level crossings and more wayside amentities and measures for a safety are to be strengthened. Projections place the cost of attaining these desired objectives at Rs. 52,000 crore. The money is worth spendings as otherwise the country loses an estimated

Rs. 15,000 crore every year because of the bad condition of roads resulting in avoidable excessive use of fuel and an increase in vehicle operating costs. This is again a problem of growth resulting in development driven increase in traffic because of economic activity. A national highway authority of India has since been constituted with a full-time chairman and three members aided by senior and technical official having expertise in various fields. In view of the massive demand for the road network cooperation of the private sector is being mobilised.

Economy's demand on ports has also gone very high. The annual growth in cargo handling has been ranging between 7.6 per cent to ten per cent. Containerised cargo which has come into vogue in recent years recorded the maximum percentage increase in 1994-95 and 1995-96. Calcutta, Cochin and Mumbai have contributed to this phenomenal growth. All the major ports handled around 1.4 million containers during the financial year 1995-96. The 11 major ports are Calcutta, Paradip, Vishakhapatnam, Chennai and Tuticorin on the east coast, and Cochin, New Mangalore, Mormagao, Mumbai and Kandla on the west coast. Development of major ports is constitutionally the responsibility of the Union government. In recent years major investments in port construction have centred on container as well as bulk facilities.

Ministry of Non-Conventional Energy Sources is endeavouring to develop alternatives to diesel and motor sprit in order to reduce their consumption and outflow of precious foreign exchange. The main alternatives are battery-operated vehicles (BOV); use of alcohol, methanol/ethanol as a fuel in diesel and petrol vehicles; and use of compressed natural gas (CNG) as a fuel. In different areas of the country, 235 battery-operated and

105 alcohol-operated vehicles have been taken up for demonstration. Apart from this, a new project to develop 100 alcohol based vehicles has been taken up in Gujarat.

FIPB had cleared in February 1994 a joint venture proposal for manufacture of solar battery car developed by M/s Frazer-Nash, UK, in India in collaboration with M/s Peerless Limited, Calcutta. It has been reported that the performance of the four wheel drive solar battery car is quite compatible to Indian autorickshaws and it can find the market potential in India among educated unemployed for rural and city mass transport, postal department, industrial sectors and various shuttle service applications.

Use of hydrogen as an energy source involves five basic issues i.e. production, storage and transportation, utilisation, safety management and economy. A 100 cc four stroke hydrogen/hydride fuelled motorcycle has been developed and development efforts to increase the range of the motor cycle is under way. The plan for hydrogen fuelled three-wheelers and motor-cars is at planning stage. The other important use of hydrogen energy is in heat pumps and refrigeration. The projects on heat pumps have been progressing well at Indian Institute of Technology, Madras. The production and storage of hydrogen has been pursued at Banaras Hindu University, Varanasi, Osmania University, Hyderabad and Rajasthan University, Jaipur.

The conversion of solar energy into chemical energy is an imortant route for tapping solar energy as it allows storage of solar energy also. As many as 50 research and development projects in the area of photovoltaic chemical cells, photovoltaics and photosynthesis have been funded and good results have been achieved in these areas. The other two areas pursued under chemical sources of energy are duel cell and electro-chemical storage batteries. A 2.5 kw phosphoric acid fuel cell (PAFC) has been developed and is under test. Plan for 200 kw PAFC has been prepared. The programme on storage batteries is for development of storage systems needed for intermittent energy sources like solar, wind, etc., and for vehicular use. Amongst commercial batteries currently available, lead acid battery seems to hold attractive position. However, lead resources in India are rather limited. The other battery systems are such as nickel-cadmium, dilver-zinc, nickel-hydrogen, etc. Materials and construction methods are too expensive fo find application.

A project on 'Development of Sodium Sulphur Batteries' suitable for electric vehicles, satellite communications, photovoltaic energy storage and submarine power etc., has been undertaken at Central Electrochemical Research Institute, (CERI) Karaikudi and NPL, New Delhi

The Ministry is actively pursuing the proposal for setting up a tidal power plant for 900 mw in the Gulf of Kachchh at an estimated cost of Rs. 4,000 crore. The tidal power potential in the country is estimated to be of the order of 8,000 mw to 9,00 mw (approximatley 7,000 mw in Gulf of Cambay, 1,000 mw in Gulf of Kachchh and 100 mw in Sundarbans). A techno economic feasibility report has been prepared by the CEA/NHPC for a 900 mw tidal power plant at Gulf of Kachchh. This project is proposed to be included as a command area development project in the state sector.

India is having large potential of Ocean Thermal Energy Conversion (OTEC) which could be of the order about 50,000 mw. M/s Sea Solar Power Inc., USA, is promoting the use of ocean thermal energy conversion technlogy and the first plant is proposed off the coast of Tamil Nadu with a capacity of 100 mw at a cost of about

Rs. 750 crore, the finance being entirely brought in by the overseas entrepreneurs. The company has signed the MOU for this project with TEDA and TNEB of Government of Tamil Nadu in January 1994.

Wave Energy Potential in India is estimated about 40,000 mw. One wave energy power plant of 150 kw (maximum) capacity based on OWC has been installed in Vzhinjam near Thiruvananthapuram by IIT, Madras under a sponsored project by Department of Ocean Development. The power plant has been commissioned and is under trial. One Swedish organisation Sea Power *(HWPC) concept. Harnessing a wave energy on this principle in India is being explored and a one mw wave energy plant is being set up in the Andaman and Nicobar Islands.

Geothermal manifestations are widespread in India, in the form of 340 identified hot springs localities, many of these having temperature near boiling point at their places of occurrence. There is considerable scope for the development and exploitation of geothermal energy resources. The ongoing activities include the survey and assessment of geothermal potential, utilization of geothermal energy for direct heat and power generation. A five kw geothermal pilot power plant has been commissioned at Manikaran in Kullu district of Himachal Pradesh. The assessment of geothermal power potential in Puga Valley Ladakh in Jammu and Kashmir has been done through Manageto-Telluric surveys and geo-scientific studies. A potential of 4-5 mw geothermal power has been estimated in the Valley. Proposal to explore this potential for power generation and utilization for nearly localities is being finaslised. The use of geothermal energy for space heating and green house effect has been demonstrated. A project on mushroom cultivation and poultry framing using geothermal fluid is under implementation at Regional Research Laboratory, Jammu.

The main objective of Indian Renewable Energy Development Agency (IREDA) is to act as a catalyst agent for accelerating commercialization of new and renewable rources of energy. IREDA has been assigned the main task of administering a revolving fund to promote, develop and finance on soft terms the NRSE technologies. The resources base of IREDA mainly consists of equity support from the Government of India, grants from foreign and international organisations, borrowings and internal accruals. The authorised share capital has been raised from Rs. 25 crore to Rs. 100 crore during 1994-95. In addition, the Government of Netherlands have already given to IREDA grant-in-aid of 17 million Guilders for assisting NRSE projects. It has further committed an amount of 23 million Guilders.

The World Bank has also agreed to provide US dollar 195 million which includes a grant-in-aid component of US dollar 30 million to be contributed by Global Environment Trust Fund and Swiss Development Cooperation for financing projects to generate power through wind energy, small hydro and solar photovoltaic schemes. IREDA has also signed an agreement with the Asian Development Bank to receive technical assistance of US dollar 3.54 lakh and a credit of US dollar 150 million is under finalisation.

The Ministry of Non-Conventional Energy Sources has established a Solar Energy Centre as an institute dedicated to the development and testing of solar energy products. The Centre has state-of-art facilities for the testing of both solar thermal and solar photovoltaic devices. Asia's largest indoor sun simulator for measurements on solar thermal collectors has been dedicated to the Centre in May 1994. In addition, there are specialised simulators for measurements on solar cells and photovoltaic modules as well as equipment for testing of systems for different applications. The Centre is coordinating cooperative activities in solar energy among G-15 countries. It is being developed as a centre of excellence of international standard.

There are 11 major ports in the country apart from about 139 minor working ports along the coastline of about 5,600 km. Major ports are the direct responsibility of the Central Government, while minor ports including intermediate ports fall in the Concurrent List of the Constitution and are managed and administered by the respective maritime state governments.

Kandla, Bombay, Mormugao, New Mangalore, Cochin and Jawaharlal Nehru Port are the major ports of west coast. The Jawaharlal Nehru Port is equipped with modern facilities having mechanised container berths for handling dry bulk cargo and service berth, etc. On the east coast, Tuticorin, Madras, Visakhapatnam, Paradip and Calcutta-Haldia are the major ports. All the major ports are administered in accordance with the provisions of the Major Port Trust Act, 1963. Each major port has a board of trustees representing various interests connected with the port operations and the shipping industry. Among the major ports, Bombay handles over one-fifth of the total traffic of the ports, bulk of which consists of petroleum products and dry cargo. Kandla is a 'Tidal Port'. A free trade zone has been set up here. It handles all types of traffic. Mormugao occupies fifth position in terms of total quantum of traffic handled. Facilities for export of Kudremukh iron ore were specially developed at New Mangalore. Cochin is a natural harbour. Tuticorin port handles mainly coal traffic.

Madras is one of the oldest ports on the east coast. The traffic handled at this port consists mainly oif crude oils and iron ore. Visakhapatnam is the 'deepest port' where an outer harbour has been developed for exporting iron ore and a berth has been constructed for crude oil and also petroleum products as well as a multi-purpose general cargo berth. Paradip handles iorn ore and some quantities of coal and dry cargo. Calcutta is a riverine port handling diverified commodities. A new mechanised dock system at Haldia with provision for deep draft vessels supplements the facilities available at Calcutta. Haldia has fully equipped coal handling oil and containerised berths. All the major ports have generated operating surpluses during 1993-94. However, the financial position of ports of Cochin and Paradip is considered to be weak. All major ports handled a total cargo traffic of 179.3 million tonnes during the financial year 1993-94 and 123.2 million tonnes upto November in the financial year 1994-95.

There are about 139 minor/intermediate ports which are in the Concurrent List of the subjects in the Consititution of India. State governments are responsible for the management and the development of these ports. Accordingly, allocation for the development is provided in the respective state sector plans by the Planning Commission. However, funds for the development of port facilities in Andaman and Nicobar Islands, Lakshadweep, etc., are provided in the Central sector plan.

The Dredging Corporation of India was set up in March 1976 and started its commercial operation from 1 April 1997. The Corporation has been rendering maintenance and capital dredging services in major ports, minor ports, shipyards, shipping harbours, navy, state governments etc. An outlay of Rs. 155 crore has been approved for Eighth Five Year Plan and Rs. 20 crore in the Annual Plan 1993-94 for the Corporation. During

1993-94, the Corporation achieved 98 per cent capacity utilisation by dredging a quantity of 531.60 lakh cu.m. of sand, silt and other material. For 1994-95, the Corporation has targetted to achieve a dredging quantity of 550 lakh cu.m.

There are four major and three medium size shipyards in India in the public sector. Apart from these, there are are about 35 small shipyards in private sector and state government sector which cater to domestic requirements for medium and small craft. Maximum size of vessels that could be constructed in Cochin Shipyard, Cochin and Hindustan Shipyard, Visakhapatnam are 86,000 DWT and 45,000 DWT respectively. Cochin Shipyard Limited has delivered two tankers out of the series of three 86,000 DWT tankers for Shipping Corporation of India, and the work on third tanker has commenced. These were constructed for the first time in the country. Small shipyards are greared up for meeting the country's requirements for small/medium size crafts and fishing vessels. Sixty two fishing vessels have been delivered so far for private entrepreneurs and 26 fishing vessels are under construction in various shipyards.

The ship-building industry is open to private sector irrespective of the size of ship. The following fiscal and financial incentives are available to the ship-building industry; (a) the shipyard constructing vessels incluing fishing trawlers under bond are entitled to duty free import of raw materials, components consumable and spares required in the manufacture of ships; (b) the shipyards registered with the Ministry of Surface Transport for constructing deep sea fishing trawlers above 20 metres in length are entitled to 33 per cent subsidy on the price of the trawler in addition to price preferntial limited to 10 per cent for indigenous trawlers.

Of the 17 dry docks in the country, 13 are available

for commercial ship repair activities. While dry docks at CSL, Cochin and HSL, Visakhapatnam can accommodate ships of maximum size of one lakh DWT and 57,000 DWT respectively, other dry dock can accommodate ships upto 10,000 DWT range. In addition, ship repair facilities have been set up at Madras Port by a private entrepreneur with two floating dry docks of 14,000 tonnes lifting capacity (TLC) and 2,400 tonnes lifting capacity respectively which can cater to ships of 40,000 DWT and 8,000 DWT respectively. In addition Western India Shipyard Ltd., is setting up ship repair facilities at Mormugao on the West Coast. A floating dry dock of 20,000 TLC has been installed which caters to ships upto 60,000 DWT. A graving dock with a capacity to repair ships upto 2,500 DWT is also under construction.

A primier national institution, namely, National Ship Design and Research Centre (NSDRC), Visakhapatnam, an autonomous body under the administrative control of the Ministry of Surface Transport, has been set up with a view to provide national technological infrastructure to assist Indian ship-building and shipping industries. It has the following objectives: (i) to assist shipping and ship-building industry with consultancy, research, maritime information and computer services; (ii) to strive for the elevation of standard of Indian maritime sector so as to keep it at par with international standards; (iii) to save foreign exchange hitherto being spent by the industries for the procurement of designs from abroad; and (iv) to offer services to the industry in matters of improving efficiency and productivity.

Ministry of Surface Transport provides grant-in-aid to the entrepreneurs who take up indigenous development of ancillaries for ship-building. The grant-in-aid available can be to the extent of 70 per cent of the total development cost. For availing grant-in-aid, the private entrepreneurs are required to apply to the public sector shipyard who, in turn, would sponsor the proposal for consideration of the Ship Ancillary Development Committee under the Ministry.

Hindustan Shipyard Limited at Visakhapatnam was set up in 1941 in the private sector Scindia Steam Navigation Company Limied. Because of difficulties faced by the owners, the Government was requested to take over the shipyard and accordingly a new company viz., Hindustan Shipyard Limited was incorporated in 1952. In 1962, the shipyard became a cent per cent public sector enterprise. Thereafter in 1971, ship repair facilities were added besides various development programmes for augmenting installed capacity of the yard. An off-shore platforms yard for construction of well-platform for ONGC was set up in 1985. The present capacity of the yard is two platforms per year. The shipyard has plans to increase the capacity to three well-platforms during the Eighth Plan period. With the completion of Stage II Modernisation and Expansion Programme, the installed capacity of shipyard was increased to the equivalent of 3.5 pioneer class vessles by 1989-90. The shipyard has produced and delivered 107 vessels of different sizes and specification viz., dumb barges, bulk carries, product carriers, passenger-cum-cargo vessels and high technology drill ships besides petrol supply-cum-support vessels in addition to off-shore well-ahead-platforms. The shipyard has successfully completed and commissioned 11 off-shore platforms in Bombay High and Godowns basin for ONGC. The 11 platforms consist of 22 structures viz., jackets and 11 decks.

Hooghly Dock and Port Engineers Limited, Calcutta (HDPE) came into existence on 30 June 1984, as a new Government public sector undertaking with a view to securing better utilisation of available infrastructure thereof, to modernise and increase the capacity for ship-building and ship repairing so as to reduce the import of ships, vessels and crafts. The company comprises of two working units in Howrah district of West Bengal-one at Salkia and another at Nizirgunge. The unit located at Salkia Works constructs various types of ships, passenger and other vessels craft, dredgers, tugs, floating dry docks, fishing trawlrs, off-shore platform supply-cum-support vessels for *Department of Lighthouses and Lightships, etc. This unit has an outfit at Kidderpore Dock Complex of Calcutta port for repairs of various types of ocean-going vessels and dredgers. The second unit Nizirgunge Works is engaged in the construction of fishing trawlers, fire floats, barges, mooring launchers, grab hopper dredters etc., and repairs of different types of vessels besides general fabrication and machining jobs.

Cochin Shipyard, set up with Japanese collaboration, is designed to have a dock for building ships upt 86,000 DWT and a repair dock to accommodate ships upto 1,00,000 DWT. The shipyard has so far built and delivered five bulk carriers of 75,000 DWT each and two crude oil tankers of 86,000 DWT each. The construction of one more oil tanker of 86,000 DWT will commence in the near future. The second tanker in this series was launched on 29 February 1992 and delivered to SCI on 29 October 1992 in a record time of eight months only. The Order Book Position of CSL has improved in so far as it has received order for construction of three tugs for Indian ports.

The Government has approved a capital restructuring plan for the ailing Cochin Shipyard Limited. The restructuring involves conversion of loans amounting to Rs. 119.14 crore into seven per cent non-cumulative preference shares and coversion of accumulated interest at normal rate amounting to Rs.

136.35 crore into interest free loans. In addition, after considering various ways and means of revival of Indian shipyards, orders on a package of reliefs to shipyards have been issued by the Government in September 1993. As a result of various measures, Cochin Shipyard, *which has been able to improve its operational performance to generate a cash margin and reduce the accounting loss, thereby eliminating the need for cash-credit facility which it had been availing of till 1990-91 against Government guarantee. As such, the yard has become a viable unit.

India has got about 14,500 km of navlgable waterways which comprises of rivers, canals, backwaters, creeks, etc. At present, however a length of 3,700 km of major rivers is navigable by mechanised crafts but the length actually utilised is only about 2,000 km. As regards canals, out of 4,300 km of navigation canals, only 900 km is suitable for navigation by mechanised crafts. About 160 lakh tonnes of cargo is being moved by Inland Water Transport Inland Water Transport (IWT) is a fuel efficient and environment friendly mode. It is also known for higher employment generation potential. IWT operations are currently restricted to a few stretches in the Ganga-Bhagirathi, Hooghly rivers, the Brahmaputra, the Borak river, the rivers in Goa, the backwaters, in Kerala and in the deltaic regions of the Godavari-Krishna rivers. Besides, the organised operations by mechanised vessels, country boats of various capacities also operate in various rivers and canals.

The Inland Waterways Authority of India was set up on 27 October 1986 as a statutory body corporate under the Inland Waterways Authority of India Act, 1985. The Authority is entrusted with the responsibility of development, maintenance and regulation of national waterways and also to advise the Central and the state governments on matter relating to development of IWT

Considering the need to develop Inland Waterways and Inland Water Transport to play its rightful role in the transport network of the country, the Government had identified 10 important waterways for consideration to declared them as National Waterways. The Ganga between Allahabad and Haldia (1,620 km) on 27 October 1986, the Sadiya-Dhubri stretch of the river Brahmaputra (891 km) on 26 October 1988 and the Kollam-Kottapuram stretch of West Coast Canal (168 km) along with Champakara Canal (14 km) in Kerala with effect from 1 February 1993 have so far been declared as National Waterways and the same are being developed for navigation by Inland Waterways Authority of India. It is also proposed to consider the declaration of some more waterways like the river Godavari, Sunderbans, waterways in Goa and the river Barak (subject to techno-economic viability) during Eighth Five Year Plan.

The Central Inland Water Transport Corporation (CIWTC) with its head-quarters at Calcutta was set up as a public undertaking in May 1967. The CIWT is mainly engaged in transportation of goods by Inland Waterways in the Ganga-Bhagirathi-Hooghly, Sunderbans and the Brahmaputra rivers. They are operating regular cargo services between Calcutta and Pandu (near Guwahati), between Calcutta and Karimaganj (Assam), Calcutta-Bangladesh, and between Haldia and Patna. The Corporation is also having a shipyard called Rajabagan Dockyard in Calcutta which is engaged in the construction and repair of inland vessels and harbour crafts. A deep-sea ship repair division with units at Calcutta and Port Blair is also functioning under CIWTC.

In the wake of the economic reforms the government has allowed private participation in facilities including building operation and maintenance of container terminals, setting up of storage and warehouse facilities;

pilot services, dredging operation and maintenance of port craft and other equipment. Two dry docks at Calcutta have been privatised. Leasing out of two berths is under consideration of the government. Also, under consideration are proposals for privatisation at other ports. Ports and highways, besides power, constitute core areas where private investment is invited to overcome capacity shortages. Major orts have identified a large portfolio of projects amounting to US $ 2 billion where private sector involvement is feasible. In addition, governments of the States with a coastline have identified such projects worth US $ 1 billion.

Since infrastructure services are central to growth, the government is keen on raising private investment in the sector substantially. The Prime Minister, Mr. Deve Gowda told a gathering of international business leaders at Destination India conference recently: "We realise the critical importance of infrastructural development to sustain economic growth. Government considers it a high priority area for investment by foreign and multinational companies. We have already initiated policy measures and programmes to attract both domestic an foreign investment in these areas. Tax holidays and other fiscal incentives are being offered for the infrastructure projects. We have gained some experience in the past couple of years with these sectors and we are aware of the need to further simplify procedures and ensure greater transparency. We are ready to examine any suggestions to improve the system"

Shipping, shipbuilding and inland water transport are other areas in charge of the Ministry of Surface Transport where growth has fuelled expansion in the last fifty years of freedom. Liberalisation measures have been taken to facilitate the growth of the shipping industry as well. A working group on shipping constituted by the Planning Commission has recommended the acquisition of an additional 3.7 million GRT at an investment of Rs. 15,000 crore during the ninth plan period to increase the total available GRT in excess of nine million. Linked to the shipping industry is the Ship-building and repair industry. In the past 50 years, four major and three medium size shipyards have been established in the public sector, there was none before.

The Hindustan Shipyard Ltd. at Vishakhapatnam and the Cochin Shipyard can construct vessels up to a maximum size of 45,000 dwt and 86,000 dwt respectively. There are about no fewer than 35 small shipyards in the private sector. The shipping industry has been declicensed and is open to private sector irrespective of the size of the ship except for the construction of war ships. Mechanised sailing vessels upto 10,000 dwt including fishing trawlers and ship ancillaries have been allowed automatic approval for foreign collaboration up to 51 per cent equity capital.

For years ship repairing facilities in the country have been far too limited. Ships have to be repaired outside the country resulting in foreign exchange outgo. The situation will change verysoon. Ports have been advised by the government to make available land and water front areas for private entrepreneurs who may be interested in setting up ship repair facilities.

In land water transport, also a responsibility of the Ministry, is a pollution free and inexpensive mode of transport and the Ministry puts a lot of emphasis on its development. Subsidy up to 20 per cent of the cost is given to private transporters in this sector. Government vessels are given to private operators for carriage of goods via inland waterways.

There are three national waterways in operation: Allahabad Haldia (the Ganga Hugly) river system; Sadiya Dubri (on the Brhamaputra system) and Kollam-Kottapuram (Kerala) Proposals have been finalised to declare Cheralta to Rajamundri on the Godavari river in Andhra Pradesh and Zuari and Mandovi rivers and Cumberjue canal in Goa and the international route between Sagar and the Bangaladesh border in Sunderbans as national waterways.

In sum, an enabling framework for private investment in the key infrastructure sector of surface transport is being made operative. This is done under the economic reforms which are currently being effected. Infrastructure development is recognized as the linchpin of Indian prosperity. Not far into the next century, deficiencies like port capacities stretching beyond their limits and road networks under tremendous pressure will be left behind, taking the development process of the last 50 years to a new credo.

Overseas shipping has an extremely important role to play in India's international trade. The country has the largest merchant shipping fleet among developing countries and ranks 17th in the world in shipping tonnage. As on 31 August 1995, the operative tonnage consisted of 460 vessels totalling to 6.84 million GRT.

Thee were 71 shipping companies in the country in operation as on 31 March 1995 including the Shipping Corporation of India, a public sector undertaking. Of these, 39 are engaged exclusively in coastal trade, 22 in overseas trade and the remaining 10 in both coastal and overseas trade. Shipping corporation of India, which is biggest shipping line of the country, had a merchant fleet of 124 vessles of 31 lakh GRT as on 31 March 1995 and operated on almost all maritime routes. Shipping Corporation of India tonnage accounts for about 49 per cent of the total India tonnage. Major private sector shipping companies which own one lakh or more GRT are: (i) Great Eastern Shipping Company Limited (5.97 lakh GRT); (ii) Eassar Shipping Limited (4.54 lakh GRT); (iii) Chowgle Steamships Limited (2.02 lakh GRT); (iv) South India Shipping Corporation Limited (2.76 lakh GRT); (v) India Steamship Company Limited (1.52 lakh GRT); (vi) Surrendra Overseas Limited (1.56 lakh GRT); (vii) Century Shipping (1.61 lakh GRT); and (viii) Varun Shipping Company Limited (1.27 lakh GRT).

National Shipping Board is a permanent statutory body established in 1959 under the Merchant Shipping Act, 1958 to advise the government on shipping matters. Ship Acquisition Licensing Committee deals with ship acquisition proposals received from shipping companies. Inter-ministerial high level committees look into problems of the shipping companies. Indian National Shipowners Association seeks to promote the interest of national shipping and other allied industries.

India's National Ship Classification Society was formed in March 1975 under the Companies Act, 1956. Its activities are: (i) to provide a faithful and accurate classification and record of mercantile shipping classed with Indian Register of Shipping (IRS); (ii) to establish and administer standards for the construction and periodical survey of ships and other maritime structure; (iii) to approve design of, to survey and to issue reports on land based installations, machinery, materials, and apparatus of all kinds; and (iv) to aid and develop marine technology in India through research and development work. Government has authorised the IRS to assign international load lines and carry out Cargo Ship Safety Construction Surveys of India Flag Ships. In order to maintain acceptable standards and provide worldwise coverage for its services, IRS has entered into agreements of mutual cooperation with all major international classification societies by virtue of which ships can also be classed dually with IRS as well as corresponding society with arrangements for survey all over the world. These agreements also enable IRS to get technical backup whenever required for its varied services from different sources.

There are three training establishments for the merchant navy officers. TS Chankya at Bombay imparts pre-sea training to navigation cadets. Lal Bahadur Shastri College of Advanced Maritime Studies and Research, Bombay conducts post-sea Instrumental Courses in Navigation and Engineering. Marine Engineering Research Institutes at Bombay and Calcutta impart training to the marine engineering cadets.

Coastal Shipping is an energy efficient and comparatively cheaper mode of transport if the carriage of bulk traffic over long hauls is involved and also particularly when origin and destination of traffic stream is located along the coast. India has along coastline of 5,560 km. Coastal shipping can play an important role in integrated transport network of the country particularly when inland modes are strained. the coastal tonnage which was 3.12 lakh GRT on 1 April 1985 (beginning of Seventh Plan) was increased to 6.93 lakh GRT on 31 March 1995.

An Inter-Ministerial Working Group set up by the Government to study the simplification of customs procedure, implementation of infrastructural facilities, financial aspects, etc., has also recently made certain recommendations for the development of coastal shipping in the country. The acceptance of these recommendations is under consideration of the Government.

At the time of Independence, there were only 17 lighthouses in India. Since then, Aids to Navigation have increased in number and variety. Government looks after general navigational aids while states, port trusts and other agenices are responsible for local aids. However, under the Lighthouse Act, 1927, the Government exercises general control over all aids through Department of Lighthouses and Lightships, which in turn maintains various navigational aids along the coast of India besides launchers and HF/VHF/radio telephone sets. At present, there are 163 lighthouses, one light vessel, twenty radio beacons, four Dacca Navigator Chain Stations, six LORAN-C stations, eleven reacons and ten lighted buoys. The Department of Lighthouses is maintaining three lauches, one mechanised lighted boad and two large ocean going vessels, M.V. Sagardeep and M.V. Paradeep for attending light stations at various places including off-shore islands. The Department is also maintining 39 Very High Frequency/Radio Telephone sets for maintaining communication with lighthouses situated in remote and isolated places.

— India has a road network covering 2.7 million kilometers which makes it the third largest road network in the world. However, this network is not adequate for speedly and efficient transportation. Half of this is made up of unsurfaced roads. The National Highways which are artirial routes have currently a network of 34,298 km. Although they carry nearly 40 per cent of the goods and passenger traffic, the national highway network constitutes less than 2 per cent of the total road network.

— Road transport is the dominant form of transport for people and goods in India. Over 80 per cent of passengers and over 60 per cent of freight move by roads. It is estimated that by the year 2000 road traffic will account for 87 and 65 per cent of passenger and goods traffic, respectively. The quality and capacity of national highway have to be enhanced consistent with the traffic expansion and overall economic growth of the country. Traffic movement on the highways is suffering from frequent stopovers and congestion as almost 15 per cent of national highways and 75 per cent of state highways are single lane roads. The problem is further compunded by inadequate road pavement thickness, poor riding quality, existence of a number of railway level crossings that need replacement, weak and distressed bridges/culverts, congested city sections, lack of wayside amenties and inadequate road safety measures. The deficiencies in the road network have contributed to safety hazards, besides entailing higher transportation cost. These highways will, therefore, require major augmentation of capacity as well as structural upgradation. About 20 per cent of national highways need widening from single to double lanes and about 50 per cent of two lane roads have to be strengthened. 30 per cent of existing two lane roads need to be four laned apart from developing expressways on selected corridors. The maintenance of roads is no less important than their expansion and the vast network of roads built over the years needs to be preserved.

The magnitude of the task on hand and the volume of funds required for this purpose are clearly beyond the capacity of the public sector. In the past, roads have generally been financed from budgetary sources and constructed by the Public Works Departments. As the budgetary allocation is not adequate to meet the challenges states above, the National Highways Act has been amended to enable the levy of a toll on selected improved sections of National Highways.

— The amendment of the Natioal Highways Act to allow the private sector to construct and charge a fee or toll will permit the private sector to participate in construction, maintenance and operation of roads on Build, Operate and Transfer (BOT) basis. Several reforms/measures taken by the Government to attract private sector participation in Highways Development are summurised and encompass land acquisition, environmental clearance, simplification of procedures, tolling of 4-lanes, by-passes and bridges, equity participation in the highway sector and sharing of force majeure risks.

— After the amendment of National Highways Act in 1995 to allow private sector particiapation, steps have been taken to initiate national highway projects through private sector participation. Two projects of bypasses (Thane-Bhiwandi in Maharashtra and Udaipur in Rajasthan) and one project or Road Over Bridge (at Chalthan in Gujarat) involving an investment of Rs. 42 crore have been awarded on BOT basis.

— The provisions relating to foreign investment in the road sector have been considerably liberalised. Automatic approval will be accorded for foreign equity participation upto 74 per cent in the construction of roads and bridges. In addition to this, automatic approval would be given for majority foreign equity upto 51 per cent in support services to land transport, like operation of highways bridges, toll roads and vehicles.

— External assistance is being obtained for the improvement of National Highways through international agencies such as the World Bank, Asian Development Bank and Overseas Economic Cooperation of Japan. The Government of India has activated the National Highways Authority, which is an autonomous body created through an Act of Parliament and has been entrusted with eh Asian Development Bank Project costing about Rs. 800 crores in 5 states viz., Haryana, Rajasthan, Bihar, West Bengal and Andhra Pradesh.

— The State Road Transport Undertakings operate a fleetk of overk one lakh buses employing 8.3 lakh workers. The undertainds, with a few exceptions, face serious financial constraints due to various factors such as the social commitment to operate even on uneconomic routes, absense of cost-based fare structures, overmanning, poor management and widespread inefficiencies.

— Indian vessels carried about 29 per cent of the total sea-borne cargo during 1994-95. The share of Indian vessels in 1994-95 in Petroleum Oil and Lubricants (POL) was 54 per cent, in bulk carriers 17 per cent, and in liner traffic 9 per cent. Long—term targets for Indian shares in bulk carriers and liner traffic are 50 and 40 per cent, respectively. The fleet strength at the end of October, 1996 was 481 vessels of 7.02 million Gross Registered Tonnage (GRT), against 468 vessels of 6.9 million GRT in October, 1995. Overseas trade during 1994-95 was 147 million tonnes against 137 million tonnes during 1993-94.

— The Shipping Corporation of India (SCI) showed a better financial performance during 1995-95 compared to 1994-95. It has earned a record net profit after tax of Rs. 323 crore in 1995-96 registering an increase of 61 per cent over 1994-95. SCI's gross internal resources rose to Rs. 554 crore in 1995-96 as against Rs. 395 crore in 1994-95. Its gross tonnages as on October 31, 1996 was 3.11 million GRT (about 45 per cent of the total Indian fleet).

— There are two major public sector ship building yards, Hindustan Shipyards Limited, and Cochin Shipyards Limited. Due to various reasons i.e. high construction cost, heavy interest burden on borrowing, low order book position, excessive manpower etc. these yards had been incurring losses. However, as a result of revival measures initiated by the Government in September, 1993 the two yards have shown an improved performance. Cochin Shipyard Limited has earned a net profit of Rs. 11.16 crores during the previous year. Hindustan Shipyards incurred a net loss of Rs. 118 crores in 1995-96.

— The International Safety Management (ISM) code, was adopted by the International Maritime Organisation (IMO) in November, 1993. This code is to come into force in 1998 for passenger ships and tankers and by 2000 for other vessels. The shipping companies are required to provide special training to on shore staff and crew on board in order to implement the Code. The Directorate General of Shipping has constituted a Sub-Committee which is in dialogue with the shipping comanies to implement the Code well before its due date.

* In order to promote the development of Indian shipping, a new shipping policy was initiated in 1990-91 and several policy reforms have since been made in conformity with the liberalisation o the Indian economy.

Inda has one of the largest road networks in the world. The country's total road length was 20,65,209 km in 1991-92. Seventh Plan laid emphasis on a coordinated and balanced development of road network in the country under (i) primary road system covering state highways; (ii) secondary and feeder road system covering state highways and major district roads; and (iii) rural roads including village roads and other district roads.

Substantial outlays were proposed for road development in the rural and tribal areas. In the first three Five Year Plans and three Annual Plans, Rs.1,121.58 crore was spent on road development. During Fourth, Fifth, one Annual Plan and Sixth Plan, Rs. 5,160.09 crore was spent on this. Outlay for road development under the Seventh Plan for Central sector was Rs. 1,019.75 crore, for state sector Rs. 3,666.98 crore and for union territories Rs. 513.31 crore. During the Seventh Plan, Rs. 6,179.75 crore was spent on *Central sector roads. For state sector roads, an amount of Rs. 1,303.25 crore was spent during 1990-91. For the Eighth Five Year plan, an outlay of Rs. 2,600 crore and Rs. 10,610 crore has been approved for Central sector roads and state sector roads repectively. During 1992-94 of the Eighth five Year Plan, an amount of Rs. 1,070 crore has been spent on Central sector roads and expenditure on the state sector aggregates to Rs. 3,709 crore approximately.

Government is responsible for national highway system. In 1947 approximately 2,500 km of missing roads links and thousand of culverts and bridges which did not exist, were required to be constructed to have an integrated and continuous network. There was an increase in missing road links with addition of new roads to the national highways system in later years. upto 31 March 1994, road links including diversions cosntructed totalled 4,624 km, widening and strengthening single lane section to double lane carriage was done in 24,574 km, widening to four-lane completed in 442 km, strengthening of weak two-lane pavement has been done in 12,365 km. In addition 507 major bridges and 2,856 minor bridges were also completed. Present natioal highway system includes a total road length of

34,058 km. An expenditure of Rs. 1,481.70 crore during the Seventh Plan and Rs. 860.50 crore during 1990-92 had been incurred on development of national highways. During Eighth Five Year Plan, an outlay of Rs. 2,460 crore has been allocated for development of national highways. During 1992-93 and 1993-94 a sum of Rs. 1,028 crore has been spent on development of national highways. Though the national highways constitute only two per cent of the total road length, they carry nearly 40 per cent of road traffic. There are altogether nine on-going external loans for the improvement of national highways. Out of these, one (US dollar 306 million) is from World Bank. Three *(total jap Yen 36,915 million approximate equivalent US dollar 369 million) are from Overseas Economics Cooperation Fund (OECF), Japan. the World Bank loan includes six NH sub-projects in the states of Punjab, Haryana, Orissa, Maharashtra, Madhya Pradesh and West Bengal and one state highway project for reconstruction of bridges in Orissa. Three subprojects in the states of Punjab, Haryana and Orissa are in progress and action for inviting tenders for the remaining three sub-projecs is under process. The first ADB loan (US dollar 188 million) provides for development of national highways in three states namely, Andhra Pradesh, Haryana and Uttar Pradesh and four state roads in three states namely, Andhra Pradesh, Karnataka and Tamil Nadu. The second ADB loan (US dollar 250 million) provides for improvement of national highways in Karnataka, Kerala, Rajasthan and of state roads in Andhra Pradesh, Orissa, Uttar Pradesh and West Bengal. The works under both these loans are in various stages of progress. The third ADB loan (US dollar 245 million) is for development of national highways in the states of Andhra Pradesh, Haryana, Rajasthan, Bihar and West Bengal. The procurement process is in progress for these sub-projects. The project for improvement of Mathura-

Agra Section of National Highway No. 2 in Uttar Pradesh in under OECF loan (Jap Yen 4827 million).

State highways and district rural roads are the responsibility of state governments and are maintained by various agencies in states and union territories. Roads are being developed in rural areas under Minimum Needs Programme (MNP). The objective of it being to link all viallges with a population of 1,500 with all-weather roads. Government also assists in development of certain selected roads in states.

Raised in May 1960 for development of roads of strategic importance in northern and north eastern border areas, Border Roads Organisation (BRO) has now spread its activities throughout the country and is presently working in states of Rajasthan, Jammu & Kashmir, Himachal Pradesh, Maharashtra, Tamil Nadu, Andhra Pradesh, Uttar Pradesh, Sikkim, Assam, Meghalaya, Nagaland, Tripura, Manipur, Mizoram, Arunachal Pradesh, Bihar and Andaman and Nicobar Islands. It has so for constructed over 24,000 km of roads and is also presently maintaining them. BRO has now diversified into construction of airfields, buildings and permanent bridges involving high degree of technical expertise, with special emphasis on mechanisation and quality control. With proven efficiency, credibility, professionalism and overall cost effectiveness, many other governmental agencies are coming forward in a big way for entrusting works to BRO and specially in those remote areas where no one else is prepared to work. The BRO is building technical institutions, schools and hospitals in far-flung places for the upliftment of the people of those regions. It has been occasionally taking up civil engineering works on behalf of other agenices in difficult areas.

Table: Road Length in India

(Km)

	Surfaced	*Unsurfaced*	*Total*
ALL INDIA	10,43,365	10,21,844	20,65,209
States			
Andhra Pradesh	81,449	71,747	1,52,896
Arunachal Pradesh	2496	5,204	7,520
Assam	10,841	58,072	68,913
Bihar	33,980	53,713	87,693
Goa	4,567	2,986	7,553
Gujarat	73,354	19,153	92,507
Haryana	26,498	3,263	29,761
Himachal Pradesh	6,971	17,859	24,830
Jammu and Kahsmir	8,325	6,104	14,429
Karnataka	86,158	50,241	1,36,399
Kerala	32,637	1,04,706	1,37,343
Madhya Pradesh	80,354	56,846	1,37,200
Maharashtra	1,47,760	98,018	2,45,778
Manipur	2,741	4,024	6,765
Meghalaya	2,931	4,901	7,832
Mizoram	1,268	2,440	3,708
Nagaland	6,842	1,963	8,805
Orissa	57,983	1,73,396	2,31,379
Punjab	47,568	8,649	56,217
Rajasthan	60,211	62,423	1,22,634
Sikkim	1,842	73	1,915
Tamil Nadu	1,18,637	67,899	1,86,536
Tripura	4,448	8,560	13,008
Uttar Pradesh	95,520	1,26,982	2,22,502
West Bengal	28,690	30,404	59,094
Union Territories			
Andaman and Nicobar Islands	807	45	852
Chandigarh	1,766	–	1,766
Dadra and Nagar Haveli	331	16	347
Daman and Diu	–	–	–
Delhi	14,952	6,846	21,798
Lakshadweep	N.A.	N.A.	N.A.
Pondicherry	1,739	1,509	3,248

Note Data given above is as on 31 March 1992.

Railways in recent years has been spurred to augment internal generation of resources through economy in working expenses and enhancing its earnings. The share of its internally generated resources has risen from a mere 25 per cent during the Fifth Plan to 58 per cent during the Eighth Plan. Railways is an important infrastructure sector and a provider of vital non-traded service which has a bearing on the overall competitiveness of the economy. It is, therefore, necessary that a distinction between the network of railway lines, and the railway rolling stock which uses this network to provide transport services is maintained. The high capital intensity and long gestation lags act as disincentives to investment in line networks. This is not, however, applicable to railway service, which can be viable and competitive. Conventional market borrowing is, therefore, restricted to funding rolling stock which is essential to sustain railway services. This has resulted in raising its liabilities on account of market borrowings through the Indian Railway Finance Corporation (IRFC). The lease charges being payable to IRFC as per budget estimates have already exceeded Rs. 1650 crore during 1996-97 and constitutes about 10 per cent of the ordinary working expenses. The resource requirements of Railways are huge and therefore cannot be adequately met through internal generation of resources and conventional market borrowings alone. This calls for greater innovations in management and in funding of assets and services provided by the Railways. A start has been made by allowing private sector participation in selected Railway projects/activities. These include Build-Own-Lease-Transfer (BOLT) and Own-Your-Wagon (OYW) Schemes. These initiatives can inject limited amount of competition in selected areas, and also ease the strain on railway ways increased from Rs. 20101 crore in 1994-95 to Rs. 22418 crore in 1995-96, representing a growth of 11.5 per cent. In 1995-96, the total working expenses (including appropriations to the Depreciation Reserve Fund and Pension Fund) were Rs. 18525 crore as against Rs. 16590 crore in the previous year. The working expenses thus showed an increase of 11.7 per cent. Consequently, the net traffic receipts of Railways have shown an increase from Rs. 3511 crore in 1994-95 to Rs. 3893 crore in 1995-96. The net railway revenue comprising the net traffic receipts and net micellaneous receipts, amounted to Rs. 4135 crore in 1995-96. The ratio of net revenue to capital-at-charge and investment from capital fund, works out to 15.2 per cent in 1995-96 as compared to 13.7 per cent in 1993-94 and 15.3 per cent in 1994-95. The ordinary working expenses, forming a major part of the total working expenses, registered a higher increase of 13.2 per cent in 1995-96 on account of interim relief, increased PLB cost, and hike in energy charges etc. After making payment of Rs. 1264 crore as dividend to general revenues, the excess amounted to Rs. 2871 crore, which partly contributed to the investment requirements of the Railways.

In 1995-96 Railways contributed Rs. 2246 crore to the general exchequer, consisting of payment of dividend of Rs. 1264 crore and net accretion of Rs. 982 crore to Railway funds kept with the general exchequer. Railways dues of Rs. 895 crore remained outstanding against certain State Electricity Boards and power houses as on 31st March, 1996. The inability to settle outstanding financial dues with Railways, bestowed on the recepient of railway services, financial accomodation without payment of interest. Railways transaction with RBI also closed with a net deposit of Rs. 908 crore in 1995-96.

The railway budget for 1996-97 envisages a surplus of Rs. 1916 crore, after providing for payment of dividend to general revenues in full. The fare and freight rate increases in the railway budget for 1996-97 consisted of the following. Freight rates of all commodities increased by 10 per cent excepting certain essential commodities. Minimum distance for charge raised from 75 kms to 100 kms; no increase in second class fares; upper class and AC 3 tier/chair car fares raised by 10 per cent; fares of Rajdhani, August Kranti and Shatabdi Express trains also increased by 10 per cent; sleeper class fares increased by 5 per cent for distance beyond 200 kms; parcel and luggage rates rationalised by replacing the existing GPA, CP1 and CP2 by new general parcel scale (GPS), concessional parcel scale (CPS) and modified luggage/motor car scales; and no increase in first and second class monthly season ticket and quarterly season ticket. They are expected to fetch an additional revenue of Rs. 927 crore. The plan outlay for railways for 1996-97, the terminal year of the Eighth Five Year Plan, has been budgeted at Rs. 8280 crore, including budgetary support of Rs. 1419 crore. Market borrowings, BOLT and OYW schemes are expected to fetch an additonal Rs. 2750 crore. The rest of the plan outlay of Rs. 4111 crore is to come from internal resources. In the plan, priority has been accorded to rolling stock, track renewals, safety works and electrificatioin.

As a carrier of 12 million passengers and over one milion tonnes of freight everyday, the Indian Railways have played a vital role in the socio-economic development of the country. However, not every effort to improve its performance has been successful, feels the author. The Indian Railways travel in one day a distance that is three and a half times the distance between the earth and the moon. In other words, the Indian Railways traverse in less than seven hours a distance that a satellite takes six days to cover. But as the world's single largest railway system under single management, which carries 12 million passengers and over one milion tonnes of freight everyday, these statistics do not come as a surprise.

At the time of Independence the first task was to integrate all 42 different lines owned by Rajas and Maharajas and British companies into one system, to give shape to the Indian Railways. Even more important was to make up as fast as possible for the manpower and other losses suffered on account of the partition on the country. A major consequence of this was that the rail link with Assam and the North-East was virtualy cut off and had to be restored at top-most speed. Once that was achieved, attention was turned to improving passenger amenities, building indigenous manufrastructure and modernizing the system.

Among the first step in that direction was to replace wooden coaches with steel-cum-aluminimum coaches which were nore durable and sturdy, were better suited to higher speed, and were less prone to catch fire. But a more significant decision was to introduce diesel engines which ran faster than the steam engines. Not everyone was happy when the first high speed diesel engine was imported from Canada but looking back it could be described as an important landmark in pushing the speed of the Indian Railways.

The country having firmly embarked on the path of planning with its accent on building a more or less self-reliant economy, almost all import by the Indian Railways was generally accompanied by agreement to transfer technology. Before long, the country was meeting several needs of the Railways indigenously with the setting up of big facilities like the Integral Coach Factory at Perambur (Chennai), Diesel Locomotive Workshop at Varanasi and Chittaranjan Locomotive Works. The Indian railways had embarked on the path of self-reliance in the early years of the young nation.

The manufacture of diesel and electric locomotives within the country was a signal that the days of the steam locomotives were going to end. It was only in the 1970s that a decision was taken not to manufacture any steam locomotives in the country. Economic considerations and the competition from the diesel and electric locomotives led to the decision to end the magnificent era of steam locos. It was a sad news for the lovers of those "black beauties" which, however, could neither match the speed nor the capacity and performance of the diesel and electric locomotives. Ecological considerations, though not in vogue then, would have also been cited as a reason for saying good-bye to the steam engine.

Incidentally, the steam locos will not disappear totally from the map of the Indian Railways. The "toy" trains of Darjeling and Ooty will continue their run into the next century. Another narrow gauge train, on the Kalka-Shimla route, however, was "converted" to diesel some time back.

The Indian Railways consist of and extensive network spread over 62,915 km. comprising Broad Gauge (40,609 km.), Metre Gauge (18,501 km.) and Narrow Gauge (3,794 km.). Electrified networks with 12,306 km. account for 19.6 per cent of the total route kilometerage. The thrust areas identified for the Eighth Plan period included replacement and renewal of overaged assets, augmentation of terminal and rolling stock capacities and gauge conversion and electrification. Indian Railways completed gauge conversion of 1,351 km. in 1992-93, 1,619 km. in 1993-94, 1,805 km. in 1994-95 and have set a target of 1,000 km. for 1995-96.

During 1995-9, the revenue earning freight traffic moved by the Railways was 390.7 million tonnes. This was 7 per cent higher than the performance in 1994-95.

The freight traffic carried during April-November 1996-97 at 260.7 million tonnes, increased by 6.3 per cent over April-November, 1995. The growth has mainly been in coal, pig iron and finished steel from steel plants, cement, foodgrains, iron ore for export and other goods, etc. However, there is a decline in fertilizers and POL both of which showed negative growth rates. The slow down in industrial production and economic activity in general in the current financial year has also, to some extent affected freight demand fron the railways in like manner. Moreover, for items such as cement, fertilizers and petroleum and petroleum products (POL), considerations of operational flexibility and continuity of arrangements already made have necessitated an increased dependence on road transport and also on pipelines in the case of petroleum.

The existing modal shares between rail and road do not conform to optimal shares as judged by the criterion of least economic cost. The Railways are trying to attract freight traffic in view of being a more energy efficient and environment friendly mode of surface transport through the Container Corporation of India (CONCOR) and various other marketing schemes.

The Railways employ about 16 lakh workers, the largest number for any undertaking in the country. A comprehensive plan for human resource development is required to upgrade skills, retrain workers and achieve higher productivity. While staff productivity in terms of the number of traffic units per employee, asset productivity in terms of net tonne kilometre per wagon day, wagon turn-around time, loco-utilisation, etc. have improved over the year, there is still scope for further improvement.

The budetary support to the Railways has declined sharply from 75 per cent of the Railway's Plan outlay in the Fifth Plan to 42 per cent of the outlay in the Seventh Plan and further to 19 per cent during the Eighth Plan. This has forced the railways to repriortise ongoing projects of line expansion, renewals, gauge conversion and electrification of key routes and has adversely affected procurement of rolling stock.

The Railways have so far met the challenge by relying less on budgetary support and more on internal generation of resources which, in future, may have limitations with increased outlay on account of the Pay Commission recommendations and growing lease rentals, ertc. Alternative sources of funding based on market borrowings are also being looked at although the servicing costs would be higher. Private sector participation through schemes like Build-Own-Lease-Transfer (BOLT) and Own-Your-Wagon-Scheme (OYWS) are also being explored. However, only limited success has been achieved in these areas till now.

For some time now, there has been considerable concern within Rail Bhawan over the resource crunch to finance the annual Plans. The Chairman of the Railway Board, Mr. C.L. Kaw, has been on record as saying that while most of the money may come from market borrowings, it was not a financially prudent way because of high market interest rates. But his concern may have something to do with the Railways' efforts, so far unsuccessfull, to receive a substantially higher budgetary support from the Government. The Railways say that the Government must pay more if all the social obligations imposed on the railway network are to be carried out.

Yet, there is something to be said in support of the railways demand for more money from the general Budget. If market borrowings continue, Indian railways may soon be engulfed in a debt trap. In 1997—98, for instance, about a third of the annual Plan of Rs. 8300 crore will have to be financed by market borrowings. Of the Rs. 3050 crore thus expected to be raised, the bulk—Rs. 2150 crore—will come from the sale of bonds and the rest, about Rs. 900 crore, from schemes like BOLT and Own Your Wagon which involve the private sector. It may also not wise to depend too much on raising money through the Indian Railway Finance Corporation which had trouble raising Rs. 1850 crore and meeting debt and interest payments last year.

The finance crunch in one manner is a peculiar problem of the Indian Railways imposed by the Government which is very keen to spread the railway network in the backward and far—flung areas. This would contribute not only to the development of these areas but also help in removing the sense of isolation among the people there.

The aim is laudable and immensely desirable. It is not good for a country of India's size and diversity to allow a sense of isolation grow among the population living in the border areas of the country. But the stark fact is that the financial health of the railways and, more importantly, the poor traffic that these far flung areas would generate, will nonly add to the problems of the Railways if the network expansion plans are concentrated in the areas of low return. There is perhaps a case for ordering a cost—benefit analysis which will help the Railways arrive at a rational pricing strategy. But it would be worthwhile only if this analysis is to be accepted and implemented.

with egalitarian considerations coming to dominate in the country, the first Janata Government had decided that Indian Railways should have only two classes, first and second. But to make the journey for the long distance traveller at least reasonably comfortable, cushioned seats were introduced in the second class coaches.

Soon, it was also decided that non-air-conditioned first class coaches will also go and their manufacture was stopped. The new second air-conditioned class came to replace the non-AC first class. The old type of first class coaches carried a maximum of 16 passengers in a compartment that resembled a drawing room with long sofa sets along the walls. It was a luxurious way of travelling, if one did not mind the heat and the dust of summers.

The new ACII generally carries 46 passengers. Obviously, the rise in passenger traffic was forcing the Indian railways to increase capacity. An attempt was made to popularize double-decker coaches. The idea could not catch on as the double-decker coaches were not considered safe enough in Indian conditions.

The Indian Railways, however, succeeded in their attempts to run faster trains, running at speeds of more than 100 km per hour. The first attempt in this direction was the introduction of Rajdhani Express between New Delhi and Howrah capable of running at 130 km per hour. The train proved to be an instant hit with the passengers and demand for similar trains on other trunk routes began to be made forcefully.

Though its implementation took an inordinately long time for reasons not seen initially, a landmark event in the history of post-Independence Indian Railways was the decision to build an underground railway system: the Calcutta Metro. Indian Railways has at least developed an expertise to execute such a project anywhere in India or abroad.

However, the country's priorities continued to be start more surface and long-distance trains like the Rajdhani Express and the next in the Rajdhani series was introduced on the New Delhi-Bombay route. Today

Rajdhani trains link Delhi and almost all State capitals, except those in the North-East. Jaipur and Ahemdabad are also not on the rajdhani map but will be included soon when the Delhi-Ahmedabad route is converted to broad gauge. It may be added here that for safety reasons the Rajdhani trains are not run at their maximum permissible speed.

A faster train, the Shatabdi series, has also been introduced from Delhi in recent years and has proved to be very popular with tourists and inter-city travellers. The travelling schedule of the Rajdhani trains enables the trveller to spend the night on the train and reach his or her destination next morning well in time for a full day business. On the other hand, the Passengers travelling by Shatabdi, which is capable of a speed of 160 km per hour, can even return to Delhi in the evening. The all air-conditioned Shatabdi trains is said to be providing a competition to the airlines flying from Delhi to destinations like Agra, Jaipur, Chandigarh and Bhopal. Of course, like the Rajdhani trains, the Shatabdi trains also do not run at their maximum permissible speed.

It is possible to introduce a still faster train or accelerate the speed of the existing trains with the induction of the state-of-the-art 6000 horse power three-phase AC electric locamotives, imported from Switzerland. But the present track, signalling and other conditions will not allow faster trains. For the time being the advantage of the new locomotives would be in boosting the hauling capacity of both the passenger and goods train. For instance, the new imported engine can haul 26 coaches or even more, against 18 or 19 in the present trains.

It is not that only faster passenger trains are envisaged. There is an equal interest in upgrading the technology and with it the hauling capacity of the more efficient wagons are also being introduced to increase the capacity of the goods trains. After all, the goods trains are the real bread winners of the Indian Railways.

Though there is no hurry to allow trains to run at speeds well in excess of 160 km per hour, some preparations seem to have already been made to plunge India into the realm of really fast trains with the recent decision to import from Germany 21 high speed passenger coaches which can be used in trains of 300 km per hour speed. The agreement to import them includes transfer of technology.

The electrification of tracks, which so far has covered 20.8 per cent of route kilometres, will also be helpful in introducing still faster trains for both passenger and goods traffic.

But it is not possible to introduce really fast trains without improving tracks and the signalling system to bring them to specified standards. A "Bullet" like train would also require a dedicated track, exclusively for such a train. It is doubtful if the present shape of Indian economy would allow such a luxury. The effort at the moment is to improve tracks and upgrade their maintenance to make them safer and comfortable for the present generation of high-speed trains. The welding of tracks will eliminate the common hazard of saboteurs removing fishplates. About 70 per cent of welding job has far been completed.

There has been an interesting by-product in this exercise. Ecologists must be quite pleased to see the wooden sleepers being replaced with concrete ones thus drastically cutting the need for consumption of wood. The amount of saving of wood can be judged from the fact that in the last 10 years or so, about 65 million concrete sleepers have been manufactured to meet the requirement and still a lot of wooden sleepers have to be replaced. It is estimated that the task would completed only towards the end of the century.

One of the travails of journey on the Indian Railways ususally begins at the very initial stage the booking of ticket for the journey. The introduction of computerized reservation, beginning with Delhi in mid-1980s, has made that task comparatively less cumbersome. But the introduction of computerisation has been bigger boon in the field of freight traffic. Today, for instance, it is possible in Delhi to trace the progress of a goods wagon almost at the drop of an eyelid; before computerisation the process would have taken several days.

The job of modernisation and speeding up the railways would not be complete without introducing a unigauge system in the country. But it is a big task, involving huge expenditure. Of the 62,800-km of route length in the Indian Railways, metre gauge accounts for 24,000 km and narrow gauge account of another 4,000 km.

The areas not served by the broad gauge often complained that their economic advancement suffered because of this Goods and passengers travelling long distances across the country required transhipment for want of a single gauge link. But in the early 1990s, the Government decided that the country has no option but to adopt a policy of unigauge. The alarming decline in freight traffic—lost to road transport—could have also forced the decision.

— Development of rail network in backward areas.
— New line from Udhampur to Baramulla and Kumarghat—Agartala, Lumding—Silchar, Harmuti —Itanagar and Bridge at Bogibeel on Brahmputra.

— Rs. 400 crore for new lines as against Rs. 220 crore in the current year.

— More than Rs. 300 crore for rail infrastructure development in North—East.

— More than Rs. 100 crore for expansion of railway system in Jammu and Kashmir.

— Originating loading of 390 MT during 1995—96. Target of 410 MT of freight loading during 1996—97.

— Computerised reservation provided at 271 locations upto 1995–96, likely to be made available at more than 300 locations by March, 1997.

— Computer reservation facility is available at Srinagar, Port Blair, Panaji, Shillong, Agartala, Imphal and Gangtok etc. which are not connected by rail. It is being made operational at Aizawl, Itanagar and Kohima.

— To provide universal facility of return and onward reservation, software is already operational at New Delhi and Secunderabad PRS. It is to be extended to Mumbai, Calcutta and Chennai.

— Satellite based telephone service on many long distance trains. This facility already introduced on Mumbai—Delhi Rajdhani Express trains during next year.

— AC 3 tier coaches operating on all Rajdhani Express trains and 51 pairs of other Mail/Express trains.

— Unreserved Second Class coaches attached ot many trains during the current year.

Catering will be provided from 01.04.97 in Hazrat Nizamuddin—Trivandrum, Hazrat Nizamuddin—Bangalore and Hazrat Nizamuddin—Jammu Tawi Express. Changes will be included in the fare itself as in other Rajdhani Expresses.

Finance

Since 1924-25 railway finances remain separated from general revenues. They have their own funds and accounts and the Railway Budget is presented separately to Parliament. However, the railways contribute to the general revenue a dividend on the capital invested. Quantum of contribution is reviewed periodically by a Parliamentary Convention Committee.

Over the years Indian Railways have made concerted efforts to achieve self-sufficiency in production of rolling stock in the country. Locomotives are build in Chittaranjan Locomotive Works (CLW), Chittaranjan, Dieseal Locomotive Works (DLW), Varanasi and BHEL, Bhopal, a public sector company which has developede capability to manufacture electric locomotives for the Indian Railways. In 1993-94, CLW manufactured 140 broad gauge electric locomotives, DLW produced 138 broad gauge diesel locomotives (including 13 locos for public sector units) and 14 metre guge diesel locos. Diesel Component Works (DCW) has been set up by the railways at Patiala for manufacturing and repairs of components of diesel locos and sub-assemblies. The project has attained the rated capacity for manufacture of components for diesel engines, its repairs and rebuilding of diesel locomotives. Bulk of passenger coaches are manufactured in Integral Coach Factory (ICF), Perambur, Madras and Rail Coach Factory, Kapurthala. Integral Coach Factory (ICF), manufactured 1,038 fully furnished coaches and the new Rail Coach Factory (RCF) set up at Kapurthala produced 1,025 coaches in 1993-94. In addition to ICF and RCF, three are two more units in public sector, viz., M/s. Jessops, Calcutta and Bharat Earth Movers Limited (BEML), Bangalore, who also manufacture coaches and electrical multiple units. A wheel and axel plant has been set up at Bangalore to cut down imports in this field. The plant performed excellently during 1993-94 and helped the railways to save valuable foreign exchange.

Railways production units are striving to develop new products for the Indian Railways. AC3-Tier coach has been manufactured by RCF which would make AC travel cheaper and comfortable. Further, production of 5000 HP electric locomotives and full efficient diesel locomotive have also commenced at chittaranjan Locomoive Works and Diesel Locomotive Works respectively. Diesel multiple units for suburban non-electrified routes and mainline electric multiple units for electrified sections have been manufactured by Integral Coach Factory, Madras.

Passenges originating had risen from 12,840 lakh in 1950-51 to 37,080 lakh in 1993-94 and passenger kilometre from 66.52 billion in 1950-51 to 296.2 billion in 1993-94. Despite constraint of resources, the railways have been able to cope with increasing demand of passenger traffic. Railways are the premier mode of passenger transport both for long distance and suburban traffic. During 1993-94, Indian Railways introduced 135 new trains, extended the run of 49 trains and increased the frequency of 10 trains in non-suburban sector. Similarly, in suburban sector, railways introduced 88 new trains and extended the run of 154 trains.

Freight Traffic

Rapid progress in industrial and agricultural sectors has generated higher level of demand for rail transport, particularly in core sectors like coal, iron and steel, ores, petroleum products and essential commodities such as foodgrains, fertilizers, cement, sugar, salt, edible oils, etc. Revenue freight traffic increased from 732 lakh tonnes in 1950-51 to 3,587 lakh tonnes in 1993-94. Transport effort measured in terms of net tonne kilometres (NTKm) increased from 38 billion in 1950-51 to 252.4 billion in 1993-94. Some of the measures taken for improvement are: (i) line capacity augmentation on certain critical sectors and modernisation of signalling system; (ii) measures such as unit train operation for bulk commodities like coal; (iii) increase in roller-bearing equipped wagons; (iv) increase in trailing loads to 4,500 tonnes; (v) operation 'UNI-GAUGE' on Indian Railways; (vi) strengthening the track structure by providing heavier and stronger rails and concrete sleepers; and (vii) production of prototype electric locomotive of 5000 HP for freight operation by Chittaranjan Locomotive Works.

Operational Efficiency

The railway Budget, presented by the Railway Minister, Mr. Ram Vilas Paswan in the Lok Sabha, took care not to increase the fare structure for the second class and suburban travellers whose reactions can be instant if not violent. Mr. Paswan made it clear that the largest public sector employer was willing to share the burden of meeting some of the development and social goals of the Government.

Thus came a clear commitment to extend the railway network in the backward regions of the country. A railway line to Kashmir, some capitals of the North eastern States and some hill region of UP is going to be a reality in the near future. Mr. Paswan also announced that while all 56,000 casual labourers would be absorbed, he would also terminate the move to engage the private sector in carrying out certain services like clearing operations so that the jobs reverted back to the employees of the Indian Railways.

As in the previous year, the upper class passengers (AC and first class) were asked to bear a 10 per cent hike in fares while the second class sleeper travellers were asked to pay only 5 poer cent extra. The night travel cost is clearly rising every year, though few would crib about it if it is accompanied by better services.

Some economists, however, have not been impressed with the decision to spare the second class traveller because it makes little sense to concentrate on higher classes alone for resource mobilisation. About 1.20 crore people travel by second class, but they account for only about 10 per cent of passenger traffic. It need not be emphasised thay even today the majority of Indians either do not travel at all or board a train very rarely.

A big hike that has already alarmed the industry was projected infreight charges: 12 per cent against 10 per cent last year. A basket of 15 items, deemed essential commodities, was exempted from this hike, though it is doubtful if these commodities would eventually manage to hold the price line.

The official estimate in Rail Bhawan is that the 12 per cent increase in freight traffic would contribute no more tan a 0.127 per cent rise in the wholesale price index. Industry is worried because it has been introduced at a time of industrial slowdown and rising inflation.

Mr. Paswan's efforts at "selective" adjustments in the fare and freight structure will yield him a revenue of Rs. 1800 crore which is almost double the amount last year. This would please rail Bhawan, though not necessarily for long if the hike in freight rates results in further loss of goods traffic to the road transport sector.

The share of the railways in the country's total freight traffic has declined drastically to 42 per cent from nearly 90 per cent in 1950—51. If the railways hope to capture at least 50 per cent of the freight traffic in the next two years or so, any further upward revision may not be wise, though it is hard to see how it can be avoided. Besides, the 12 per cent hike in freight has come in the wake of 10 per cent hike announced just seven months ago when Mr. Paswan presented his first budget.

It is a argued that the periodic steep rise in freight and passenger fares could be avoided, or minimised, if the railways improved their efficiency and functioned purely as a commercial propositon. This may not be such an easy task in Indian conditions where, for instance, the demand for more trains goes on mounting even when in other countries the number of trains is being brought down. There has been a steadyu deterioration in the operating ratio of the Indian railways which is an indicator of how the revenues are used to meet operating expenses.

Possibly because introducing new trains has now become so common, the budget did not have a long list of new trains, except a modest number of five "golden jubilee" and seven other trains. Frequency of 10 trains was also increased. Of the 17 new lines announced, the Planning Commission has given clearances to 12. But a generous number of surveys—37—for new lines would be taken up in 1997—98, apart from five for gauge conversion and three for doubling.

The budget might have included many more new schemes if only the size of its Plan had been kept at Rs. 11,000 crore, as demanded by the Railways, and not pegged at Rs. 8300 crore. The budgetary support at Rs. 1831 crore works out to 22 per cent when the railways had pressed for a hefty 40 per cent support.

The budget has set a target of carrying the highest ever freight trafic of 430 million tonnes in 1997—98, projecting the figure on the success of meeting the previous year's target of 410 MT. However, it is to be remembered that much of the freight carried in the previous year was low revenue yielding traffic as a result of which the financial target was missed by Rs. 325 crore. This was made up partly because the passenger traffic earnings went up by Rs. 130 crore. The Railways also carried more coal and ffodgrain, though the latter is low income yielding traffic.

The activities of Civil Aviation are broadly divided into three areas; operational, infrastructural and regulatory-cum-developmental. On the operational side, Indian Airlines Ltd. and private airlines (scheduled and non-scheduled) provide domestic air services. Air India Ltd. provides international air services. Indian Airlines Ltd. Also provides air services to neighbouring countries. Pawan Hans Helicopters Ltd. provides helicopter support services primarily to the petroleum sector. Infrastructural facilities are provide by the Airports Authority of India (AAI). The two authorities viz. International Airports Authority (NAA) were merged on April 1, 1995 to form a single authority viz. Airports Authority of India (AAI) as a result of enactment of Airport Authority of India Act, 1994. The regulatory and developmental functions are lookded after by the Ministry of Civil Aviation and the Directorate General of Civil Aviation.

With the repealing of the Air Corporation Act, 1953, on March 1, 1994, the monopoly of Indian Airlines, Air India and Vayudoot over scheduled air transport serivices came to an end. Seven private operators, who were hitherto operation as air texis, have been granted the status of scheduled airlines. In addition, 21 air taxi operators have been given the permit for charter/non-schedule air transport services. A new policy for private investment in civil aviation has been announced allowing for 40 per cent foreign equity in domestic airlines.

Domestic air services are operating in a competitive

environment and this has effectively been in existence since April, 1993. By September, 1996, 34 aircrafts in the 120 plus category belonging to the private airlines were in operation. The natural consequence of creating a competitive environment in this sector was that, by March 1996, 41.1 per cent of the domestic air transport was being catered to by private air services. The number of passengers carried by private operators has increased from 15,000 in 1990 to 4.1 lakh in 1992, 29.2 lakh in 1993, 36 lakh in 1994 and 48.9 lakh during 1995. The ushering in of competition in domestic services has two major implications for Indian Airlines. First, it had to share the market on its profitable trunk routes with private operators. Second, it had to contend with the loss of critically skilled personnel to private operators who offered much higher emoluments. This affected its ability to optimally deploy its existing aircraft capacity. India Airlines has since geared itself towards coping with the challenges brought forth by competition.

Several measures which have been taken by the public carriers mainly centered on making the organisation adopt a market oriented approach to decision making and to considerably improve the quality of its product. It has improved its passenger facilities both on board and on the ground, on time performance, flight safety measures and has also increased employee participation to provide better services.

For Indian Airlines Ltd, the year 1995-96 has been considerably better than the last few years. The Company made an operating profit of Rs. 156.51 crore in 1995-96 as against Rs. 36.24 crore in 1994-95 i.e. an increase of 332 per cent. The Company has laid stress on passenger facilitation by increasing the seat pitch on the Boeing-737. It has also increased the number of seats in the Executive class of A-320. Other measures include improvement of flight service, adoption of convenient time schedules and agreements with Global CRS companies to enable passengers to have access to flight schedules globally. These measures taken by the Company have started yielding positive results, and the seat load factor increased to 73.4 per cent in 1995-96 as against 69.7 per cent in 1994-95.

Indian Airlines laid stress on cargo promotion in association with M/s. GATI and its earnings from cargo have increased from Rs. 89.7 crores in 1994-95 to Rs. 112.7 crore in 1995-96. The company also provided the ground handling services to various foreign and domestic carriers. As a result, the company's profitability increased and the net loss came down from Rs. 188.7 crore in 1994-95 to Rs. 110 crore in 1995-96. The Company carreid 7.7 million passengers and performed 722.8 Revenue Tonne Kilometers in 1995-96.

Indian Airlines still incurred losses due to the heavy incidence of depreciation, interest and financing charges associated with its A-320 fleet. It has also had to contend with increases in overhead costs, increases in exchange rates, etc. During 1995-96, the company increased its domestic fares effective from 1.10 1995 on an average by 20 per cent and dollar fares with effect from 1, January 1996. But this was not sufficient to meet the increasing costs of operations.

The price of ATF was revised from 3rd July, 1996 and the annual impact of this has been estimated to be Rs. 60 crore in 1996-97. Consequently the company has increased its domestic fares effective from 22nd September, 1996 and proposes to increase dollar fares effective from 1st March, 1997 to offset some of its losses. Constant efforts are being made to monitor the uneconomical routes and to improve its market share by aggressive marketing strategies.

Air India Ltd. incurred a net loss of Rs. 271.8 croie in 1995-96 as against profit of Rs. 40.8 in 1994-95. According to provisional estimates the company also incurred a net loss of Rs. 195 crore during April-September, 1996. While the total operating revenue of the company increasd by 14.6 per cent from Rs. 2980 crore in 1994-95 to Rs. 3,426.5 crore in 1995-96, the total operating expenditure of the company increased by 24.9 per cent from Rs. 2,920 crore in 1994-95 to Rs. 3,647.5 crore in 1995-96. The resumption of losses was due to factors such as flights and disruption of flight schedules; the incidence of depreciation and interest on account of acquistion of four Boeing 747-400 aircraft; increase in expenditure by 24.9 per cent due to insurance, fuel and oil, landing lease, rental and hire charges; increases in allowances payable to the employees and payment of additional perquistes as per the Memorandum of Understanding reached with the Unions, associations, guilds; and the drop in its yield. Air India's overall load factor of 62 per cent is also low compared to other international airlines. Air India's share of international traffic originating from India came down from 42 per cent in 1981 to 35 per cent in 1991 and 20.4 per cent in 1994. However, in 1995 Air India's market share had improved marginally to 22 per cent.

In addition four B-747-400 aircraft which were acquired recently, Air India acquired two more B-747-400 aircraft in December 1996. To provide for growth in the short-term, Air India wet-leased a few aircraft. Five new stations were added in 1995 i.e. Manchester, Amsterdam, Tel-Aviv, Entebee and Perth. With the acquisition of two new aircraft, new destinations like Chicago and Zurich are being introduced. Air India has formulated a four pronged revitalisation strategy comprising the following: (i) growth in fleet, capacity, passenger carriage and market share, (iii) increase in efficiency and greater productivity, and (iv) development of human resources. There has been an improvement in on time performance of Air India which is over 85 per cent in 1994-95. While profits have declined, most of the physical parameters have improved in 1995-96 as compared to 1994-95.

Pawan Hans Helicopters Limited (PHL) basically provides helicopter support services to the petroleum sector i.e. ONGC and Oil India Limited and connects remote and inaccessible areas. It also provides air support services to several customers which include the Governments of Punjab, Madhya Pradesh and Arunachal Pradesh, Lakshdweep Administration, GAIL, BSF, and the Revenue Department. The total revenue flying hours during 1995-96 were 18,582, as compared to 18,458 during 1994-95. The revenue earnings and net profits during 1995-96 were Rs. 156.68 crore and Rs. 37.26 crore respectively, compared to Rs. 134.25 crore and Rs. 39.97 crore respectively in 1994-95. The flying hours during April-September, 1996 were 10470 and revenue and net profit were Rs. 87.72 and Rs. 26.50 crore respectively.

The International Airports Division (IAD) of Airports Authority of India (AAI) manages, operates and develops five internaional airports at Mumbai, Calcutta, Delhi, Chennai and Thiruvanthapuram. IAD earned a net profit of Rs. 113.59 crore in 1995-96 as compared to a net profit of Rs. 97.7 crore during 1994-95. During 1995-96, expenditure grew by 35 per cent whereas revenue increased by 27 per cent. Passenger and Cargo traffic at 256.4 lakh and 561582 tonnes during 1995-96 were higher by 12 per cent and 14.2 per cent respectively than in 1994-95. IAD has declared a divided of Rs. 22.72 crore (20 per cent of post tax profit) for 1995-96 as against Rs. 15.28 crore (25 per cent of paid up capital as on 31.3.1195) for 1994-95.

A number of projects like modernisation of air traffic

services at Mumbai and Delhi airports, installation of Airport Surveillance Radar/Monopulse Secondary Surveillance Radar at Ahmedabad, Guwahati, Hyderabad and Thiruvananthapuram, development of 12 model airports for upgradation of facilities and improvement in the quality of the services at the airports have been taken up. Although investments in airports of the North Eastern region are not economical, a large number of operations have been taken up there. Sixty per cent of investment on projects which have the prior approval of NEC is borne by the North Eastern Council. Development work in other areas like Jammu & Kashmir, Lakshadweep, Himachal Pradesh, Andaman & Nicobar are also under way.

The Civil Aviation Sector has two functional divsions–operational and infrastructural. On the operational side, Indian Airlines, Vayudoot and private air taxis provide domestic air services and Air India provides international air services. Pawan Hans provides helicopter services ONGC in its shore operations and to inaccessible areas and difficult terrains. Indian Airlines operations also extend to the neighbouring countries, South East Asia and Middle East. Vayudoot Limited is in the process of being merged with Indian Airlines. Its network which linkds the remote places in the North Eastern Region is being taken over by the newly created Short Haul Operations Department of Indian Airlines. India has been a member of International Civil Aviation Organisation (ICAO). India got elected to the council of ICAO in the triennial elections held in September 1992 at Montreal by a record margin of votes.

The Department of Civil Aviation is responsible for the formulation of national policies and programmes for developmnt and regulation of civil aviation and for devising and implementing schemes for orderly growth and expansion of civil air transport. Its functions also extend to overseeing the provision of airport facilities, air traffic services and carriage of passengers and goods by air. The Department is also administratively responsible for the Commission of Railway Safety, a statutory body set up under the Railway Act.

Policy Initiatives

In a major policy change, the Government has ended the monopoly of Indian Airlines and Air India on the scheduled operations by repealing the Air Corporation Act, 1953. The Government has also converted Indian Airlines and Air India into public limited companies to enable these airlines to tap the capital market to meet their growth requirements and also to give them greater autonomy in order to face the challenges of stiff competition. There are at present six private scheduled airlines operating on the domestic network rendering the passengers a wider choice of flights. Apart from this, 15 air taxi operators are providing non-scheduled air services. The existing policy on air taxi services provide for a route dispersal plan to ensure operation of a minimum number of services in the north eastern region, Andaman and Nicobar Islands, Lakshadweep and Jammu and Kashmir.

In order to help the Indian exporters and make their exports more competitive, the Government had introduced in April 1990 an 'open sky policy' for cargo. Under this policy any foreign airlines or association of exporters can bring freighters to the country for upliftment of cargo. The Government have also permitted market forces to determine cargo tariff, with IATA rates as the floor rates.

The charter flights bringing foreign tourists in the country are now allowed to operate to certain domestic airports cleared for tourist charter operations in addition to the international airports. The minimum payment to the Indian tour operator by the foreign charter operator is 350 US dollars per person for a seven days package for the period from 1 October to 31 March ana 300 US dollars for the period from 1 April to 30 September. However for tourist from SAARC countries, the amount to be remitted is 50 per cent of the aforesaid amount.

Air taxi services can be operated as non-scheduled flights both on chartered and non-chartered basis to 93 airports in the country open to civil operations. The seating capacity of aircraft used for air taxi operations is so regulated as to ensure an orderly growth of air transport services in the country. The air taxi operators are free to charge any fare in their own commercial judgement. The procedure for import of aircraft for air taxi services has been simplified by dispensing with the requirement of licences for import of aircraft, components, etc.

Directorate General of Civil Aviation (DGCA) is the regulatory organisation for enforcing civilian regulations, air safety and airworthiness standards. It is responsible for (i) regulation of air transport services to/from/within India; (ii) formulation and implementation of standards of airworthiness applicable to all civil aircraft registered in India; (iii) certification of aircraft operators and licensing of air crew, engineers and airports; (iv) investigation of air accidents and incidents; and (v) rendering advice on matters relating to air transportation and processing of aviation legislation. DGCA also coordinates all regulatory functions with the International Civil Aviation Organisation (ICAO).

Bureau of Civil Aviation Security (BCAS) is a nodal body on all civil aviation security matters. It is responsible for the formulation of the National Civil Aviation Security programme and its application. It sets the guidelines/standards of the security measures and monitors their enforcement at the airporst through periodical/surprise inspections and conduct of dummy checks and also imparts training in aviation security on a regular basis. It has four regional offices at Bombay, Delhi, Calcutta and Madras, which have a bomb detection and disposal squads.

The Airports Authority of India formed on 1 April 1995 by merging the International Airports Authority of India and National Airports Authority, is responsible for providing safe, efficient air traffic services and aeronautical communication services for effective control of air traffic in the Indian air space.

The Authority manages 92 civil airports and 28 civil air terminals at defence airfields in the country. It controls and manages the entire Indian air spce extending even beyond the territorial limits of the country, as accepted by the International Civil Aviation Organisation (ICAO). The Authority comprises of a National Airports Division and an International Airports Division. Air Traffic Control (ATC) Services, Communication Services and Radio Navigational aids are provided by the National Airports Division at all the airports including the five internationals airports viz.,Delhi, Calcutta, Madras, Bombay and Thiruvananthapuram. It has a Civil Aviation Training College at Allahabad which imparts training to various operational cadres like communication, ATC/radar controllers. The College is being modernised under a UNDP plan and will emerge as an important training establishment in the South-East Asia conforming to ICAO standards. It also has a Fire Service Training School at Narayanpur near Calcutta for imparting training and conducting refresher courses in fire fighting and rescue services.

The International Airports Division of the Authority

is responsible for providing services and facilities for efficient operation of air transport at the five international airports of the country. The Division is also responsible for the planning, construction, maintenance of terminal buildings, airfield pavements, visual ground aids, passengers and cargo handling, airport fire services etc., at the international airports. It has established an Institute of Aviation Management and the Fire Training Centre at New Delhi to impart training in aviation management and fire fighting/rescue services.

India has bilateral air services agreements with 74 countries. Air India Limited is the major international carrier of the country. It operates services to USA, Canada, Europe, the Russian Confederation, the Gulf/ Middle East, East Asia, Far East, Africa, Australia. Air India owns a fleet of 26 air craft consisting of nine B747-200, two B747-300, four B747-400, three A300-B4 and eight A310-300 aircraft. Air India has also plans to augment its fleet through the induction of three A310-300 aircraft in 1995-96 and two additional B747-400 aircraft in 1996-97. During 1993-94, Air India carried 19,77,668 passengers as against 21,81,000 in 1992-93. The drop in carriage of passengers has been due to flight engineers strike and changes in scheduled deployment due to induction of Boeing 747-400 aircraft and training of pilots.

Indian Airlines is the major domestic air carrier of the country. It also provides services to 11 countries viz., Pakistan, Maldives, Nepal, Sri Lanka, Malaysia, Bangladesh, Thailand, Singapore, UAE, Oman and Kuwait. Its operations cover 66 destinations including 14 abroad. The Airlines owns a fleet of 10 Airbus A300, 30 Airbus A320 and 18 Boeing B737 (excluding 2 Boeing 737 set aside for disposal) and 2F-27 (leased out). Presently six private scheduled airlines and 15 air taxi operators are supplementing the air transport services provided by Indian Airlines on the domestic sectors.

Pawan Hans Limited has been providing helicopter support services to the petroleum sector including ONGC, Oil India Ltd., and Enron Oil and Gas, USA at Bombay. Apart from this, it also provides services to certain state government and public sector undertakings. The company presently has an operational fleet of 20 Dauphin, one Bell 206L4, two Robinson R 44 helicopters, as also two leased MI 172 helicopters. Out of these, 11 Dauphins and two MI 172 helicopter are presently deployed with ONGC for their offishore oil exploration work. One Dauphin each is operating with NTPC, Government of Punjab, Lakshadweep Administration and Enron Oil and Gas, USA at Bombay. One Robinson helicopter is leased to Oil India Limited. One bell 206L4 and one Robinson R 44 are being used for business charters for which there is a growing demand. In addition, the company has undertaken operational and maintenance contracts of helicopters belonging to Government of Madhya Pradesh, Gas Authority of India, Border Security Force and a private party. It achieved total flying task of 19,270 hours during 1994-95 as compared to 18,812 hours in the previous year. The average monthly deployment of helicopters has also improved.

Indira Gandhi Rashtriya Uran Akademi located at Fursastganj (UP) is an autonomous body established to provide an opportunity to commercial pilots to achieve higher standards in flying and ground training. The Akademi is equipped with modern and sophisticated trainer aircraft, flight simulators, computer based training system (CBT) and excellent audiovisual training aids. Commercial Pilots Licence courses with multi-engine endorsement and instrument rating are conducted on a regular basis. The Akademi has trained 248 fixed wing pilots and 20 rotory wing pilots till now. Besides there are 35 flying clubs/institutes which impart ab initio training and 11 gliding clubs/wings in the country.

Research and Development

Research and Development Directorate of DGCA is responsible for; (i) type certification of civil aircraft, engines, propellors and equipment: (ii) approval of modifications and repair schemes of civil aircraft; (iii) development testing of indigenous aircraft materials, parts and equipment; (iv) scientific laboratory investigation work on failed aircraft/power plant; sructural parts and components; (v) design and development of gliders, light trainer aircraft, glider launching winches; (vi) quality control monitoring and testing of fuel samples, etc; and (vii) economics of aircraft operation and performance evaluation.

With our large pool of skilled technical manpower, relatively low manpower costs and extensive manufacturing base, we should be in a position to have a much larger share of aerospace market from the West, says the author. Aviation in India strarted witha special flight by the grand old man of Indian aviation Mr. J.R.D. Tata and since then, aviation has never looked back though this vital means of transport has not been without its periods of glory and setbacks.

Standing as it does now at the threshold of the 21st century, India can boast of new planes like the spanking new 747—400s, but it has to accept the blot of unfortunate crash of the Saudia plane and Kazakh Airlines aircraft, which is a pointer towards what needs to be done.

Aviation is one of the most significant technological advances of our time. Apart from its strategic importance, it has a major role in economic development.

Our country has been fortunate in having started aeronautics related activities as early as the 1940s when Hindustan Aircraft Ltd., forerunner of today's Hindustan Aeronautics Ltd. was established in Bangalore. Over the years, a number of academic and R&D institutions have also been set up which have created an extensive range of skills and capabilities. The strong domestic base contributes to the capacity of our aerospace industry to generate significant economic activity.

India's industry is reaching out of forge new partnerships as our economy is opening up. This applies to the aerospace industry as well. With all our experience and skills, India's share is only 0.1 per cent in the world aerospace market which is valued at Us $ 300 billion per annum.

Prospects

With out large pool of skilled technical manpower, relatively low manpower costs and extensive manufacturing base, we should be in a position to have a much largest share of the market from the West. The strengths of our academic and R&D institutions and the extensive capacity of our industry in both the public and private sectos have to be put together to meet our nation's requirements as also to develop an international presence.

By the year 2010, it is projected that passenger traffic will more than double, Aisa-Pacific being the fastest growing region. Airport infrastructure requirements upto the year 2010 are expected to be of the order of US $ 350 billion. Large investments will also be required in air traffic management, communication, navigation and surveillance systems and upgrading of other systems at airports.

Within the country, over the next 10 to 15 years, a

number of new aircraft may have to be inducted for a variety of uses. Airport systems will have to be upgraded and manpower will hve to be trained on a large scale.

We have had notable success in a number of areas such as making training and combat aircraft, as also space vehicles and satellites. New knowledge and skills have been acquired in the curse of design and development of launch vehicles, the Light Combat Aircraft and the Advanced Light Helicopter. Using these skills, we can provide internationally competitive products and services.

To our friends from other countries we can say that there are ample oportunities for cooperation in the growing Indian economy and in the aviation sector. India would welcome mutually beneficial partnership in which we share knowledge, skills and resources. The cooperation can be in a manner in which the strengths of two sides are drawn on and commercial benefits shared equitably.

During the year 1995-96 the domestic air transport operations in the country witnessed appreciable growth in traffic as the total traffic carried by Indian Airlines and private operators reached the 12.8 million mark. Seven private operators were granted status of scheduled operators and 18 companies are holding air taxi operator's permit.

Better Performance

During the said period scheduled airlines operated 67,908 flights carrying 49,71,064 passengers and air taxi operators have operated 8,609 flights carrying 1,16,153 passengers. Tourist charter flights had brought in 84,811 tourists by 844 flights during the year.

Air India introduced four new destinations during 1995-96–Manchester, Amsterdam, Entebbe and Tel Aviv.

Also the airline operated 182 flights from different points in India carrying 18,513 Haj pilgrims.

Indian Airlines improved its operating profits form Rs. 36.24 crore in 1994-95 to Rs. 114.35 crore in 1995-96.

Pawan Hans Limited increased its net profit to Rs. 51.58 crore during the last year. The company started helicopter services to Arunachal Pradesh in the North-east in December thereby meeting a long standing demand for airlinks from the State. It has also finalised the purchase of two Bell helicopters and part of its fleet expansion programme.

Alliance Air (Airline Allied Services Ltd. a wholly owned subsidiary of Indian Airlines) started its airline operations from 15 April' 96 after the transfer of one Boeing 737 aircraft from Indian Airlines.

The second aircraft was transferred by Indian Airlines on 25 April, followed by two more planes in July and August this year. The route network was further expanded when Alliance Air took over services of the fifth and sixth planes in the first week of September. It has taken all its senior personnel from Indian Airlines adding upto 183 employees.

The on-time performance of Indian Airlines has significantly improved with the passenger load factor going up from 68 per cent in 1994 to 72.3 per cent in 1995. The Average number of passengers carried by Indian Airlines has also increased by about 5 per cent during 1995.

Special marketing efforts have been initiated, which include setting up of special counters, Computer Based Automatic Information System, KERB squads to inform passengers of delays and cancellations, introduction of J class in all A 320s and improvement in inflight service and improved safety. The airline also added Kaula

Lumpur and Yangon (Rangoon) to its international network. The year ended with Indian Airlines getting the best airline award against the stronger contenders in the private sector.

Last year saw the process of stablisation and substantial presence of the private airline operators in the domestic transport industry.

Twenty-four aircraft were sanctioned to the private airlines, including 13 Boeing aircarft. The total seats carried by both Indian Airlines and private operators add up to 50,000 seats a day.

While Indian Airlines has a capacity of 28,000 seats, the private operators have 21,000. The total passengers carried per day has been around 36,000 representing an overall load factor of 73.6 per cent. Private operators carry 40 per cent of the traffic with their fleet. The domestic airline traffic has increased dramatically from 7.5 million in 1990 to about 12 million by 1995.

As far as international airlines are concerned, more than 2 million additional seats have been offered to international passengers and Air India entered into unique code sharing agreements with four airlines.

Air India has seen a great deal of transition and consolidation. The main thrust areas of the airlines were expansion of routs, introduction of new destinations, better product, more productive utilisation of resources and improvement of image. After a gap of a decade or so, Air India expanded its fleet by inducting four B747-400 aircraft, orders were placed for two more and were delivered in November this year.

New destinations like Perth, Johannesburg, Durban, Manchester and Amsterdam were opened, as have Madrid, Entebbe and Tel Aviv. More international operations were introduced from Chennai, Thiruvananthapuram and Bangalore and the number of direct point services increased.

An ambitious programme of fleet renewal is being taken up to achieve growth of operation. Though Air India's profits had dwindled this year because of increased interest and depreciation burden due to acquisition of new aircraft and increase in cost of operations, the health of the airline is improving.

Determination and dedication to regain its lost place of pride amongst the international carriers is making the airlines forge ahead. The passenger load factor has increased from 59 per cent to 68 per cent. The number of passengers carried showed an upward trend too.

Several measures have been taken by India to upgrade its product and services. These include introduction and use of Malayalam language for the Gulf sector, upgraded inflight services in long-haul sectors and setting up of special counters and multiple check-in facility at Delhi and Bombay airports. Airport lounges at major centres like Hong Kong, Bangkok, New York and London have been upgraded.

Air India has entered into code sharing arrangement with Scandinavian Air Services, United Airlines, Finnair and Kuwait Airways. It has also entered into joint venture agreements with Gulf Air, Malaysian Airways and Air Mauritius.

In 1995 the profits of Air India declined considerably due to reduction in overally yield, increade in expenditure and hiring of aircraft, higher material consumption and outside repairs due to aging fleet, world-wide increase in insurance rates and increased depreciation and interest due to acquisition of new aircraft.

The process of acquiring the Medium Capacity Long Range aircraft is in an advanced stage. The year ended with the hope that Air India will expand its network dramatically, once it inducts new aircraft by phasing out the aging aircraft.

Another major development was the merger of National Airports Authority of India and International Airports Authority of India into a single entity called Airports Authority of India to give a unified direction. During the year 1995, tremendous work has been done in the construction of terminal buildings, providing navigational aids and installation of sophisticated radars at Thiruvananthapuram and Hyderabad. Special thrust has been given to the North-eastern region, Jammu & Kashmir and smaller airfields in Uttar Pradesh.

New Terminal buildings have been completed at Jaipur, Lucknow, Vadodara and Calicut airports. Sophisticated communication facilities were provided at many airports—Agartala, Belgaum, Jorhat, Tezpur, Tirupati, Jammu, Varanasi, Bangalore and Calicut. Over Rs. 440 crore are planned to be spent in the coming year for the development of airport infrastructure.

Lucknow and Jaipur model airports have already been inagurated and work on the other ten airports is in an advanced stage of completion. Work has also been undertaken for construction of new airports at Kargil in Jammu & Kashmir, Taru in Meghalaya, Lengpuri in Mizoram and Androth in Lakshdweep.

A big boost was given to private investment in airport construct with a cabinet clearance on the proposal for Calicutt airport. A memorandum of understanding was signed between the Government of Karnataka and private consortium for constuction of an international airport in Balgalore in December last year. It is hoped that all 12 model airports would be ready by the end of the financial year 1996-97, Providing better and safe services to the discerning traveller.

Pawan Hans Limited has completed 10 years ofits service to the nation. The organisation has earned a profit of Rs. 40 crore during 1994-96. The company has started helicopter services in Arunachal Pradesh from December, 1995 by deploying on Dauphin helicopter having a capacity for 8 passengers. Next year, it will substitute Dauphin helicopter by a large 25 seater helicopter.

The company is planning expansion of its fleet to meet the demand of ONGC and other customers. It is purchasing 2 Bell 206 L4 helicopters to meet requirements of Customs Department and 2MI-172 helicopters to meet ONGC requirements. The company proposes to add upto 10 more helicopters to its existing fleet by March '97.

Proper dissemination of requisite information in a disaggregate and easy-to-understand manner is an effective means to plug many leakages in the delivery system. In fact, such information concerning development works at grass roots level should be made available without any favour or fear, it need be, against small payment for photocopies, etc. so that action may be taken against the erring persons concerned. This leads to the issue of decentralization and dissemination of information on development and welfare activities programmewise and villagewise, including the financial inputs, implementing authority, method, sources of funds and information and so on. Broadly, the areas to be covered for dissemination of information includes, inter alia, subjects asigned to the local bodies as well as basic minimum services in an easy to understand language and through accessible media, modern and\or traditional. Since the programme and schemes differ from place to place, the relevant information requires to be area-specific. In short, the right type of information to be made available and accessible to the people is desired in a disaggregate and comprehensible manner. Hence the whole process should be people-based and people-oriented. It should not be that unnecessary and unwanted information gets piled up. The need-based open house information system is a powerful tool in the hands of the people which will go a long way to achieve greater transparency, accountability and resultant efficiency in functioning at all levels—Central, State and sub-State—down to the village level.

It should be mandatory on the part of the government to release such information at all levels not only sectorwise but also workwise and villagewise. Kerala has reportedly brought out some 600 booklets on plan schemes in local language for dissemination among the Panchayats. On a very limited scale, the Maharashtra-based voluntary organization like the Foundation for Research in Community Health (FRCH) does so in Marathi and even Dr. Chitra Naik's voluntary organization has also attempted in this direction. Thus, in this great endeavour, besides the government and Panchayati Raj, the voluntary organizations, and committed social workers like Anna Hazare play a predominant role in carrying out such widespread awareness campaign and bringing out transparency in activities.

In this context, resource mapping may be a useful exercise for total resources available at various levels which will provide a broad spectrum of the resource deployment. It would not be impossible to bring out such information on a massive scale in this hi-info-tech age.

The delivery channel, open house information system, Panchayati Raj and such organizations are only means to achieve the absolute end of poverty. This calls for the strengthening of productivity potential of the economy and creating space for involving the poor in the development process through decentralization ensuring participatory democracy with proper institution and organization and empowerment of the deprived ones. Most of the present poverty allocation programmes are relief oriented rather than development oriented to achieve a sustainable growth with egalitarian bias. But the alleviation approach will never be able to root out poverty within a reasonable time-frame even with a higher growth.

It is common knowledge that even a good organization can be badly run. Ultimately, it may be emphasized that an individual can, make or mar the system. Here the character counts. And charity begins at home. How prophetic, today, are the words of Dr. S. Radhakrishnan uttered on 14 August 1947, "A free India will be judged by the way it will serve the interests of the common man in the matter of food, clothing, shelter and the social activities.... Unless we destroy corruption in high places, love of power, profiteering and black-marketing, we will not be able to raise the standards of efficiency in administration as well as in production and distribution of the necessary goods of life."

Even on the eve of the recent Republic Day, President Shankar Dayal Sharma emphasized, "I feel convinced that India's need today is for a profound moral and ethical rejuvenation.... Simultaneously, there must be a forthright and outright rejection of casteism and communalism with its sinister nexus with corruption and criminality.... Our approach will have to be value-based and people-centred."

In a developing country like ours, the new economic policy aiming at more market-oriented liberalization, privatization, and globalization does not, as the experience of other countries in a similar situation suggests, appear to be very friendly to the backward areas and the weaker sections of the society. It is something like a five-star hotel, open to all without any distinction of caste, creed, colour or status. But actually who can avail of it? Thus, without adequate infrastructure facilities and purchasing power, the poor often get marginalised in the process of development and the spatial and income disparities get widened. It is also implicitly agreed that the reform process would hurt the poor most and, therefore, there is need for a 'human face' approach which would make the process less painful. Hence, this calls for an effective State intervention with poverty alleviation and other welfare measures.

Funds

Keeping in view the above fact, even the Ninth Plan (1997–2002) approach paper is reported to have envisaged an outlay of Rs. 60,000 crore for rural development which is double the amount allocated for the purpose in the Eighth Plan. So far so good. But mere more allocation of resources will not solve the problem. In fact, there is a dearth of a scientifically co-ordinated approach to rural development, management, organization and involvement of the people in the development process. So the most important question is: How will this amount be spent and how far their benefits will percolate down to the grass roots level? Our past experience so far has not been so encouraging. Even after five decades of Independence, one-third of our people (310 million) live below the poverty line. They do not have sufficient food to meet the calorie requirement of their bodies. Out of a rupee spent by the government, it is borne out, hardly 10 to 15 paise reach to the poor at the end, the remaining paise absorbed by the administration and leaked out to vested interest. If such is the state of affairs, out of Rs. 60,000 crore envisaged for rural development, only Rs. 6,000 to 9,000 crore is likely to be spent during the five years, erosion in the inductory value due to inflation apart.

In the absence of a sound delivery system, the financial allocations are not often fully fructified and their benefits do not reach out unto the last poor in the expected way. Investments sans proper organization go awry. So far the delivery organisation has been one of the weakest links in our planning process. However, there is a silver lining to the dark clouds. The recently re-incarnated Panchayati Raj institutions (PRIs) can delivery the goods, provided they are empowered with adequate funds, authority, accountability and requisite information on village-level workers concerned and programmes for development and welfare. Today the poor illiterate villagers do not know fully the details of development works carried out in their villages. They do not get information on the money spent on such works and the copies of bills, vouchers and the muster roll of the workers in respect of construction of schools, health centres, community halls, roads, wells, houses, etc. to verify the facts. Sometimes the works reported to have been completed are only on paper. In a sense, information is power. The suppression of information from the people, breeds embezzlement, misappropriation and corruption. Over the years, enormous amounts have been spent in the name of village uplift and welfare of the poor and crores of rupees have been misappropriated. Taken together the amount involved in such decentralized corruption can total up to a huge scam of the meanest type looting the poor. Today even mute animals are not spared as in the reported 'fodder-scam.

Communication

With the number of telephones in India aggregating to a

mere 5.8 million to service a population of over 850 million people, telecommunications is an industry of tremendous growth potential. It is also one of the most profitable business areas in India today with the pay back on a line being only two years.

The new Ministry of Communication has drawn up a very ambitious 26 point program for this Industry. Some of the highlights are that private participation has been invited for building and operation of telecom networks in 'growth centres and satellite towns'.

In the new Industrial Policy, telecom equipment was delicenced and thrown open to foreign investment. Several joint ventures came up- GPI and K.K. Birla, Ericcson with their long term collaborators the Jiwarajkars, AT&T with Tata Telecom, Fujitsu with the Punjab State Electronic Production and Development Corporation and Alcatel with B.K. Modi. Of these companies gearing up to meet the indigenous requirements, the last two are near ready to commence production of equipment to meet the specifications set out by the Department of Telecommunications.

The Ministry of Communication has in October this year allowed eight private companies to establish cellular telephone systems in the four metropolitan cities kof Delhi, Bombay, Calcutta and Madras. In each of the four metros, the two private companies would operate the system along with their two foreign partners. Tenders are expected to be floated soon inviting private manufacturers to set up value-added celluler telephone systems in other secondary cities in the country. Mobile telephones will be made available against foreign exchange payment. Video conferencing, Email, Radio Paging and other value added services and manufacturing of ten thousand line exchanges, will be available to joint/private sector without licensing (capacity) regulation.

Until now only terminal equipment and PABX manufacturing was permitted in private sector subject to lecensing.

New Import Export Policy

A new Import-Export Policy was announced on 1st April, 1992. The policy statement eliminated a number of import categories, exceptions and exemptions, special lists, open lists etc. The new 5 year exim policy makes trade "free" subject to a small negative list. Even the short negative list which prohibits import of certain items is likely to be curtailed further during the year.

The Finance Minister, Dr. Manmohan Singh, while inaugurating the International Asia Pacific Conference on private sector has stated that "bureaucratic controls would be fully dismantled, quantitative import restrictions phased out and customs tariff reduced to international levels to make the private sector vibrant."

Collaboration by non-Small Scale Industrial units for items reserved for the SSI sector is allowed subject to the condition that the firms concerned would undertake to export at least 75% of its output. Applications for 100% EOUs are cleared by the SIA and those for 100% Export Processing Zone (EPZ) units are cleared by the Development Commissioner of the particular EPZ, subject to the guidelines aplicable to such units.

Export obligations are no longer imposed in other cases of collaboration. Instead, the export offers made by the applicants are taken note of as being in the nature of a gentlemen's agreement, and are not linked to legal or bank guarantees. Their fulfilment is a matter of trust, and not compulsion.

The Government has liberalised the guidelines for * automatic approval in 30 days for all cases involving an equity of upto US $ two million.

The Government has initiated steps to deregulate the domestic civil aviation industry and bring an end to the public sector monopoly in domestic civil aviation. The Ministry of Civil Aviation has proposed to withdraw the three major constraints on private taxi operators namely:

- Restriction on level of fare.
- Route restriction.
- Flight time restriction.

The ministry has given support to the 'open sky policy' for air taxi licenses in India. Selling Indian airlines or Air India is however not on the immediate agenda.

Liberalisation and 'open sky policy' has opened the vast domestic market to new scheduled airlines in India. There are 22 registered private airlines of which a few are already operational. The most notable being East West Airlines which has already acquired 3% of the total domestic market, that was till now monopolised by Indian Airlines.

The ministry of Civil Aviation and Tourism has recently invited foreign capital and technology for 'collaborative partnership' for an "integrated development of the Indian aviation industry".

'Liberalisation window to opportunities was the theme of the 41st annual convention of the Travel Agents' Association of Inida, held at Hydrabad recently.

Many interesting facts emerged during the convention. Partial convertibility has made visiting India and even shopping an inexpensive proposition. For example, there is a charactered flight every day from Uzbekistan carrying 240 passengers stopping at New Delhi for a day of shopping!

In a radical departure form the Industrial Policy of

1956, the Union Government has announced that it will allow 100% foreign equity participation for setting up of power plants in India. It has also permitted substantial modification in the Electricity (Supply) Act 1948 to hasten the private sector's participation in the ailing power sector.

These two decisions have been taken by the cabinet and the bill containing the amendments in the Electricity (Supply) Act and the 100% foreign equity participation proposals will be tabled soon before the Parliament.

The 100% foreign equity participation proposals allows free repatriation of profits and other incentives. Besides, it will facilitate foreign parties to set up power plants without time delays, which are solely responsible for the cost escalation in the power projects.

Proposals from foreign investors for new power units are expected to be cleared through a high powered committee. The domestic private company's proposals will be cleared through a single window to minimise bureaucratic and other delays. The Government is likely to invite various foreign consortia including non-resident Indians (NRI's), particularly those in Japan and the UK to come forward.

Since the 1960's, the two public sector companies, Oil & Natural Gas Commission (ONGC) and Oil India Limited have held a monopoly over oil exploration in India. ONGC is seeking a change of its status to an autonomous corporation with the freedom to raise its resources directly from markets in India and overseas. It is prepared to enter into new projects such as country wide gas grid in collaboration with the private sector. It is understood that 73 drilling and exploratory blocks have been offered to international oil companies through international tendering. The Government has invited offers for joint ventures to develop designated medium-sized as also small sized oil and gas fields offering a range of incentives. Companies may singly or as a consortium bid by the 31st December 1992. Major tax concessions are made both for Indian and foreign companies engaged in oil exploitation. Income Tax will be levied at a flat rate of 50% without surcharge as against 65% now applicable to foreign companies in other businesses.

The Government has accorded status of importance to the Bombay High oil producing belt in the Arabian Sea and initiated highly sophisticated defence procedures for safeguarding the rigs from aggression.

Potential estimates claim that India should produce 70 metric tonnes of crude per annum by 1999 and will be considered a major economic power of the next century.

The rate of tax applicable to foreign companies continue to be 65%. Surcharge is not levied in the case of non-resident assessees.

Section 80 HHC of Income Tax Act 1961 provides for 100% exemption from income tax if the entire business income is generated from exports. The deductions available to an assessee involved in exports in now to be calculated on a new formula. The formula makes a distinction between a manufacturer exporter and a trading exporter. The actual deduction is calculated taking into consideration the FOB value of the exports as against the turnover and profits/gains of the business.

Under the provisions of Section 80-0, 50% of technical services fees, royalties etc derived under an approved agreement are deductible from income. This concession which was available to Indian corporate bodies has now been extended to non corporate bodies. This concession has been granted with the prupose of encouraging professionals such as architects, accountants etc to earn foreign exchange for the country. Further clarifications are expected from the Government on how this scheme would be applied to professionals as prior approval of agreements may be very difficult to administer.

Some immediate effects of the changes outlined above can be seen from the following events:

— As early as April 1992, a 1243% increase in foreign investment has been registered in India since the announcement of the liberalised industrial policy in July 1991.

— Foreign Collaborations in India recently approved by the Indian Government include companies like General Motors, General Electric, Coca Cola, Suzuki, Leasaffre (French), GERB (German), Buhler (Swiss), IBM, BMW, Ford etc. In the communication sector, AT&T, Siemens, France and British Telecom have shown keen interest in bidding for setting up cellular phone networks in India.

— 100 senior Japanese business executives spent a week in India in February 1992 and Nomura Securities Company has established a presence in Delhi. The opening of a trading office of a securities house in known to be a major jumping off point for further investment in India.

— 200 foreign participants attended the Euromoney conference in Delhi on "Business, Finance and Investment in India" in the last week of March, 1992.

New Horizons

In the recent few months, with the Bombay Stock Market Scandal in which banks and financial institutions stand to lose upto Rs. 30 billion, inflation running upto 13% on occasions and other regional and national political problems, the feeling has been that the Government is now in the danger of letting opportunities slip away. The Government did announce de-licensing of the electronic industry, liberalisation which would permit foreign financial institutions to invest in India and permission to open branch offices by foreign companies in the last few months to counter the allegations that there has been a slow down in the economic reform process. Although there may be some truth in this allegation the process of liberalisation has certainly not stopped. The Government has given an assurance that it will endeavour to proceed with the intended further liberalisation as promised.

On the whole, along with devaluation of the rupee in June 1991, the new trade policy and the further reforms promised includding full convertibility of the rupee, if the new Industrial Policy and its effect does turn out to what it promises to be, new horizons will open. This should lead to faster growth of industries in India. Indian industries would be open and accessible to the world. The opening up of new areas such as air transportation and power generation for private sector participation will result in opportunities for contractors and financial institutions to bid for project and asset work. The feeling in India is that a clear signal has been sent to industrialists, both local and foreing, that the government really means business. The radical nature of the industrial policy has met and continues to meet some resistance from the bureaucratic machinery which it seeks to dismantle. Its fine print still requires further clarifications. But more important than the fine print is the inescapable fact the political power has finally recognised that it is time for a new order to emerge. For some, their efforts may have fallen short of expectations, but the Government has acted, at last.

This update has been prepared by Thakker & Thakker Solicitors & Advocates, Bombay, for the AIJA 1992 conference in Bombay on "Emerging Investment Opportunities in India". The Update is necessarily of general nature and seeks to provide information only on some of the major changes announced by the Government and cannot be regarded as legal advice.

Status of the Indian Telecom Network

India today operates one of the largest telecom networks in Asia comprising

— Over 20 172 telephone exchanges;

— About 118 400 route kms of coaxial terrestrial UHF/ microwave radio relay systems up to 140 Mbit/s apart from analogue systems;

— 23 300 kilometres of optical fibre systems comprising of systems up to 565Mb/s;

— 50 per cent of Transmission network is digitalised.

About 7 700 cities and towns are connected to the National Subscriber Dialling (NSD) network and the Department of Telecommunications (DOT) plans to extend the facility to all automatic exchanges by 1997.

Fully automatic International Subscriber Diallilng (ISD) service is available to 237 countries through two international earth stations and submarine cable systems. Trunk manual service is also available to all countries.

To meet the low speed data communication needs of Business/industrial units in Remote and far flung areas, a Business. Message Network (RABMN) with a hub-station near Delhi, having a capacity of 1000 subscribers has been commissioned. About 456 Very Small Aperture Terminals (VSAT) are deployed in this network for providing data service at maximum speeds up to 9.6kbits.

A dedicated Packet Switched Public Data Network

(PSPDN), with international access for computer communication services is available in the country with speeds up to 2Mbit/s.

For providing international connectivity, a Gateway Packet Switching System (GPSS), is available which offers the capability of sophisticated telecommunication networking terminals and computers internationally.

INSAT satellite systems are being used to provide over 4126 two-way speech circuits through 165 earth stations across the length and breadth of the country. In 1975, the government of India took a decision to have its system for meeting domestic communication needs of the country and approved the scheme in 1977 for the multi purpose Indian National Satellite System (INSAT).

The INSAT-I series of satellites, comprising four satellites were launched in 1982, 1983, 1988 and 1990 respectively. INSAT-II series of the satellites comprising four satellites in orbit and one ground spare, are being manufactured indigenously. Under this series, INSAT-IIA was launched in July 1992 and INSAT-IIB Satellite was launched in July 1993.

The present space segment comprises of * INSAT IIA and IIB Satellites in orbit. The ground segment of INSAT-ID & INSAT-IIA, IIB comprises of 82 fixed Satellite earth stations. In addition to the above, 29 satellite earth stations have been commissioned as captive networks to meet the telecommunication needs of Government undertakings.

Besides above fixed satellite earth stations the ground segment also comprises 23 mobile terminals including three Flyaway Terminals. These terminals are capable of being transported to different parts of the country by road/air to restore the telecommunication services as well as to meet an urgent telecommunication

Profile

Capital	–	New Delhi
Area	–	3,287,560 sq km
Population	–	915 million (1995)
Urban Population	–	27% (1994)
Population Growth	–	1.9% (1994)
GDP	–	USS 231,870 million
GDP, per Capita	–	USS 257 (1993)
Currency	–	Ruppee
TelephoneDensity		
Rural	–	0.25%
Overall	–	1.07% (1995)
Waiting list for Telephone Lines	–	2,496,850 (1993)
Cellular Subscribers	–	-
Facsimile Machines	–	50,0000 (1994)
Telex Subscribers	–	49,063 (1993)
International Outgoing Traffic (million mins)	–	614.2 (1994)
Network Digitization		
Switching	–	53.9% (1994)
Transmission	–	29.8% (1994)

need from any part of the country. There are also nine special routes/networks.

About 185000 villages out of 604 734 villages are provided with telecommunications facililties;

There were 2.5 telephones per 1000 population in the rural areas at the end of march 1995, as against the figure of 107 in the country as a whole. These figures are expected to become 3.00 and 15.00 respectively by the year 1997 as per the modest government investment. Private sector participation, which is expected shortly, will raise telephone density considerably.

The total equipped capacity of the Indian local network is 12 million with over 10 million main lines. There has been a rise of 25 per cent in telephone traffic in 1991-1992 and 35 per cent in 1992-1993 as compared to the previous year.

The pending demand however is 215 million and is growing at over 20 per cent per annum. In the past the registered demand has grown at a rate of 10 to 13 per cent per annum while the supply remained between 9 to 10.5 per cent. As a consequence the waiting list has grown. Over the last two years, we have stepped up the growth rate to 15 per cent per annum to see a slight dip in the demand.

The Indian Telecommuinications network provides nearly 400 000 Long Distance Switching Circuits with 94 per cent digitization.

A number of state-of-the-art switching technologies have been inducted in Indian network, ie FETEX 150, EWSD, AXE 10, No.5 ESS, OCB 283, System X, NEAX 61E and the indigenous CDoT.

Enhancement of capacity and digitalization of the transmission network is being carried out with optical fibre, digital microwaves and satellite.

A great emphasis is being laid on R&D of sophisticated digital switching and transmission equipment to meet india's urban and rural needs. The Centre for Development of Telematics (C-DoT) has successfully designed a family of digital-SPC switching systems from small to large main automatic exchanges.

Technology for several transmission products such as 10 channel UHF-600 MHz, 2/8 and 8/34 Digital mux, Satellite Based Rural Telegraph Network (SBRTN) Single Channel VHF and 2/8 Mbit/s OLTE has also been indigenously developed by CDoT and technology successfully transferred to a large number of local manufacturers. CDoT technology has also been offered to other countries as well.

Value added services are being indigenously developed exchanges through introduction of better signalling features such as Common Channel Signalling No. 7 and through ISDN.

The ultimate goal of R&D units is however to lead to the development of an Intergrated Services Digital Network (ISDN) and eventually to Broadband ISDN (B-ISDN) through Synchronous Digital Hierachy (SDH). Digital Access Cross Connect System (DACCS), Asynchronous Transport Module (ATM) etc.

There is a Telecommunications Engineering Centre (TEC) for issuing of specifications, type approvals, interface approvals and evaluation of new telecom products and for standardisation.

Over the years, the Department of Telecom, have built up extensive training facilities starting at the apex with Advanced Level Telecommunications Training Centre, near Delhi, set up with the systems and support of the UNDP and ITU.

The Telecommunications Training Centre at Jabalpur and 11 Regional and 25 State and District Level Training Centres also provides extensive training facilities. India has been extending assistance to Asia and Pacific countries too in meeting their training needs in the high tech areas of telecommunications.

Through DOT's consultancy group known as Telecommunication Consultancy India Limited (TCIL), India has been offering a wide spectrum of consultancy services in the international arena.

These include technical and management support, training, inspection, rehabilitation, modernization of existing systems, techno-economic studies in the core sectors of engineering and design studies, besides construction management and electronic data processing etc.

The consultancy services, include feasibility studies, network design studies, software support, installation, testing and commissioning of switching systems and transmission systems, operation and maintenance of networks.

TCIL has executed various contracts abroad and has been operating in about 28 countries.

The Indian Telegraph (Amendment) Bill, 1995

The National Telecom Policy 1994, has inter-alia laid emphasis on achieving the universal service, bringing the quality of Telecom service to world standard, provision of the widest permissible range of services to meet the customer's demand at reasonable price and participation of the companies registered in India in the area of basic telecom services as also making arrangements for protection and promotion of consumers' interest and ensuring fair competition. The Department of Telecomomunications feel that to achieve these objectives, there is need to separate regulatory functions from service providing functions which will be in keeping with the prevailing general trend in the world. It has, therefore, proposed to set up an independent Telecom Regulatory Authority to be called 'Telecom Regulatory Authority of India' which, to begin with, will be non-statutory in character but will have well defined functions and responsibilities and powers to play the role of a watch-dog body for the Telecom sector in an effective manner.

The Indian Telegraph Act, 1885 regulates the functioning of Telecommunications services in the country. Under Section 4 of the Indian Telegraph Act, 1885, the Central Government has the exclusive right of establishing, maintaining and working telegraphs and under the first provision of this section, it may grant a licence on such conditions and in consideration of such payment as it thinks fit to any persons to establish, maintain or work a telegraph within any part of the country. Under Section 4(2) of the Act, the Central Government may by notification in the Official Gazette delegate to the Telegraph Authority all or any of its powers under the first proviso to subsection (1). Section 3(6) of the Indian Telegraph Act, 1885 describes Director General (Posts and Telegraphs) as the Telegraph Authority and includes any officer empowered by him to perform all or any of the functions of the Telegraph Authority under the Act. Presently, the Secretary, Department of Telecommunications who has been notified as the Director General Telecommunications in his capacity as a Telegraph Authority exercises regulatory powers and performs regulatory functions as delegated by the Central Government under the Indian Telegraph Act, 1885. In order to vest the powers of the Telegraph Authority with the proposed Regulatory Authority in respect of certain assigned functional areas. It has become necessary to amend Section 3(6) of the Indian Telegraph Act, 1885 by including "any statutory or non-statutory authority".

The secretary, Department of Telecommunications stated in evidence that at present all the regulatory authority under the Indian Telegraph Act is exercised by the Secretary, Department of Telecommunications. This power of the telegraph authority can be further delegated by him to another officer of the Government. It cannot be delegated to a statutory or a non-statutory authority as such. So, the basic purpose of the proposed amendment of Section3(6) of the Indian Telegraph Act, 1885 is to delegate certain regulatory powers of the Telegraph authority to the proposed Telecom Regulatory Authority.

The Secretary, Department of Telecommunications further clarified that the reasons for not coming up with a comprehensive Bill to setup a statutory with independent powers at this stage, are that the Government would like to watch the working of such an authority for a year or two and learn from such an experience. After getting the feed-back from the Chairman and Members of the authority and various interest groups viz, operators and subscribers etc., it would frame a comprehensive law to make it a statutory authority. Then the authority will derive its powers directly from an Act of Parliament.

The witness further told the Committee that "the need for amendment is based not only on Government perceptions of the local market but also arises from the international experience that wherever there has been a situation of more than one player in the market scene, a need has been felt for an independent umpire. The current trend in the telecommunication sector the world-over is to distance policy making functions, operational functions and regulatory functions from each other and to entrust regulatory functions to an independent Regulatory Authority for regulating Telecom services".

The Secretary, Department of Telecommunications informed the Committee that in due course the proposed authority would be independent and autonomous; it would operate outside the Government, at arm's length from the Government so that it could inspire the confidence of various operators as well as the subscribers. He further added that for this purposes the intention of the Government is to ensure that it is manned by people of eminence and independent views. Therefore, the Cabinet has decided that it would be chaired by a retired or a serving Chief Justice of a High Court or a retired or a serving Judge of the Supreme Court and it will have two members who should have worked in the State Government or the Central Government in a position not lower than the position of an additional Secretary to Government of India for a period of three years. These Members would enjoy the status of Secretary to Govt. of India. It was further stated that the tenure of the Chairman and the Members would be secure and protected. Their removal will require the same safeguards as are available to Judges of the Supreme Court. Similarly their emoluments and other terms and conditions of service would not be changed to their disadvantage. The Secretary Department of Telecommunications stated that the apparent idea was to send across a strong signal that there would be an authority who would act independently, impartially, in an objective manner to protect the interests of the operators as also of the subscribers.

Clarifying the position further in reply to a query by the Committee, the Secretary, Deptt. of Telecommunications stated that soon after the amendment of law, two things would follow. Firsts that Department of Telecommunications would set up this authority by means of a Resolution of the Government. Secondly the Department would issue a notification that the authority set up under that Resolution is vested with the powers of the Director-General of Telecommunications under Section 4 of the Indian Telegraph Act in respect of certain matters. Once that is done, the authority would be clothed with the powers of Telegraph Authority in relation to its are a of work. However, it would still be a creature of the executive arm of the Government. Later after an year or so it will come before the Parliament with a comprehensive Bill.

In reply to a query regarding the impact of Telecom Regulatory Authority after its inception on working of Telecom Network in the country, the Ministry informed that it was excepted that the Telecom Regulatory Authority would have healthy impact on the working of telecom services in the country, since it will act as a watch dog for telecom sector, ensure level playing field as also monitor quality of services and protect and promote the consumer interest.

Asked whether after setting up the Authority, it would be possible for Government to set aside any decision of the proposed Authority, the Secretary Deptt. of telecoommunications replied in negative. He further added that the intention was that there would be not right of appeal to the executive wing of the Government. The orders issued by the proposed Telecom Regulatory Authority can only be challenged before the High Court or the Supreme Court.

In the light of the Government view known to the Committee, the Committee agree with the amendment of Section 3(6) of Indian Telegraph Act, 1885 for inclusion of any statutory or non-statutory authority within the definition of Telegraph Authority and support the Bill. The Committee hope that steps will be taken to set up a statutory Authority.

Science & Technology Development

The investment in Research and Development. (R & D) has increased from a paltry Rs. 20 crore in the First Five Year Plan. Presently there are 214 universities, 400 national laboratories and 1300 in-house R & D centres in the industrial sector. Several Science & Technology departments have been set up in the areas of environment, non-conventional energy resources, bio-technology, ocean development, industrial research, space, atomic energy, defence, health, agriculture and electronics.

Identification and promotion of priority areas in R & D is done by Science an Engineering Research Council (SERC) set up under the Department of Science & Technology (DST). DST supports 12 autonomous research insitutions as well, for furthering research work in several discipline. Technology Information, Forecasting and Assessment Council (TIFAC) has been set up for generating technology forecasting and technology assessment documents and enabling a technology information system that is interactive and nationally accessible.

Industrial research in several diverse fields of scientific activity is being undertaken through a network of 40 laboratories and 81 field stations set up by the Council for Scientific and Industrial Research (CSIR). In the field of bio-technology, more than 24 specialised R & D centres have been developed for pursuing state-of-the-art research. Identical efforts for promoting new avenues of research are being undertaken in the field of ocean development as well.

The Union Budget for 1996-97 has taken various measures to promote R & D facilities. A matching one time grant has been awarded to CSIR and the Indian Council of Agricultural Research (ICAR) for modernisation of laboratories and institutes. The Technology Development and Application Fund created in 1995-96 has been proposed to be strengthened by Rs. 30 crore. A Five Year Tax Holiday under Section 80-IA of the Income Tax Act has been allowed to companies exclusively create for participation in R & D activities. The existing procedure for awarding weighted deduction under Section 35(2AA) of the Income Tax Act on sums paid for scientific research to a National Laboratory or a University or an IIT has been amended, by deleting the condition of approval by an outside body. In order to encourage R & D efforts, goods developed and patented in India and concurrently in specified countries have been exempted from levy of excise duty for a period of 3 years. The exemption procedure for customs duty on import of equipment and consumables for R & D institutions has been rationalised as well.

Private Sector Partcipation

The Value added service sector has been open to the private sector since 1992. In respect of value added services, except radio paging and mobile telephony services, companies registered in India are permitted to operate under licence on non exclusive basis. In the area of Radio paging and Cellular Mobile Telephone Services, however, a policy of selection is being followed in the granting of licences through a system of tendering.

A tender for operation of radio paging services in 27 cities was earlier invited and 14 companies have been granted operating licences. For other areas of the country comprising 19 territorial telecom circles, tenders have been invited, and licensing is being progressively done. Commercial service has been started in 22 cities by one or more operators to over 48,000 subscribers and in the rest of the five cities the service will start very soon.

Eight companies have been selected for the franchises of cellular mobile service in the four metro cities namely Bombay, Delhi, Calcutta and Madras. In respect of rest of the country, a tender had been invited. The evaluation of 33 bids for the 20 telecommunications circles, is expected to be completed shortly. Service has commenced in Calcutta and Delhi in September 1995.

With a view to supplement the efforts of Department of Telecommunications in providing telecommunication services to the people, 81 bids received for grant of licence for operation of basic services in 20 telecom Circles are now under evaluation.

The government has decided to create an autonomous Telecom Regulatory body called the Telecom Regulatory Authority of India (TRAI). This will have well defined functions, responsibilities and powers to play the role of a watch-dog body for the telecommunications sector in an effective manner. The Authority will regulate its procedure for conduct of business with the approval of the government and will be expected to ensure transparency and accountability.

Profound changes are taking place in Telecommunication sector the world over and India is no exception. The Government of India has taken bold initiatives to liberalise and expand the telecom network in the country.

Some of the milestones in this direction are:

— 1984

Manufacture of Customer Premises Equipment delicensed.

— 1991

New Industrial Policy permitting private sector to manufacture all types of telecommunications equipment.

Other salient features are:

No industrial Licence is required;

Automatic approval of foreign equity investment up to 51 per cent in the case of manufacturing projects:

Automatic approval of foreign collaboration in the

case of telecommunications sector with technology fees up to Rs. 10 million net of taxes and/or royalty up to five per cent for domestic sales and/or eight per cent for exports.

The possibility for more than 51 per cent foreign equity and higher technology fees/royalty in manufacturing projects through special approvals;

All foreign investment proposals for telecommunications services require the specific approval to the Government of India.

1992

Value added services thrown open to private sector participation.

1994

New National Telecommunications Policy allowing private sector participation in basic services announced.

The National Telecommunications Policy announced by the Government would be instrumental in bringing about phenomenal expansion and improvement in the telecom sector.

The objectives of the Telecommunications Policy are:

— providing Telecommunications for all and Telecommunications within the reach of all;
— Universal Service Obligation at affordable and reasonable price;
— Providing telecommunications services of world standard;
— To ensure that India emerges as a major manufacturing base and major exporter of telecom equipment.

The targets laid down in the policy are as follows:

— Telephones to be available on demand by 1997;
— All vjillages to be provided with telecommunications services by 1997;
— In urban areas a Public Calling Office (PCO) should be provided for every 500 persons by 1997;
— Special emphasis on the quality of telecoommunications services provided to the customers will be given;
— All value added services available internationally to be introduced in India, preferably by 1996.

The other important aspects of the policy are:

— Private initiative would be used to supplement the departmental efforts to raise additional resources both through increased internal generation and adopting innovative means, like, leasing, deferred payments, build-operate-and-transfer, build-lease-and-transfer.
— A suitable funding mechanism for indigenous R&D is proposed to be set up;
— Pilot projects will be encouraged directly by the government in order to access new technologies, new systems in both basic as well as value added services.

With low telephone penetration rates, India represents one of the world's most attractive markets for telecommunications service providers and equipment manufacturers. Service sector opening of the basic telecom services to the private sector is the biggest opportunity for foreign direct investment. The growth potential in the basic telephone service in India is tremendous taking into consideration the low telephone density at present.

The challenge in rural telecommunications in India is indeed quite formidable. Out of the 604 734 villages in the country, only 185000 have telephone facility. Over 420,000 villages are still without a telephone facility.

Under the National Telecommunications Policy, one public telephone will be provided in each of the over half a million villages by 1997. Provisioning of a single telephone in each village, as per the telecom policy, may involve an investment of the order of S billion US Dollars. The sub-sector of value added services is already open for private investment. This sector in India represents one of the world's largest opportunities for supply of services and equipment.

The Indian Switching market, which is estimated to increase from about 2.5 million lines now to over 3.00 million lines in 1996-1997 represents-one of the largest market in the Asian region. The digital switching markets in India has witnessed a true metamorphosis since 1991 when the new Industrial Policy was announced by the Government.

A number of foreign companies attracted by DOT's liberalised procurement policies, have set up local production ventures in India. The opening up of the Import Policy in 1992 has opened this largest market to international competition.

The market for providing private networks is also growing very fast. Major international companies have already announced their plans for making an entry in this market.

The Radio Transmission Equipment market in India has undergone extensive changes in the post industrial liberallization period. With the diversification or production of transmission equipment which was earlier limited to the public sector companies, the present production base has expand with the setting up of the manufacturing facilities in the private sector.

With the opening up of Microwave Radio systems to competition, a number of multinational companies have entered the radio equipment market. The digital microwave radio equipment market has potential for large investments since most of the radio frequency spectrum in microwave is still available for deployment.

The investment opportunities in the optical fibre cable and equipment as well as infrastrucure equipment for value added services such as cellular and paging are immense. With the possibility of the entire long distance network being converted to optical fibre media, a number of international companies are getting their products validated at present. The investment opportunities in this area are extremely good.

Another area expected to sustain great demand in the coming decade is VSATs with voice transmission. The steady increase in the number of customers demanding high bit rate data transmission and separate corporate networks has given spur to VSAT development.

With increased availability, VSAT services are likely to get a big push and, therefore, the opportunities in this sector are excellent.

— The gross receipts of the Department of Post during the year 1995-96 were Rs. 1150 crore. Gross working expenses were Rs. 2472 crore and net working expenses Rs. 1810 crore. there was, therefore, a deficit of Rs. 660 crore. During the year 1996-97, as per budget estimates, the gross receipts are expected at Rs. 1350 crore and gross working expenses at Rs. 2616 crore. With net working expenses at Rs. 1962 crore the deficit is estimated at Rs. 612 crore for 1996-97. (BE).

— The Budget of Department of Post has been in deficit continuously over the years, and no dividend is being paid to the general revenue. Modernisation activities, through inductin of new technoloy, has been initiated on a modest scale during the current plan. Its further expansion and spread during the next plan, are likely to improve the service efficiency. A modernised postal system should also be able to provide new value added services to yield revenue. Low tariff on most of the postal services for many years, and inadiquate agency charges for agency functions, are the main factors for the deficit. However, a moderate increase in some of the services i.e., printed postcard from 60 paise to 100 paise and registration fee from Rs. 6.00 to Rs. 8.00 and introduction of cmpetition postcard at Rs. 2.00 each is expected to yield additional revenue to the tune of Rs. 76 crore in a full financial year. The degree of subsidy, as indicated in Table 2.11 ranges from about 1 per cent in respected of money orders to 92 per cent on postcard.

— The network owned and operated by the Department of Telecommunications (DOT) has been generating surpluses, which is utilised for further exapansion of the net work. Net receipts increased to Rs. 4951 crore in 1995-96 (RE) from Rs. 3936 crore in 1994-95 reflecting an increase of 25.8 per cent. Net receipts are estimated at Rs. 5213 crore in 1996-97 (BE). The dividend contribution to the general revenues increased to Rs. 279 crore in 1995-96 (RE) from Rs. 270 crore in 1994-95. The operating ratio, which is a percentage of net operating expenses (excluding the provision for redemption of bonds) to operating revenue earned (excluding registration fee) has come down to 48.7 in 1995-96 (RE) from 48.8 in 1994-95. The plan outlay for Telecommunication Services (including all PSUs) for the year 1996-97 (BE) is marginally higher at Rs. 9874 crore from Rs.

9830 crore in 1995-96 (RE). The entire outlay (except Rs. 5.00 crore pertaining to WMo etc. which is by way of budgetary support) is to be financed from the internal accruals and extra budgetary resources of the Telecommunication sector. Internal accruals amounting to Rs. 7491 crore account for 75.9 per cent of total resources against 79.6 per cent in 1995-96 (RE).

— Though the telecom network in India is fairly large in absolute terms, (in 1994 it was ranked fourteenth in the world) yet the tele density was 1.4 per cent in March, 1996. An advanced and efficient telecommunications system can enhance international competitiveness of the economy. The DOT has been increasing the quantum of resources deployed for the development of the telecom infrastructure, although the pattern of financing has undergoes a sea change. During the first plan DOT received budgetary support which accounted for around 79 per cent of the total resouces deployed it. In the Eighth Plan, 78.7 per cent is expected from internal accruals, 21 per cent from borrowings and other sources, and only 0.3 per cent from budgetary support. In the coming years, substantial investment would be required to upgrade and expand the existing telecom network. The aggregate resource requirements for the provision of basic and cellular mobile telecom services as estimated bny the Expert Group on Commercialisation of Infrastruture Projects is placed at Rs. 1,91,500 crore by 2006. Thee estimates are at todays prices and duty structure.

— Of late, DOT has primarily relied on internal accruals. However, to meet its targets of network expansion, DOT will have to look to a larger resource pool. It will have to devise a tariff structure which largely reflects the cost oriented approach, subject to country's social obligations and thrusts.

— A corporate structure for the DOT will enable it to leverage its substantial assets and raise adequate funds to meet all its investment needs. Corporate structure would make DOT into an autonomous entity owned by the Government. In the short and medium term, the government will remain the dominant operator and provider of telecom services in the countrty. However, with the advent of private operators, the present tariff regime should orient as quickly as possible towards a costbased structure. It is imperative to have the tariffs reviewed to allocate costs for various services and identify the need, if any, of subsidies.

— As per the revised estimates for 1995-96, the total expenditure on Broadcasting was Rs. 974 crore as against total receipts of Rs. 549 crore. This shows an increase of 19 per cent and 20.4 per cent in total expenditure and receipts, respectively. As a result, the ratio of total receipts to total expenditure improved from 55.8 per cent in 1994-95 to 56.4 per cent in 1995-96. The rising trend in commercial receipts in broadcasting activity over the past few years is indicative of efforts being made in this direction. Commercial receipts were Rs. 426 crore in 1993-94, Rs. 450 crore in 1994-95, and Rs. 540 crore in 1995-96 (RE). Further break up of commercial receipts brings to the fore the overwhelming contribution of Doordarshan towards revenue generation. The commercial receipts in case of Doordarshan were Rs. 363 crore in 1993-94, Rs. 384 crore in 1994-95 and Rs. 460 crore in 1995-96.

— The important place commanded by India in world trade in coffee, tea, leather and spices on a historical basis has continued in recent years as wll. In 1994, India accounted for 2.4 per cent, 13.6 per cent, 2.5 per cent and 9.1 per cent of world trade in coffee and coffee substitues, tea and mate, leather, and spices, respectively. Furthermore, there has been a significant progress in export diversification, and India has emerged as an important exporter of iron ore and concentrates, and pearis, precious and semi-precious stones. In 1994, India accounted for 6 per cent or world exports of iron ore and concentrates and 10.9 per cent of world exports of pearls, precious and semi precious stones (Source: 1994 United Nations International Trade Statistics Year Book, 1995).

— During 1950, India accounted for about 1.8 per cent (1.85 per cent of exports and 1.71 per cent of imports) of world trade. After gradually declining to 0.57 per cent by 1980, India's share improved marginally to 0.63 per cent by 1985. The reason for improvement in the share was that while world trade declined in the period 1980-85, India's trade continued to grow. However it came down again to 0.53 per cent by 1991. The first half of the nineties witnessed a sharp increase in India's exports and imports have grown in dollar terms annually by 12.4 per cent and 9.4 per cent, respectively. The corresponding growth rates of world trade was about 5.7 per cent. The secular decline in India's share in world trade has been arrested and reversed, and the years ahead are likely to see a continuation of this increasing trend.

— The trade policy components of the reform process undertaken since July 1991 have been motivated by a full recognition of the important role that trade can play in promoting growth. The utilisation of the expanded scope for specialising in areas of comparative advantage is manifest in the improved growth performance of the economy. Furthermore, while exports have vigorously responded to the removal of the anti-export bias of a protectionist environment, domestic industry appears to have been stimulated by the expended availability of imported inputs and capital goods as well as the challenge of competing in the international market place. The positive response of Indian industry to liberalisation is amply demonstrated by the capital goods sector. The tariff on capital goods was as high as 85 per cent in the pre-reforms period. This has been reduced to about 25 per cent covering about 80 per cent of capital goods in 1995-96. The capital goods industry which witnessed a negative growth of 12.8 per cent in 1991-92, registered an average growth of about 23 per cent during 1994-96.

— The terms of trade, which measure the terms of exchange between a unit of exports and a unit of imports, have been improving in the post-reform period. Two common ways of measuring the terms of trade are the net terms of trade (NTT) and the income terms of trade (ITT). A time series indicating all parameters of terms of trade (TOT) for India since 1969-70 with the base of 1978-79 = 100 Indicates that there have been wide fluctuations in the TOT. The NIT (1978-79=100), which is an index of export prices divided by an index of import prices, improved from 109.3 in 1990-91 to 152.4 in 1994-95. It is

— It may be mentioned that India s purchasing power of exports as reflected thorough ITT has been improving continuously since 1985- 86. The value index of exports at 484 stands much higher than that of imports at 351 and hence, in terms of value, india has gained.But in terms of volume, the index of exports has been much less at 384 in comparison to that of imports at 515. This means that the volume of imports is increassing faster, though India is getting a better price for her exports.

— Compared to the experience of other developing countries, the improvement in the terms of trade for India has been very impressive. The NTT (1990=100), as presented in the UN's International trade Statistics Year Book, 1995, is reproduced below:

— Developing economies, with exports dominated by primary products, lost out to developed econoies,. Relavtive abundance of supply of primary products as well as the superior bargaining strength of developed countries have often ben adduced as two major reasons for the deterioration in the terms of trace. Gains in the terms of trade for India in the comparable period perhaps reflects her diversified export base as well as the relatively low international prices of oil in the relevant period.

Economies	*1980*	*1985*	*1990*	*1991*	*1992*	*1993*	*1994*
Developed	90	91	100	100	102	104	104
Developing	125	109	100	98	99	100	96
India	65	92	100	91	114	NA	NA

India is committed to further liberalisation of its import regime, notwithstanding the dismantling of licensing controls over a wide area. At the same time, there are concerns whether developed nations of the world are implementing in letter and spirit their part of the obligations under the Uruguay Round Agreements. Many contries are resorting to protectinist devices in the guise of environmental hazards and exploitation of labour such as child labour. The obligations of providing access to imports of developing countries, especially textiles and garments, are being circumvented under one pretext or the other, even under the back-loaded integration of Textiles and Clothing into the World Trading System. Such restrictions are designed to keep out cheaper imports.

By virtue of the radical shift from a highly-regulated to an outward-oriented economy, India has attracted immense interest abroad, at both Governmental and private investor levels. India is one of the largest emerging markets, second only to China's, and the country has been experiencing inflows of foreign portfolio and direct investments—thought not as large as in China and a few other countries—which were unthinkable in the world of even 1980s. Economic strength has become the principal determinant of a nation's standing in the international community, and even the most powerful country, the United States of America, looks for market opportunities all over, more especially in the dynamic Asia-Pacific region, as the best shield of security.

With the end of the Cold War, the East-West barriers have broken down. The rapid spread of liberalisation and globalisation is a historic development which has blurred both East-West and North-South divisions. Developing countries have been compelled to adapt themselves to conditions of global interdependence although in the process they run grave risks in the medium-term and rare not assured of international safety nets.

In the rapidly changing world environment, each developing country must certainly concentrate on building its inherent strength and developing areas of comparative advantage and forge alliances with neighbours and, where promising, enter regional blocs which offer greater opportunities of trade and other exchanges to enhance national arena, disadvantaged nations must make common cause and unite to advance their pressing needs more effectively than what has been witnessed over the last fifty years in the post-decolonisation era. This is the only way of securing a post-cold war order which is just and equitable.

India has a long way to go before it could emerge as a strong global player, as currently it occupies the 32nd place as a leading exporter of merchandise, well below several countries in East and South-East Asia. It has to make up for the time lost in its inward-looking route to development which left the cuntry far behind in the international league, despite building a strong industrial base and possessing highly technical manpower, the third largest in the world. Indian planning did not take sufficient note of the gathering pace of global intergration with the frowth of merchandise trade exceeding the growth of output in virtually every year of the post-war period.

In recent years, India has begun to look East, is now a full dialogue partner in ASEAN (the 7-member Association of South East Nations) and excepts to find a place in the Asia Pacific Economic Forum (APEC) by 1999. These should promote greater intra-Asian trade and investment flows even as India strives to gain an increasing share of exports into developed economies of the West such as the European Union and North America. Trade with Russia and Eastern Europe as well as Central Asian States holds prospects of considerable expansion over present levels and a more promising development is the initiative taken by 14 states of the Indian Ocean Rim for an economic cooperation grouping with a Charter expected to be signed in March 1997.

The bilateral and pluralistic approaches cannot, and

should not, in any way dilute India's firm commitment to multilaterialism which is the best safeguard against' domination of the global economy by a few powerful nations. India's immediate responsibility is to solidify South Asian cooperation through SAPTA and ensure its early graduation to becomes SAFTA (South Asian Free Trade Area) to make it a region of good neighbourliness less prone to confliilcts than at present. With 16 per cent of the world's population, India's weight in the international economy remains negligible, and the building up of internal strength with determination through higher saving, and investments and greater efficiency in the use of resources is a pre-requisite for the country to claim its due share in the global market-place.

Looking Ahead

The fifth decade of Independence has triggered investment interest in India as never before. Policymakers should now bring in a lot more clarity on their objectives.

The rules of international trade have changed. Witrh trade barriers getting dismantled by the day, there is need to infuse a very high degree of competitiveness. A major development is the evolution of regional trade groupings like the European Community (EC), the North American Free Trade Association (NAFTA), ASEAN, APEC etc.

Though the south Asian countries have formed the SAARC, progress achieved in free trade among these has been slow. Apart from mere trade flows, potential benefits in terms of the phasing out of poliltical animosities and more cohesive regional developments are immense.... The EC experience proves this. Over the last 50 years Britain, France and Germany, who have been bitter adversaries for centuries, have been bonded together on the strength of mutuality of economic interests. The SAARC union could grow to include

China, the Central Asian Republics and the Indian Ocean rim countries, including South Africa, and forge close links with ASEAN and APEC in course of time. The comparable levels of economic development of most of the countries in this region would help in co-ordinated growth.

There is a huge market for such equiptment: there are capabilities in these countries to produce entire range of such equipment–generators, turbines, boilers, transformers, switchgears, motors etc.

The Korean automobile manufacturers—Daewoo Motors and Hyundai—indicate plants for developing India as a major centre for their global operations. Like we did in regard to Maruti, in the assimilation of mass production technology, India should attempt absorption of the high productivity levels of the Koreans, Americans and others; combine this with the strength of the massive availability of skilled manpower to win global markets.

With the progress of economic reforms in many countries of the world and deregulation of financial markets, the importance of private capital flows into Asia has increased from US $ 76.8 billion in 1994 to US $ 98.0 billion in 1995, while net official flows increased marginally from US $ 5.6 billion to US $6.4 billlion during the same period. Similarly, while there were considerable official flows to Mexico and the transition countries in 1995 in support of their comprehensive adjustment programmes, net private capital flows to the developing countries increased from US $ 140.4 billion in 1994 to US $ 166.6 billion in 1995. India has has modest, but increasing, success in attracting a growing part of these private capital flows. Furthermore, much of these private capital inflows into India has been of the non-debt creating variety, and helped to boost the balance of payments as well as the availability of investible resources in the economy.

The international financial community is appreciative of India's economic performance in the last years, but concerns continue to be expressed about the high fiscal deficit, the slowing down of structural reforms, continued restrictions on consumer goods imports, and tariff levels considerably higher than in other countries. Also, references are often made to India's move towards capital account convertibility (with some observers advocating a cautions approach), high level of subsidies, inadequate disinvestment in the public sector, need for further relaxation of rules to attract foreign investment and the continued high stake of the government in the public sector banks. On the whole, the international community is very positive about India's effort to achieve a high rate of growth.

Participants in the India Development Forum (IDF) meeting in September 1996 acknowledged the strong performance of the Indian economy and appreciated the new Government's declaration to continue reform measures to strengthen the social programmes as set out in the Common Minimum Programme (CMP). Various delgates stressed the importance of (i) fiscal consolidation, (ii) sustaining programmes in the social sectors, (iii) infrastructrue, (iv) provety eradication, (v) reforms in agriculture, public sector, and financial sector, and (vi) strengthening of legislation against child labour. In support of India's economic development, the donor countries pledged official assistance in 1996-97 of US $ 6.7 billion. Inclusion of US $ 400 million in long-term finance, promised on a bilateral basis at market rates, will raise this total to above US $ 7 billion. About 33 per cent of the total could be in the form of grants and interest-free loans.

With effect from January 1, 1997, India subscribed to the Special Data Dissemination Standards (SDDS) of the

International Monetary Fund (IMF). by subscribing to the SDDS, India ha committed itself to streamilining the tatistical system of the country to produce most of the data categories with a much shorter time lag, improved quality and coverage by December 31, 1988.

By virtue of the radical shift from a highly-regulated to an outward-oriented economy, India has generated immense interest abroad, but it has a long way to go before emerging as a strong global player, opines the author. India's development strategy launched in the 1950s, soon after Independence, aimed mainly at strengthening the industrial base of the country, especially in basic goods and heavy machine-building, and adopted the import-substituation model to achieve self-reliance. Exports were not viewed as an integral part of overall economic development, and such imports as became unavoidable were financed by drawing down foreign exchange reserves that had accrued to India at the time of Independence, in the form of sterling balances held in its favour for goods and services provided by this country during the Second World War.

Export pessimism dominated the mood of the early planners as it was rightly assumed then that until India's manufactures began to be diversified, there was little possibility of exporting manufactures while primary products and traditional manufactured goods faced poor demand .prospects in the world market. It was during the later half of the fifties, when the Second Five Year Plan was under way with its emphasis on heavy industry, largely in the public sector, that it began to be realised that India needed to export to be able to finance at least part of the maintenance and developmental imports.

The foreign exchange crisis that was looming by mid-1957 reinforced the importance of export growth as part of planned development. The pessimistic view about the potential for export earnings gave way to a more positive approach in the Third Plan (1961-66) with the introduction of export promotion measures without deflecting from the thrust of import subsitution and industrialisation. It was clear by mid-estimated the import content of the inward-looking path of development opted by India. Pressures on balance of pyaments had already brought into existence the Aid-India-Consortium comprising the World Bank and developed countries interested in providing assistance to India. Renewed emphasis on exports was laid in the Fourth Plan (1969-74) which envisaged porogressive elimination of dependence on foreign aid while the Fifth Plan (1974-79) identified certain sectors such as engineering goods, garments, leather manufacture and marine products for achieving increases in exports.

Thus, as agianst virtual stagnation in the 1950s, export performance improved to an average growth of 3 to 4 per cent in the 1960s, and was more impressive in 1970s with an average growth of 6.3 per cent in volume and 15.9 per cent in value terms.

But in the three decades, India's share in world exports had declined throughout from about 2 per cent in 1950 to 0.65 per cent in 1970 and dropped further to 0.42 per cent in 1980. This was the period when there was impressive growth in world trade and the opportunities were seize by many smaller Asian developing countries as well as the industrialising economies in Latin America to great advantage.

Paradoxically, even as india's export growth was being maintained or marginaly improved upon, her share of world exports was declining. Over the three decades ending the Seventies, the share of exports in Gross Domestic Product (GDP) ranged from 4 to 6 per cent. In a continental economy of India's size, the role of external sector in the development process was under-played so much that it took a successions of droughts, oil price shocks and balance of payments difficulties in the first two and a half decades of planning before the country could begin to see import substitution and export promotion as two sides of the same coin. But heavy reliance on quantitative restrictions on trade through import and export controls and detailed industrial licensing kept India a closed economy.

The Primary issuance of securities has a long history in India. The Indian bond market, measured by the estimated value of bonds outstanding, is next only to the Japanese and the Korean bond market in Asia. By January 31, 1995, the outstanding value of the Indian securities market was estimated to have reached Rs.3000 billion, almost 3.5 times its size in 1986. The size is deceptive as, despite attractive yields, secondary market trading has remained poor with virtually no quotation even in respect of listed securities. The estimated outstanding amount accounts for about 42% of GDP, as at the end of January 1995. Partial deregulation of interest rates in the early nineties and increasing emphasis on monetary policy in stabilization are the first major steps towards the emergence of an active debt market, with government securities spearheading the process. With the issuance of government securities at market determined coupon rates and the use of innnovative products, it has become possible, for the first time, for other issuers to offer debt products priced off the yield on government securities.

The process of financial sector reforms initiated in 1991, is far from complete. The Growth of the Indian Capital Market since Independence has been phenomenal. The number of stock exchanges increased from 7 in 1947 to 23 in 1994. Likewise the number of listed companies on stock exchanges grew from 1125 in 1946 to 7811 at the end of 994. Similarly, the quantum of listed capital registered a growth of about 565 times from Rs.270 crore in 1946 to Rs.152,322 crore at the end of March, 1994.

The basic objective of financial sector reforms is to promote a diversified, efficient and competitive financial system by a policy shift from detailed regulation and controls to one based on market forces. Alongwith dismantling administrative regulation, the goal is establishment of a system of prudential regulation, supported by a mechanism for reporting, monitoring and supervision of the compliance.

Another major plank of reform is injection of new competition into a hitherto virtually government owned financial system. For the first time in many years, six new banking licences have been granted to the private sector all of which have been implemented. The new banks are permitted to have financial joint ventures with fgoreign baks, particularly for accessing modern systems and technology. There has been a mushrooming of Non-Banming Finance Companies (NBFCs), some of whom have already built up a large net-work. Several well known investment banks have established a presence in India. Since April 1993, nearly 300 Foreign Institutional Inestors (FIIs) have been registered with the regulatory authority and quite a few are active investors in the domestic capital market which has been opened up to foreign portfolio investment in a limited way. Several new mutual funds have been set up by the private sector including some by global fund managers. The most spectacular growth has been registered when we compare the share of market capitalization to gross domestic products (GDP) which was 12.9% in 1946, while in 1991-92 it was 57.2% and further increased to 68.8% during 1993-98.

Trade Policy

Side by side with the announcement of New Industrial Policy for Promoting Small Tiny and Village Enterprises, the Government have also announced major reforms in the Trade Policy. The main objective of the trade policy have been to progressively reduce the system of administrative controls and lilcences and to link import except in the case of essential items. The major reforms in the Trade Policy are given below:

Exports were in the past allowed replenishment to provide for essential inputs required for the manufacture of products exported. To allow flexibility to enable diversification of export products and also as an incentive for exports, the REP licenses so issued, were allowed to be freely sold. The entitlement for REP licenses also varied from item to item. In view of the flexibility of the REP Licenses Government realise that to treat it as licence is an misnomer, under the new policy the REP licences have been replaced by a new instrument named 'Eximscrips'. Eximscrips will be issued on the basis of FOB value of exports or Net FOreign Exchange (NFE) earnings from exports as indicated below. The main features of the new systems are:

The basic rate at which Eximscripts will be issued against exports will be 30% of FOB value. Exports to hard currency areas will be eligible for Eximscrips valid for hard currency imports while exports to rupee payment areas will be issued Eximscrips valid for imports from these areas only. However, as a measure of transition, exports to rupee payment areas may continue to avail of REP licences valid for hard currency imports at the rate prevailing prior to 4th July, 1991. This transition facility will be available only for exports effected upto 31st December 1991.

Products such as gems and jewellery, handcrafts, newspapers, journals and periodicals and cinematographic films, which enjoyed higher rated of REP will receive Eximscrips at the same rates as before.

The Basis rate of 30% is inadequate for exports of certain products such as value-added agricultural projects, electronics, bulk drugs and marine products, formulations and certain categories of advanced engineering goods. These products will be eligible for an additional Eximscrips entitlement of 10 percentage points, taking the total Eximscrips rate to 40% of FOB value.

For exports made on the basis of duty free imports obtained against Advance Licences, Eximscrips will be available at the general rate of 30% but this will be applied to the net foreign exchange earnings. On the same principle. Eximscrips at 30% of NFE will also be available for all EOU and EPZ units.

The 30% of NFE rate of Eximscrips is also applicable to service exports, including software exports which is a thrust area. The definition of services covered under this category is being ratinallized and extended to include other services such as services of architects, textile designers, artists, management consultants, lawyers etc. The benefit will be available to services exported by resident Indians for which remittances are made to India. The details are being notified separately.

Eximscrips issued to exporters will be tradeable and can be used to import any item in the limited permissible list (Appendix-3), the non-sensitive canalised list (Appendix-5A) and for all OGL, items for actual users (Appendix-6, List 8, Part I and List 10). Eximscrips earned by exporters on their own exports can also be used to import non-OGL capital goods other than those on the restricted list (Appendix-1A). All REP licences issued against exports prior to 4th July, 1991 will continue to be valid for the life of the licence and will have the same import entitlement as the new Eximscrips. Additional licences issued to export houses/trading houses, which were earlier valid for a more limited range of imports, will also be valid for the same range of imports as Eximscrips.

With the introduction of Eximscrips, the system of issuing supplementary licences of raw material, components and spares listed in Appendix-3 will be discontinued except for small scale industries and for manufacturers of specified life saving drugs and equipment. In future, all import requirements of these items (with the exceptions indicated above) will be made through Eximscrips, Similarly items in Appoendix-4 and Appendix-9, which were earlier importable against supplementary licences, will henceforth be importable only against Eximscrips. Import of items appearing in Appendix-2 Part B (list of Restricted Items) and Appendix-8 (List of Scientific and Measuring Instruments Restricted for Import) of the Import-Export Policy 1990-93 will continue to require licences. Such licences as well as licences required for small scale industries and manufactures of life saving drugs/equipment will be called Special Licences as these will be limited and include special cases.

As a measure of import compression and to strengthen the linkage between import capability and exports, two further changes have been made. The category of unlisted OGL has been abolished and these items have been shifted to Appendix-3. They are now importable only against Eximscrips (except for SSI and manufacturers of life saving drugs and equipment). In the case of units subject to the Phased Manufacturing

Programme (PMP), many of which benefit from concessional duty on their imports of OGL items, all such items will henceforth be importable only against Eximscrips.

Eximscrips will be issued only after export proceeds have been realised. The procedure for issue of Eximscrips has been streamlined and Government will ensure that Eximscrips are issued within 48 hours of the receipt of the application accompanied by single document, namely, the bank certificate for the realisation of export proceeds.

Advance Licences

The system of advance licences is designed to provide exporters with duty free access to the inputs they need to produce competitively for world markets. This is an important instrument of trade policy especially in our situation where tariff levels are still high. The Government has taken the following steps to strengthen the system of Advance Licences as an instrument of export promotion:

(i) The procedures for considering Advance Licence applications have been simplified to ensure that advance licences will be issued within 15 days of application in all cases where input-output norms have been fixed. Where norms have not been fixed, the licence will be issued within 45 days.

(ii) The number of documents accompanying an Advance licence application has been reduced from 9 to 3 where norms are prescribed and to 4 where chey are not prescribed.

(iii) Ar present norms have been prescribed for 540 items. This will be increased to over 1000 items by 31st October, 1991 and more items will be covered thereafter.

(iv) Substantial Manufacturing Activity as a necessary condition under the Advance Licence Scheme will no longer be applicable for exports to the general currency area. However, the value addition norms will remain in force. A large number of exporters will benefit under this scheme.

(v) A new Scheme of Transferable Advance Licence has been introduced for GCA exports in selected thrust areas, namely textiles, leather goods and engineering industries. Under this scheme exporters can undertake exports based on duty paid inputs obtained from the market and subsequently obtain advance licences for replenishment of these inputs by duty free imports. These advance licences will be freely transferable. The coverage of the scheme will be extended on merits.

(vi) Advance licence will specify values in free foreign exchange both for the purpose of import and export. The currencies in which such values are denominated will be limited to those notified for this purpose by the RBI.

(vii) The Existing procedure for obtaining Bank Guarantee (BG) and Legal Undertaking (LUT) from different categories of exporters in being streamlined and liberalised as follows:

(a) Export/Trading/Star Trading House and Public Sector Undertakings will have the facility of obtaining advance licence against LUT only without any monetary limit.

(b) All manufacturing units having an annual turnover of at least Rs. 5 crores (including both domestic and exports turnover) during the previous 3 year would also be able to avail of the LUT facility up to a value limit of 50% of their annual production.

(c) A new unit without any production or export performance to its credit would also be allowed LUT facility provided it is promoted by an existing company with an annual production of Rs. 5 crores for more than three years. In such a case, both the new company and the promoting company would have to provide LUT.

(d) Bank guarantee and/or LUT obligation will be concurrent to the fulfilment of export obligation.

(viii) Exporters would be allowed to dispose of the materials imported against advance licences by way of replenishment without seeking prior permission of the licensing authority in cases where no MODVAT facility has been availed of on the domestic material used in exports.

(ix) Adjustment needed on account of fluctuation of prices of imported individual items would be permitted within the overall CIF value of advance licence.

(x) The power of revalidation which presently vests in the Licencing Committee at the Headquarters has been delegated to the Licensing Authorities.

(xi) In case where applications for an advance licence are turned down, the exporter will be permitted to convert to the Duty Drawback regime by the Collectors of Customs so that shipments made in advance can be imported on payment of duty subsequent claims of duty drawback.

(xii) Exporters can obtain advance release orders for domestic supply against advance licences under which the domestic supplier gets the benefit of deemed exports. Henceforth, release orders will be issued across the counter without requiring the name of the domestic supplier, which could be given later.

The adoption of these procedures would reduce discretionary controls and delays and afford much greater freedom to exporters in procuring essential duty free raw materials to maintain their competitiveness in the would market thereby promoting exports from the country.

The export Processing Zone scheme and the 100% EOU scheme were introduced to provide for duty-free enclaves, which would enable entrepreneurs to concentrate on production exclusively for export. However, with increasing liberalisation in the DTA, the duty advantages enjoyed by EPZs/EOUs have become less important. While the procedures of Customs Bonding are very onerous. The schemes have not therefore taken off as expected and they have also not attracted foreign investment aimed at tapping export markets to the extent that was expected. The working of these schemes has been reviewed and the following changes made:

(i) All EOUs/EPZ unit will be eligible for Eximscrips at the basic rate of 30% applied to net foreign exchange earning.

(ii) The duty applicable on DTA sales from EOUs/EPZ units is being reduced to 50% of the normal customs subject to the duty payable not being less than the excise duty on the same product. The extent of DTA sales allowed will be accordance with their entitlement. DTA sales will be permitted in the ratio of 25:75 in relation to export sales in case of units while use of indigenous raw material is more than 30% of production. In all other cases the ratio of permissible DTA sales to export sales will be 15:85. The procedures for clearing goods from the EOU/EPZ units for DTA sales are also being streamlined.

(iii) In order to encourage exporters to set up EOUs or

EPX units the net foreign exchange earned by EOUs or EPZ units can be clubbed with the earnings of their parent/associated companies in the DTA for the purpose of according Export House. Trading House of Star Trading House status for the latter.

(iv) The IPRS scheme for supply of steel to exporters will also be extended to EOUs and EPZ units. The Development Commissioners are being empowered to issue "payment authorities" in lieu of JCCI & Es.

Under the New Industrial Policy, most industries do not require an industrial licence except for a defined list. With a view to bringing about comparable streamlining in the procedure for EOU/EPZ approvals, a systems of automatic approvals is being established for all proposals which fall within certain parameters. Capital goods imports will be allowed under the automatic approvals procedure if they are fully covered by foreign equity or if they do not exceed 50% of the value of plant and equipment subject to a ceiling of Rs 3 crores. All proposals within the automatic approval parameters will be cleared within two weeks. All other proposals will be submitted to the Board of Approvals for consideration and decisions including issue of licences will be taken within 45 days.

A large number of issues relating to the operation of EOUs/EPZ units required centralized clearance in the Ministries of Commerce and Industry. Powers are being delegated to the Development Commissioners so that these approvals can be given on a decentralised basis. The specific approval of the Development Commissioner would not be required in cases of broad banding by EPZ units, where value addition is being maintained. The unit concerned would need only to provide relevant information to the Development Commissioner.

The following specific concessions to EOUs/EPZ units have also been extended:

(i) Allowing entry of imported raw material on "Provisional Assessment" basis, to expedite customs clearance.

(ii) Permitting units under the EPZ and EOU schemes to supply/transfer finished goods among themselves.

(iii) Replacement of multiple bond by a single bond, for obtaining import clearance.

(iv) Increasing the list of items under the "Special Imprest Licence Scheme" on selective basis.

(vi) Clarifying that containers stuffed in EPZ and EOUs are not to be reinspected at other points, as long as seals are intact.

Government have also decided to allow private parties to establish bonded warehouses within EPZs for stocking and sale of duty free raw materials, components, consumables and spares to EPZ units and EOUs. This will cut down delay in obtaining supplies of duty free materials which are in constant and regular demand by exporters. The details of this scheme will be notified shortly.

Other steps announced in the new Trade Policy have been the simplification of procedures for import of capital goods, decanalisation of number of items which were previously canalised, permission to allow established exporters to open foreign currency accounts in approved banks, raise external credits, pay for export related imports from such accounts and credit export proceeds to such accounts, its decision to re-designate the office of the Chief Controller of Import and Exports as Directorate General of International Trade with the principal function being to promote of exports, and facilitation of imports to promote export trade.

The policy changes now being implemented imply substantial reduction in the extent of licensing and in the number of types of licences. Supplementary licences for import of items in Appendixes-3 (except for SSI and manufacturers of life saving drugs and equipment), 4 and 9 of the Import-Export Policy 1990-93 have been abolished. Additional licences which were issued as an incentive to Export Houses and Trading Houses will stand abolished with effect from 1st April, 1992 and the incentive will take the form of an additional Eximscrip entitlement.

To achieve optimal import containment in the context of the present Balance of Payments situation, several steps have been taken. One of these is the shift of many items which are on OGL to the limited permissible list.

With these changes, the policy for import of raw materials components and other inputs needed for production has been simplified. Most raw materials and other inputs (except for those on the Restricted List) can be freely imported either against Eximscrips or on OGL. Some raw materials continue to be canalised but in more of these cases requirements beyond those provided by the canalising agencies can be met through Eximscrips.It is the policy of the Government to move to a situation where imports of essential raw materials and components needed for industrial production are regulated through appropriate tariffs. However, in view of the Balance of Payments position which necessitates continued import containment, this cannot be done immediately. Many items must therefore remain on the limited permissible list, with imports permitted only against Eximscrips.

The medium term objective of the Government is to progressively eliminate licensing and quantitative restrictions on capital goods and raw materials/

components so that all these items can be placed on OGL save for a small carefully defined negative list. This shift is proposed to be achieved over a 3 to 5 year period. The Government will appoint a High Level Committee to work out the modalities of achieving this transition keeping in mind the Balance of Payments position and the need to rationalise the reduce tariffs progressively to provide Indian Industry with an appropriate environment to develop international competitiveness.

Industrial Policy and Trade Policy of the Government of India

Over the years the Government of India has been adopting various measures for the liberalisation of the Industrial Policy, for streamling the licensing and foreign collaboration procedures, for reducing the number of agencies which the prospective investors have to approach to get the necessary approvals, etc., with the objective of attracting more investment and technology transfer. On the 24th July, 1991 the Government tabled before Parliament the Statement on Industrial Policy, 1991, which was followed by the issuance of a Notification by the Department of the Industrial Development to implement the Policy Statement and a series of Press Notes to set out the changes in the existing system and procedure for obtaining industrial licenses and approval of proposals for foreign and for foreign testing of indigenous raw materials and products and indigenously developed technlogies.

The new Industrial Licensing Policy of the Government of India has exempted form the requirement of obtaining industrial licence all industries, except those reserved for the Public Sector (Schedule I to the the Notification), those in respect of which Idustrial Licensing is compulsory (Schedule II to the Notification) and those relating to the items reserved for exclusive manufacture in the small scale sector (Schedule III to the Notification).

The exemption from Industrial licensing is also subject to:

The proposed project (except in the case of a project relating to electronics, computer software, printing industry, industry located within an area designated as 'industrial area' by a State Government before the 25th July, 1991 or the small scale or the ancillary sector) being not located with 25 kilo meters form the periphery of the standard urban area limits of a city having a population of more than one million according to the 1991 census; and of the Central and the State environmental laws and regulations including local zoning and land use laws and regulations.

Units qualifying for exemption from industrial licensing in accordance with the foregoing conditions are required only to file a Memorandum in the prescribed form, before establishement of the project, with the Department of Industrial Development (Secretariat for Industrial Approvals) together with a crossed demand draft for rupees one thousand in favour of the Pay and Account Officer, Department of Industrial Development and another Memorandum in the prescribed form at the time of commencement of commercial production.

Small scale and ancillary units are required, as before, to be registered with the Director of Industries of the concerned State. Manufacturing units with an investment in plant and machinery up to Rs. 60 lakhs, ancillary units with an investment in plant and machinery up to Rs. 75 lakhs and units which are willing to undertake an export obligation to the extend of 30 per cent of their annual production by the third year with an investment up to Rs. 75 lakhs are eligible for small scale registration.

The new industrial policy of the Government of India has announced major liberalisation for attracting foreign investment in respect of a list of high priority industries (Annexure III to the Statement of Industrial Policy, 1991). Foreign equity investment up to 51 per cent will be allowed subject only to the condition that;

— The requirement of imported capital goods should be covered by the foreign equity;

— Remittance of dividends should be covered by earnings of the company from export of items in Annexure III to the Statement of Industrial Policy , 1991. The amount of dividend payment may be converted by export earnings of such items recorded in Years prior to the payment of dividend or in the year of payment of dividend. This will be monitored by the Reserve Bank of India. However, such balancing will not be required beyond a period of seven years from commencement of production.

In all such cases the Reserve Bank of India has been authorised to issue automatic approvals of foreign investment and also grant exemption from the operation of the relevant sections of the Foreign Exchange Regulations Act, 1973.

3

Shipping

The salient features of India's Shipping Policy continue to be :-

(a) increasing self-reliance in the carriage of country's overseas trade, and

(b) reservation of 100% coastal trade for National Shipping.

To achieve this, and in line with our new economic policy aimed at liberalisation of controls, the acquisition of certain categories of vessels have been put under open General Licence (OGL) with effect from 1.4.1997. With the favourable market freight rate, the Indian shipping grew steadily and achieved the 8th plan target of 7.00 million GRT in December, 1995, ahead of time. However, the impressive growth has slowed down during the year 1997-98. The volume of trade is expected to double in the next 5 years and to cater to that kind of business, Indian tonnage should also double to 14 million GRT from 7 million GRT. However, keeping in view the pace of development in the last few decades and on account of financial constraints, it has been proposed to achieve a net growth of 2 million GRT taking the total tonnage to 9 million GRT at the end of the 9th Plan with the acquisition of 3.7 million GRT (2 million on additional account and 1.7 million on replacement account) at an investment of Rs. 15,000 crs. approximately.

Indian Shipping tonnage which was only 1,92,000 Gross Tonnage owned by Indian Lines on the eve of Independence now stands at 6.77 million Gross Tonnage. 27 vessels totalling 21.3065 GRT have actually been acquired and added to the Indian fleet and 23 vessels totalling 319430 GRT have been deleted from Indian fleet during the year 1998.

The details of the Indian Tonnage Category-wise for coastal & overseas is at Appendix-III & IV respectively.

Tonnage on order

59 ships were on order with Indian Yards as on 30th November, 1998 i.e. 26 Tugs of 4554 GRT, 4 Bulk Carriers of 55810 DWT, 1 Passenger vessel of 4650 DWT, 1 Tanker of 92400 DWT, 6 Barges of 17700 GRT and 26 vessels of other categories of 4554 GRT.

3 vessels were on order with foreign Yards as on 30th November, 1998 i.e. 1 Crude Oil Tanker of 105500 DWT, 1 Product Tanker of 30,000 DWT and 1 Anchore Handling Tug of 2100 GRT.

Ship acquisition licensing committee (SALC)

During 1998, the Committee held 4 meetings and approved acquisition proposals for 19 Spl. Vessels aggregating to 9600 GRT approximately in respect of private sector shipping companies. Sanction has invariably been issued within 45 days of the receipt of application. As per the new Import Export policy effective from 1.4.1997, certain categories of vessels have been placed under OGL and no permission is required from this Ministry for import of vessels. In addition to above, the various shipping companies had submitted papers under OGL scheme for acquisition of 18 vessels comprising about 501003 GRT. Further, DG(S) has issued technical clearance for these vessels.

Fishing trawlers development fund

The scheme of granting subsidy in respect of fishing trawlers built by Indian shipyards was continued during 1998-99. However, during the last 2-3 years, no claim of subsidy from Indian Shipyards has been received. A token provision of Rs.1 lakh has been provided in the Budget for disbursement of subsidy.

Directorate genernal of shipping, Mumbai

The Director General of Shipping (DG(S)) is a statutory authority appointed under the Merchant Shipping Act, 1958 and is responsible for implementation of the provisions of the Act. The Directorate also ensures implementation of various International conventions relating to safety requirements for prevention of oil pollution and other mandatory requirements of International Maritime Organisation (IMO).

Following are the allied and the subordinate Offices of DG(S):

(i) Mercantile Marine Departments at Mumbai, Calcutta, Chennai, Jamnagar, Mormugao, Port Blair, Cochin, Tuticorin and Visakhapatnam.

(ii) Seamen's Employment Offices at Mumbai, 3 Calcutta and Chennai.

(iii) Shipping Masters office at Mumbai and Calcutta.

(iv) Training Institutes viz. (i) L.B.S. College of Advanced Maritime Studies & Research, Mumbai (ii) Marine Engineering and Research Institutes at Calcutta and Mumbai (iii) Training Ship 'Chanakya', Mumbai.

(v) Regional Offices (Sails) at Jamnagar, Mumbai and Calicut.

Shipping Masters Offices are located in Mumbai/ Calcutta. Their main functions include supervision of the engagement and discharge of seamen, navigational Officers, issuance of Continuous Discharge Certificates to persons eligible under M.S. (C.D.C.) Rules. From Jan. to Nov. 98, 1552 officers & 6111 Seamen were engaged and 1655 officers and 5780 seamen were discharged. As many as 4945 CDCs were issued during the period. 42 death cases were reported and 663 inward & 665 outward clearances were granted. The total Revenue earnings were Rs. 21.10 lakhs.

Seamen's Employment Offices have been set up at Mumbai, Calcutta and Chennai to regulate recruitment of Seamen in India. Since 1992, instead of Rotational Employment Scheme`Retainer Scheme' for employment of Indian Seamen is in force. During the period under review, against 5669 available jobs, 14137 were registered with SEOs for jobs.

The Regional Office (Sails) are responsible for the welfare of the sailing vessel industry in the respective regions. During the period under review, 477 fresh identity cards and 158 duplicate identity cards were issued and 1333 identity cards have been renewed.

National welfare board-for seafarers

As provided in section 218 of M.S. Act. 1958, the Government of India constituted a National Welfare Board for seafarers headed by the Union Minister of Surface Transport for advising the Government on the measures to be taken for promoting the welfare of seamen whether ashore or abroad.

Seamen's provident fund organisation

The Seamen's Provident Fund Organisation has been set-up under the Seamen's Provident Fund Act, 1964 to provide institution of Provident Fund for Seamen w.e.f. 1st July, 1964.

National shipping board

The National Shipping Board is a permanent statutory body established in 1959 under Section 4 of the Merchant Shipping Act, 1958 to advise the Government of India on matters related to Shipping including the development thereof. The National Shipping Board has played an important role in the maritime development of the country. The Board has thus contributed immensely in the evolution of a sound and pragmatic National Maritime Policy over the years.

The Chairman and other members of the Board hold office for a period of two years. The Composition of the Board is as follows: -

(a) Six Members elected by Parliament, four from the Lok Sabha from among its members, and two from the Rajya Sabha from among its members;

(b) Such number of other members not exceeding sixteen as the Central Government may think fit to appoint on the Board to represent -

(i) The Central Government,

(ii) Shipowners,

(iii) Seamen, and

(iv) Such other interests as in the opinion of Central Government ought to be represented on the Board.

The Act provides that one of the members of the Board shall be nominated by the Central Government to be the Chairman of the Board.

In the current year, i.e. 1998, two meetings of the Board were held as per details below: -

1) 98th meeting of the National Shipping Board held at Kandla on 17th April, 1998.

2) 99th Meeting of the National Shipping Board held at Cochin on 19th August, 1998.

National shipping policy committee

A National Shipping Policy Committee under the Chairmanship of Director General of Shipping was constituted by Govt. The Committee in its report submitted in July, 1997, made 31 recommendations. The Empowered Committee subsequently constituted to examine the report, recommended acceptance of 26 recommendations and rejection of 5 recommendations. After detailed examination, Govt. have taken a decision to implement 15 recommendations with immediate effect.

The matter relating to acceptance of the remaining 11 recommendations is under active consideration by Government and final decision will be taken in due course.

India's delegation to IMO

The IMO is a specialised agency set up under the United Nations dealing with technical aspects of Shipping relating to Maritime Safety, Protection of Marine Environment, Standard of training and related legal matters. The ILO has a maritime wing which deals with various aspects of employment of seafarers. The UNCTAD deals with commercial and economic aspects of Shipping with involvement of regional - UN bodies like ESCAP. Lately the World Trade Organization (WTO) meetings concerning Maritime Transport Services are taking place regularly in which India has a big stake.

International conventions and protocols

IMO has developed 40 instruments (22 Conventions, 17 Protocols and 1 operating agreement). Out of 22 Conventions and 17 Protocols, 20 Conventions and 10 Protocols are in force internationally. One Operating Agreement is also inforce internationally. India has ratified 19 instruments (13 Conventions, 5 Protocols and 1 operating agreement). India has ratified the following Conventions/ Protocols,

Conventions ratified

(i) International Convention for the Safety of Life at Sea, 1974 as amended [SOLAS (Amended) 1974].

(ii) Convention on the International Regulations for Preventing Collisions at Sea, 1972 as amended [COLREG (Amended) 1972].

(iii) Convention on Facilitation of International Maritime Traffic, 1965 as amended [FAL (Amended) 1965].

(iv) International Convention of Load Line, 1966 (LL 1966).

(v) International Convention on Tonnage Measurement of Ships, 1969 (TONNAGE 1969).

(vi) International Convention on Civil Liability for Oil Pollution Damage, 1969 (CLC 1969).

(vii) Special Trade Passenger Ships Agreement, 1971 (STP 1971).

(viii) International Convention on the Establishment of an International Fund for Compensation of Oil Pollution Damage, 1971 (FUND 1971).

(ix) International Convention for Safe Containers, 1971 as amended [CSC (Amended) 1972].

(x) Convention on the International Maritime Satellite Organization (INMARSAT) as amended [INMARSAT (Amended)].

(xi) International Convention on Standards of Training, Certification and Watch keeping for Seafarers, 1978 (STCW 1978).

(xii) International Convention on Salvage 1989 (SALVAGE 1989).

(xiii) International Convention on Oil Pollution Preparedness, Response and Cooperation, 1990 (OPRC 1990).

Conventions under consideration

(i) International Convention on Maritime Search and Rescue, 1979 (SAR).

(ii) Convention for the suppression of Unlawful Acts against the Safety of Maritime Navigation (SUA 1988).

(iii) International Convention relating to Intervention on the High Seas in cases of Oil Pollution Casualties, 1969 (INTERVENTION 1969).

(iv) Convention on Limitation of Liability for Maritime Claims, 1976.

(v) Convention on the Prevention of Marine Pollution by Dumping of Wastes and other matters 1972 as amended [I.C. (Amended) 1972].

Convention not to be ratified

(i) Convention relating to Civil Liability in the field of Maritime Carriage of Nuclear Materials, 1971.

(ii) The Athens Convention relating to the Carriage of Passengers and their Luggage by Sea, 1974.

Protocols ratified

(i) Protocol of 1978 relating to the International Convention for the Safety of Life at Sea, 1974.

(ii) The Protocol relating to the International Convention for the Prevention of Pollution from Ships 1973 as amended [MARPOL (Amended) 73/78)].

(iii) Protocol to the International Convention on Civil Liability for Oil Pollution Damage, 1969 (CLC PROT 1976).

(iv) Protocol on Space Requirement Special Trade Passenger Ships, (SPACE STP 1973).

(v) Protocol to the International Convention on the Establishment of an International Fund for Compensation for Oil Poll Damage 1971 (FUND PROT 1976)

Protocols under consideration

(i) Protocol for Suppression of Unlawful Acts against

the Safety of Fixed Platforms located on the Continental Shelf (SUA PROT 1988).

(ii) Protocol of 1992 to amend Convention on Civil Liability for Oil Pollution Damage 1969.

(iii) Protocol of 1992 to amend the International Convention on the Establishment of an International Fund for Compensation of Oil Pollution Damage, 1971.

(iv) Protocol to the Conventions on the Prevention of Marine Pollution by Dumping of Wastes and Other Matters, 1972.

(v) Protocol of 1988 relating to International Convention for the Safety of Life at Sea 1974.

(vi) Protocol of 1988 relating to the International Convention on load lines.

(vii) Protocol relating to Intervention on the High Seas in cases of Pollution by Substances other than Oil, 1973.

Protocols not to be ratified

(i) Protocols to the Athens Convention relating to the Carriage of Passengers and their Luggage by Sea, 1974 (PAI.PROT 1976).

(ii) Protocol of 1990 to amend the Athens Convention relating to Carriage of Passengers and their Luggage by Sea, 1974.

(iii) Torremolinos Protocol of 1993 relating to the Torremolinos International Convention for the Safety of Fishing Vessels, 1977 Revised.

(iv) Protocol of 1996 to amend the Convention on Limitation of Liability for Maritime Claims, 1976.

Operating agreement (ratified by India)

(i) Operating Agreement on the International Maritime Satellite Organization (INMARSAT), as amended [INMARSAT OA (AMENDED)].

The following Conventions/Protocols, which have been adopted by IMO recently have not yet entered into force internationally as requisite number of countries have not yet ratified. These Conventions/Protocols will be taken up for consideration only after there is an indication that they may come into force.

Convention

1. International Convention on Standards of Training, Certification and Watchkeeping for Fishing Vessel Personnel, 1995 STCW-F.
2. International Convention on Liability and Compensation for Damage in connection with the Carriage of Hazardous and Noxious Substances by Sea, 1996 (HNS, 1996).

Protocol

1. Protocol of 1997 to amend the International Convention for the Prevention of Pollution from Ships. 1973 as modified by the Protocol of 1978 relating thereto (MARPOL PROT 1997).

Amendments to merchant shipping act., 1958

A Committee constituted under the Chairmanship of the Director General of Shipping in February, 1991 to review the various provisions in the M.S. Act, 1958 and to suggest the suitable amendments submitted its report in 1992. This committee suggested about 180 amendments to be made in the M.S. Act, 1958.

An internal high level committee was formed to examine these recommendations for implementation of the Report. Meanwhile, some of the amendments suggested by the Committee were taken up for legislation on account of its urgency and importance in the order of priority. Accordingly, Section 21, 42, 45, 51, 412 and 414 were amended with effect from 17th Jan., 1994 to facilitate implementation of current policy of liberalization of economy and relaxation of Govt. control. Subsequently, amendments to few other Sections (89, 132, 138A, 369 and 436) were also taken up and an ordinance was promulgated on 26th Sept., 1997 to give effect to the proposed amendments in pursuance of Govt.'s ratification of ILO Convention 147. This has since become law and Ordinance has been replaced by an Act of Parliament passed in June, 1998 (No. 6 of 1998). Similarly, amendments to Sections 76 and 95 were also taken up. A revised amendment Bill incorporating the consequential amendments in the relevant sections was introduced and passed by the Rajya Sabha in the winter session.

Comprehensive amendment proposals are under finalization after which approval of, Cabinet will be sought before seeking approval of the Parliament.

Multimodal transportation of goods act, 1993

The Multimodal Transportation of Goods Act, 1993 was enacted on 2nd April, 1993. The Act provides for the regulation of the Multimodal Transportation of Goods from any place in India to a place outside India on the basis of a multimodal transport contract and for matters connected therewith or incidental thereto.

In the light of the experience gained during the course of implementation of this Act and the discussions held with various organisations, concerned shipping lines, Chambers of Commerce and Industry and the Directorate General of Shipping, there is a proposal to amend certain provisions of the Act to ensure its smooth implementation and achieve the stated objective.

Registration of MTOs : According to the existing scheme of the Act, the DG(S) has been notified as the completent authority for the purpose of registration of Multimodal transport operators.

Ship acquisition

The number of licences issued during the period 1st Jan.,`98 to 30th Nov., '98 is given below :-

1 .	General Trading Licence	90
2.	Specified Period Licences for Indian Flag vessels.	06
3.	Specified Period Licences for Offshore vessels.	27
4.	Specified Period Licences for Foreign Flag vessels.	176
5.	Specified Voyage Licences.	50
		349

The Directorate has given following permissions for chartering in of foreign flag vessels from 1st Jan., '98 to 30th Nov., '98 for export/import of cargoes and also for transportation of cargoes in the coastal trade of India.

1.	Voyage Charter	419
2.	Time Charter	93
3.	Bareboat Charter	05
4.	Space Slot/Space Charter	21
5.	Feeder Service	

Merchant navy training

LBS college of AMS&R

The Lal Bahadur Shastri College of Advanced Maritime Studies and Research is a premier post-sea Maritime Education and Training Institute offering a comprehensive range of courses for 'Merchant Navy Officers. The college was established by the Ministry of Transport, Government of India, in 1948.

The College attracts a large number of students for maritime education and training. In terms of student turnover, this is one of the largest Marine Training institutions in the world. It offers about 30 post-sea courses which run almost concurrently. The courses meet the standards of International Maritime Organisation (IMO) as well as those of Government of India. There are over 1200 students on the rolls at any given time. The college is fully equipped to meet the requirements of marine officers afloat and ashore. About 70% of Indian Officers afloat are employed on foreign flag ships. This is because of the high quality of maritime education imparted to them in this institute and the subsequent high level of professionalism and competency maintained by them.

During the year 1998, there has been a spurt of foreign nationals attending courses in this college. Hence, the Government approved a proposal to charge fees from them in US dollars for each modular course. The revenue earned by the college from 1st April to 30th November, 1998 is about Rs. 2,45,50,089 which includes US dollars 25,303 received as fees from foreign students.

Teaching faculty

The total number of faculty members in this College is 57 of which 47 are deputed by MMERT (Merchant Marine Education and Research Trust). The break up is as follows :

Nautical	Engineering	Radio	Academic	Electronics	Instructors
27	8	3	9	3	6

The College has a well-equipped video-cum-book library having nearly 8,000 technical books. A large number of Indian and foreign technical periodicals are subscribed for. This library is manned by well qualified and experienced personnel and it is fully computerized. The College is an institutional member of the British Council Library and the I.I.T. Library.

T.S. Chanakya

T.S. Chanakya is a Shore-Based Academy established in 1993 after the de-commissioning of 'T.S. Rajendra'. It conducts two streams of training courses - (1) 3-year B.Sc. (Nautical Science) Degree course and (ii) 3-months pre-sea training course for Deck Cadets approved by D.G. Shipping. The intake capacity per year is 80. During the current year, for the degree courses there are 96 cadets in the first year batch (including 7 Ethiopians), 76 cadets in the second year batch (including 3 Ethiopians) and in the third year batch 66 cadets (including 2 Ethiopians). In the 3-months pre-sea course, 115 cadets have been trained during this year as under:

XIV Batch - 39 Cadets' (from 01.04.98 to 29.06.98).

XV Batch - 76 Cadets' (from 05.08.98 to 02.11.98)

Marine engineering & research institute (MERI)

Marine Engineering & Research Institute, erstwhile Directorate of Marine Engineering Training (DMET), with its Headquarters at Calcutta and Branch at Mumbai, was established in the year 1949 to impart training to the Marine Engineering Cadets. The Headquarters of the Institute is headed by the Director and the Branch by the Dy. Director. The MERI, Calcutta conducts 4-year Marine Engineering course equivalent to Degree course in Marine Engineering. The intake capacity of the above course is 120 per year. Similarly, MERI, Mumbai, conducts Trainee Marine Engineering Course (TME) of 6 months duration in which about 120 Graduate Mechanical Engineers undergo training in various subjects. Both institutes are fully equipped to impart effective training in all the branches of Marine Engineering. The graduate engineers are sponsored by various Indian and foreign shipping companies through the MMERT for admission at MERI, Mumbai whereas the cadets for admission to MERI, Calcutta, are selected through a combined all India entrance examination conducted by IITs, all over the country.

India's delegation to international bodies

The Ministry of Surface Transport participates in the international Conferences and meetings convened by the International Maritime Organisation (IMO), the International Labour Organisation (ILO) and UNCTAD. From April, 1998 India has participated in the following international meetings : -

(i) 77th Session of Legal Committee from 20th April, 1998 to 24th April, 1998. at IMO London.

(ii) 69th Session of IMO Maritime Safety Committee from 11th May, 1998 to 20th May, 1998 at London.

(iii) Second Preparatory meeting on the formation of regional Port State Control in the Indian Ocean region from 1st June, 1998 to 5th June, 1998 in Pretoria, South Africa.

(iv) 80th Session of IMO Executive Council from 15th June, 1998 to 19th June, 1998 at IMO, London.

(v) Steering Committee meeting of the Ballast Water Project of IMO from 29-30th July, 1998 in Cape Town, South Africa.

(vi) Conference on Maritime Search & Rescue (SAR) and Global Maritime Distress & Safety System (GMDSS) at Fremantle, Australia from 21 st Sept., 1998 to 25th Sept., 1998.

(vii) 81st Session of IMO Executive Council from 16th November, 1998 to 20th November, 1998 at IMO, London.

(Viii) 5th Session Of the Sub-Group on Transport of the Indo-Russian Joint Commission from 24th November, 1998 to 25th November, 1998 at Moscow.

(ix) ESCAP IMO Regional Policy Level Seminar on Safety of Coastal and Inland Navigation from 23rd November, 1998 to 26th November, 1998.

Shipping agreement

During the year 1998-99, no new shipping agreement has been concluded by India. However, proposals for bilateral shipping agreement with the following countries/organisations are under active consideration: -

"Ukraine, South Africa, European Union, Latvia, Romania, Morocco, Vietnam, Lithuania, Egypt, South Korea, France".

Shipping corporation of India

The Shipping Corporation of India Ltd. (SCI) was formed on 2nd October 1961 by the amalgamation of Eastern Shipping Corporation Ltd. (ESC) and Western Shipping Corporation of India Ltd. (WSC). The paid up capital of the company then was Rs. 23.5 crores.

The present authorised capital of SCI is Rs. 450 crores and the subscribed and paid up capital is Rs. 282.3 crores. The equity capital disinvested by Government of India remains at 19.88%. The status of SCI has changed from Private Limited Company to Public Limited company with effect from 18th September, 1992. The shares of SCI are listed and traded regularly.

Fleet strength

As on 15th Dec., 1998, SCI owns and operates 116 vessels of a total Gross Registered Tonnage (GRT) of 29.86 lakhs (50.09 lakh Dead Weight Tonnage (DWT)). The highly diversified fleet of SCI includes Bulk Carriers, Crude & Product Tankers, General Cargo Vessels, Cellular Container Vessels, Offshore Supply Vessels, Ammonia/ LPG Carriers, Phosphoric Acid/Chemical Carriers, Passenger-cum-Cargo Vessels and Timber Carriers. The

SCI also mans and manages 27 ships on behalf of Government Organisations/Departments,

Financial performance

SCI has a track record of making profits and has been earning substantial returns on investment. For the year 1997-98, the Gross Earnings increased to Rs. 2521.5 crores from Rs. 2442 crores in the previous year showing an increase of 3.25%. The Net Profit after Tax in 1997-98 was Rs. 246.2 crore. The company paid out a dividend of 20% for the year 1997-98.

Services operated by SCI

The SCI operates a number of general cargo liner services, passenger-cum-cargo services, overseas and coastal dry bulk cargo services, overseas tramp services and tanker services. The SCI also operates specialised vessels for carriage of LPG/ Phosphoric Acid.

Tonnage acquisition

SCI took delivery of one new bulk carrier of 42,750 DWT built at Hindustan Shipyard Ltd. during 1997-98, and one product tanker of 32,940 DWT from Hyundai Shipyard in November 1998. SCI has also purchased one second hand cargo liner vessel of 20,435 DWT during 1997-98. Vessels on order include one product tanker at Hyundai Shipyard, one double hull crude oil tanker at Cochin Shipyard, both scheduled for delivery in the first quarter of 1999 and two bulk carriers at Hindustan Shipyard Ltd.

Keeping in view, both the trade opportunities and the replacement requirements, the company has chalked out an ambitious acquisition programme to strengthen and modernise its fleet during the 9th Plan period. During the year 1998-99, it plans to acquire 16 vessels of 6.53 lakhs GRT. The vessels proposed to be acquired include crude and product tankers, general cargo vessels and LPG/Ammonia carrier.

Memorandum of understanding (MOU)

The profitability and performance of SCI is being periodically reviewed and evaluated on the basis of criteria agreed in the MOU signed with the Government every year. The MOU for the year 1998-99 was signed on 28th April, 1998. SCI has consistently been achieving "Excellent" rating as a MOU signing PSU in the past and expects to continue the trend in future.

Energy conservation

SCI is very conscious about conservation of energy and has been looking at ways and means to conserve energy. The main consumption of energy in ships is fuel oil. SCI has been trying to replace its old vessels with new hull designs, self polishing paints and other improvements in the propeller machinery which reduce resistance giving more speed per horse power to the ship resulting in the conservation of energy.

Human resource development

SCI lays great emphasis on training and retraining its personnel. SCI's Maritime Training Institute (MTI) at Mumbai is recognised as a branch of World Maritime University (Sweden) and also as a Regional Training Centre by UNCTAD. Extensive training programmes in consultation with Indian Government both for Navigating/ Engineering Officers, and also for shore based personnel are regularly conducted at MTI. During 1997-98, in all 389 courses were conducted, training 8429 personnel. MTI, as a branch of World Maritime University, is not only serving our nation but also the developing countries in the Asia-Pacific region. MTI is the first & only Maritime Institute in India to acquire Quality standard of ISO 9001 :1994 certificate for Design, Development, Delivery & Assessment of Marine Education & Training Research. It commissioned India's first GMDSS laboratory in January 1998 and was awarded the "Golden Peacock National Training Award" for excellence in training in June, 1998.

Implementation of official language policy

SCI continues to make efforts to promote and popularise the use of Hindi in the day-to-day official work. The company makes arrangement to provide in-service training in Hindi to non-Hindi speaking employees and also to provide training in typing and stenography in Hindi. The company organises quarterly Hindi workshops as well as various programmes such as Hindi competitions, Hindi fortnight, Hindi Kavi Sammelan etc. to create consciousness towards use of Hindi as an official language.

Welfare activities

The Company has always had the welfare of its employees and their families as one of its prime concerns. The welfare activities undertaken include educational scholarships to the children of the employees, loan assistance to pursue higher studies, provision of recreational facilities, subsidised canteen facility, dispensary facility, post-retirement medical scheme, incentives for adoption of small family, healthy baby competition etc. These activities are conducted in close co-ordination with the employee's forum and a welfare officer looks after these matters.

Assistance to weaker section of society and representation of reserved categories.

SCI makes constant efforts to improve the representation of SC/ST/OBC categories in the employment. Recently, a committee has been formed to extend financial assistance to the weaker sections of the society to encourage them to pursue education and come up in life.

1rano hind shipping company

The Irano Hind Shipping Company, a joint shipping venture established in 1975 in Iran earned in 1996-97, a pre-tax profit of Iranian Rials 22621 million (US$ 12.93 million) and a net profit of Iranian Rials 16688 million (US$ 9.54 million). It is expected that this joint venture company would make a pre-tax profit of Iranian Rials 15475 million (US$ 8.84 million) and a net profit of Iranian Rials 9891 million (US$ 5.65 million) during the year 1997-98. The company owns a fleet of 8 ships aggregating 0.167 million DWT.

Chartering

The Chartering Wing (Transchart) of the Ministry is responsible for making shipping arrangements for the ocean transportation of the Government owned/ controlled cargoes as per the policy of buying FOB/FAS and selling C&F/CIF. The shipping arrangements are centralised with Chartering Wing. The Wing undertakes shipping business on behalf of the private sector as well.

This Wing makes shipping arrangements on internationally competitive freight rates and in the process gives cargo preference to Indian bottoms. This Wing also advises the concerned indenting Departments/ PSUs/ Projects on various aspects of shipping and post-shipment issues.

Highlights of 1998-99

During the year 1998 (Jan. to Dec. '98), the quantity of Govt. Cargoes for which the Chartering Wing made shipping arrangements was about 218.82 lakh tonnes. The cargo handled during the year were Coking Coal, Lime Stone, Petroleum Products, Fertilizers, Fertilizer Raw Material, Iron-Ores, Steel Materials and other liner cargoes. Of the cargoes for which shipping arrangements were made by Transchart during the year 1998 a quantity of about 130.95 lakh tonnes about 59.84% was through Indian flag vessels. Efforts were made to ensure shipments as per the requirement of the indenting Departments/ PSUs and utilise Indian flag vessels to the maximum extent possible in ocean transportation of governmental cargoes.

A statement indicating the quantities of Government owned/controlled cargoes for which shipping arrangements were made by this Wing during the year 1997 and 1998 is at Appendix-V.

In addition to fixing vessels for shipment of cargoes, Chartering Wing also arranged charter of a specialized vessel for, XVIIIth Indian Scientific Expedition to Antarctica Account Department of Ocean Development. Besides Coal, Contract of Afreightment (COA)'s were also included for import of CPP, LPG in bulk account IOC and Caustic Soda account NALCO.

Government of India has an agreement with the IPBC (India, Pakistan, Bangladesh Conference) which caters to trade from U.K. and Continent to India. The agreement has been reviewed in consultation with Indian member shipping lines. As a result of negotiations with Conference members, it has been agreed to increase the rebate over tariff from present level of 15 & 17% to 22.5% in respect of break bulk cargoes and 35% in full container loads (FCL) w.e.f. 1.1.1999. There is a similar agreement with other conference under the title "INDPAKCON" (India, Pakistan, Bangladesh, Ceylon and Burma Outward Freight Confernece) which covers trade with US Gulfs and Atlantic Ports to India which has been further extended till 31 st January, 2000.

Service charges

Levying of 1% Chartering Service Charge on freight/ dead freight/demurrage/charter hire earned by Indian companies on vessel fixed through Transchart for carriage of import/export cargoes was made applicable from Feb.'93. Since then the earnings on this account have already totalled Rs. 35 crores (approx.). The total amount deposited into public exchequer during 1998 is Rs. 6 crores approximately.

Freight market 1998-99

In general the freight market has been weak and in a very bad shape throughout the year for dry bulk trades. Freight indications for handymax and large bulkers have dropped 20/34 per cent respectively since last December. The general view seems to be that the low levels will continue well in to the New Year 1999. The BFI (Baltic Freight index) at the end of 1998 is at 752 points corresponding to its level of 1231 points at the end of 1997. This reflects the shipping market for dry bulk sector.

The tanker market when compared to the bulk cargo market, though remained steady during the year in contrast to last year, showed weakness during the year.

4

Shipbuilding and Shiprepair

The nodal responsibility for the entire Shipbuilding and Shiprepair Industry, including the Fishing Vessels Industry and Floating Craft Industry vests with the Ministry.

There are 32 shipyards in the country including 23 private sector shipyards, the break-up of which is as under :-

Under the Central Public Sector	Under the State Govt.	In the Private Sector	Total
7	2	23	32

The break-up of 7 Shipyards in the Central Public Sector and 2 in the State Government is as under :-

Under the administrative control of minisrty of surface transport

1 Hindustan Shipyard Limited, Visakhapatnam
2. Cochin Shipyard Limited, Cochin.
3. Hooghly Dock & Port Engineers Limited, Calcutta.
4. Central Inland Water Transport Corporation, Calcutta.

Under the administrative control of ministry of defence

1. Mazagon Dock Limited, Mumbai.
2. Garden Reach Shipbuilders & Engineers Limited, Calcutta.

3. Goa Shipyard Limited, Goa.

Under the control of state governments:

1. Alcock & Ashdown Co. Ltd., Gujarat.
2. Shalimar Works Ltd., Calcutta.

Shipbuilding and Shiprepair (SBR) Wing, headed by the Development Adviser is the apex technical organisation connected with the development of Shipbuilding and Shiprepair Industry, ancillary development and related R&D activities. This Wing renders advice on matters relating to the development of facilities for Shipbuilding and Shiprepair, Fishing Trawlers, Ship Ancillary and R&D activities. Development Advisor also renders advice to other Ministries and Government Departments on such matters.

Important Achievements of this Sector during the year are as under:-

(a) Modernisation of Shiprepai facilities at Calcutta Port (Phase-I) has been completed at a total cost of Rs. 507 lakhs. Phase-II relating to modernisation of KIP Dry dock and NS Dry dock at a cost of Rs. 3.10 crores is under progress under delegated powers of Calcutta Port Trust.

(b) Modernisation of Shiprepair facilities at Mumbai Port is under implementation and is expected to be completed by end of March, 1999. The revised cost is Rs. 25.50 crores.

Budgetary matters relating to release of funds to Calcutta Port Trust and Mumbai Port Trust for the above schemes have been transferred to Ports Wing.

(c) The Ship Ancillary Development Committee set up by the SBR Wing has rationalised policy framework for progressively substituting import by indigenous material and equipment of acceptable quality and reliability. There is a scheme for providing grant-in-aid to Ship Ancillary Development Projects sponsored by the Central Public Sector Shipyards and Ministry of Surface Transport.

Entrepreneurs who take up the indigenous development of Ancillaries used in shipbuilding can avail Grant-in-aid up to the extent of 70% of the total development cost. The entrepreneurs are required to apply with full details of their proposals to the public sector shipyards who in turn would sponsor the proposal for the consideration of the Ship Ancillary Development Committee under this Ministry for approval of the project for Grant-in-Aid. Shipyards have also been requested to make sincere efforts to activate the vendors for developing Ancillary items indigenously. Copies of guidelines have also been circulated to the Shipyards/ Port Trusts, Shipping Corporation of India, Indian National Shipowners Association, Indian Shipbuilders Association & Shipyard Association of India. A Workshop is also being organised regarding Ship Ancillary items.

(d) This Ministry has a scheme of giving Grant-in-Aid to Educational and Research Institutions for carrying out R&D activities. There are at present, nine (9) on-going R&D projects, sanctioned at an estimated cost of Rs. 127.12 lakhs. Out of these nine schemes, two schemes viz. 'SAIL as an auxiliary propulsion by NSDRC and also 'Development of Computer Software for Ship Design & Operation by NSDRC are expected to be completed by the end of January/March 1999 respectively. Till date, an amount of Rs. 66,79,995/- has already been released by Ministry of Surface Transport on these schemes.

The R&D Schemes on "Development of Manual Software on 3-D Finite Element Analysis of Ship Structures by IIT, Kharagpur was completed in May 1998, The Final Report received is being circulated to Shipyards, IRS, DG (Shipping).

(e) An Apex Committee on Shipbuilding under the Chairmanship of Director General of Shipping has been constituted by this Ministry to look into the problems of Shipyards and prepare a strategy for making the Indian Shipbuilding industry competitive.

(f) A study has also been entrusted to the Bureau of Industrial Costs & Prices by this Ministry regarding pricing/costing of ships and problems of shipbuilding industry in general. The BICP is also expected to prepare a strategy for International Competitiveness of Indian Shipbuilding Industry.

(g) One of the recommendations of the National Shipping Policy Committee accepted by the Government encourages the State Governments to create suitable infrastructure for ship repair by State Governments. Chief Ministers of Maritime State Governments have been requested to initiate action in this regard by the Hon'ble Minister (SFT).

National ship design & research centre, Visakhapatnam

The National Ship Design & Research Centre (NSDRC) has been set up at Visakhapatnam as a Registered Society under the Registrar of Societies Act, 1860 under the administrative control of the Ministry and is managed by a Governing Body constituted by the Government with Secretary (SFT) as Chairman. The total cost of NSDRC Project was Rs. 2489 crores including 19 Million Dutch Guilders provided by Government of Netherlands as grant-in-aid. The Centre has become fully operational since May, 1993.

NSDRC is designed to provide support to the Indian Shipbuilding Industry in the field of Ship Design, Research in Hydrodynamic structures, noise and vibrations, ocean/water transport economy, shipyard management, operation of vessels etc. 4.1.6 An integrated Projects Division has been set up at NSDRC comprising of Ship Design, Marine Consultancy & Maritime Economic Specialisation to meet the above objectives.

Major projects completed by NSDRC

1 Modification of ICC Jetty at Kandla. The project was completed in record time and the soundness of modified design was proved in the recent cyclone.
2. Feasibility Study for restructuring of M/s Hooghly Dock & Port Engineers Ltd., Calcutta completed as a part of SCICI Project.
3. Conceptual Design of Water Front facilities for Vepac at Ennore Port.
4. Design of Hopper Barge for Mumbai Port Trust.
5. Design of one number Multipurpose Vessel for Calcutta Port Trust.

Hindustan shipyard limited, Visakhapatnam

H.S.L. was set up in 1941 in the Private Sector and was taken over by the Government of India in January, 1952. Its authorised capital is Rs. 100.00 crores and the paid up capital is Rs. 90.81 crores.

The investment made by the Government up to 31 st March, 1998 for development of the Yard is Rs. 221.16 crores. The Yard has the following activity centres and production facilities:-

(a) Shipbuilding:

The present capacity is 3.5 pioneer vessels of 21,500 DWT. It can undertake construction of ships of 50,000 DWT. For quality assurance, it has obtained ISO:9001 in respect of ship design and industrial structures. The shipbuilding facilities include slipways, a covered building dock, wet basin, shops equipped with good and adequate infrastructural facilities. So far, HSL has constructed and delivered 111 vessels, Naval Vessels and other small crafts, etc. The Yard has to its credit construction of high technology oriented and sophisticated drill ship for the Oil and Natural Gas Commission, which is first of its kind built in India.

(b) Shiprepairs

This complex was added in 1971. The Yard has undertaken repairs of variety of vessels including Naval Ships, Merchant Vessels, Dredgers, Tugs and also Submarines. The facilities include a modern dry dock supported by modern infrastructural facilities to undertake any type or repairs of ships up to 70,000 DWT. HSL is making profit on ship repairs. Yard has also equipped itself for undertaking the repairs of submarines.

(c) Offshore platforms construction yard:

This Yard came in 1985 as a major step towards diversification. The Yard constructed, installed and delivered 11 sophisticated platforms of various types to ONGC. The OPF Yard is another profit-making centre. After delivering the last platforms in March, 1995 there is no order on hand. However, the Yard's capacity is being used for shipbuilding.

(d) Structural fabrication - diversification project:

This activity was taken up in 1985 to gainfully utilise the steel shop to the fullest possible extent. During this year,

HSL has taken up structural fabrication work of Visakhapatnam Steel Plant and Railways to the tune of Rs. 1 crore. HSL has plans to strengthen this activity into full fledged work centre.

Performance of the company

Financial Results for the last three years.

Year	*Turnover*	*Profit/Loss*
	(Rupees in crores)	
1995-96	180.07	(—) 118.16
1996-97	132.86	(—) 150.80
1997-98	104.99	(—) 62.19

The Company has been incurring losses on shipbuilding since 1980-81 for the following reasons :

(a) Cost-price gap in shipbuilding;
(b) Heavy interest burden on Government and Bank loans;
(c) Excessive manpower.
(d) Reduction in turnover for want of fresh orders for shipbuilding and OPF, as well.

Steps taken for improving the performance of, the company: -

The following specific policy decisions taken by the Government of India assist the company in the process of improving its performance :-

(a) reintroduction of subsidy scheme; and
(b) restructuring of capital base of the Company Shipbuilding subsidy scheme which has been reintroduced w.e.f. 14th August, 1997 for a period of 5 years both for domestic and export orders of ocean going vessels. It envisages grant of shipbuilding subsidy of 30% on Ocean-going vessels; permitting shipping companies to raise

funds for acquisition of ocean-going vessel from Indian Public Sector Shipyards through ECB.

Capital restructuring of the company.

Government has approved the capital restructuring of the Company, with cutoff date as 31st March, 1995, which has resulted in writing off of Govt. loans and interest accrued thereon to the tune of Rs. 470.93 crores and conversion of Govt. loans to the tune of Rs. 120.20 crores into equity.

In addition, it has also provided for conversion of outstanding of SBI's cash credit with interest thereon into 'Term Loan' payable in equal yearly instalments over a period of 10 years with an initial moratorium of 3 years. The said loan is secured against the Government guarantee.

Impact of capital restructuring would be reflected in the Company's records only after receipt of approval of MAT exemption from the Government.

Steps taken by HSL to improve performance.

Company has undertaken the following measures within the organisation to improve the performance of the company.

(i) Securing new shipbuilding orders with aggressive marketing efforts.

(ii) Improved utilisation of production facilities.

(iii) Better industrial relations - (not even a single man-day lost due to any strike/lock-out).

(iv) Reduction of surplus manpower (from 7400 to 5300) through VR Scheme. It is proposed to bring manpower at the optimum level of 4200 employees by 2000 AD.

(v) Upgradation of quality standards through accreditation of ISO : 9001.

(vi) Diversification into related areas like structural fabrication for steel plants, railways, pelletization plants and exploring possibilities into new areas like petro chemicals, manufacture of ships i equipment etc. with the assistance of experts in the field.

IX five year plan outlay

Govt. of India have allocated Rs. 77.50 crores towards additional investment for the yard during IX Plan Period. A provision of Rs. 15 crores has been made for the Annual Plan 1998-99.

Future outlook:

The Company is facing challenges. The series of measures initiated by the Management have started yielding results in both Shipbuilding and Shiprepair Division and productivity has shown improvement. The Shiprepairs Division is operating at 100% capacity utilisation. Company has also emerged as the largest unit to undertake repairing of Naval vessels. Exclusive facility has been set up for repairing of submarine, which has good potential of order book in future. Remunerative Shipbuilding orders from the Indian Navy and the Coast guard are being pursued with full force. Emphasis on increasing Shiprepair Turnover will be continued. Prestigious order for repairs to the Floating Dock FDN 1 of the Indian Navy against tough international competition was received. H.S.L. is planning for concluding Annual Maintenance Contracts with the Navy and the Coast Guard for the selected class of ships. This is in advanced stage of negotiations. Action for procurement of Floating Dock to augment the docking facilities has been initiated. By concentrating on Shiprepairs and remunerative Shipbuilding orders coupled with shedding excess manpower, HSL should be able to turn around in 3-4 years' time.

Cochin shipyard limited (CSL)

Cochin Shipyard Limited was incorporated as a Company fully owned by the Government of India in 1972. The Authorised Capital of the Company is Rs. 220.00 crores and paid-up capital is Rs. 217.93 crores as on 31st March, 1998.

The Yard has two major divisions; one for shipbuilding and the other for shiprepair. Designed capacity of the Yard is to build vessels up to 95,000 DWT and repair vessels of sizes up to 125,000 DWT. The Yard has so far constructed 7 ships - 5 Panamax Type Bulk Carriers of 75,000 DWT each and 2 Crude Oil Tankers of 86,000 DWT each. Construction of an 83,400 DWT Double Hull Crude Oil Tanker is in progress in the Yard now. Besides this, the Yard has constructed 23 Nos. of small Crafts of different descriptions. On the Shiprepair side, the Yard has repaired about 700 vessels of all descriptions.

Performance

Performance of the Yard has improved significantly during the last three years. Overall performance of the Company in financial terms is given below :

(Rs. in crores)

Year	*Value of production*	*Profit/Loss*
1995-96	129.82	18.46
1996-97	131.80	12.56
1997-98	124.73	31.72

Estimated profit for the current financial year is Rs. 11.00 crores.

Order book position

The present Order Book Position of the Yard for new building is one Crude Oil Tanker of 83,400 DWT, for the

Shipping Corporation of India, and 4 Tugs from Port Sector (3 from Kandla Port Trust and 1 from New Mangalore Port Trust).

Human resource development

The manpower strength of the Company as on 31st March, 1998 was 2493 as detailed below:-

in Nos.)

Sl. No.	Category	Total	Reservation status: Scheduled Castes	Reservation status: Scheduled Tribles
1.	Executives	285	29	2.
2.	Supervisors	284	25	3.
3.	Staff &Workmen	1924	253	44
	Grand Total	2493	307	49

Total Nos. indicated above includes:

Physically handicapped	127
Other Backward Communities	814
Women	180

In addition 331 Trainees were undergoing training in various disciplines including 67 Mechanical Engineers for specialisation as Marine Engineers for the Merchant Navy.

The Company maintains cordial industrial relations.

Government directives with regard to reservation of posts, implementation of Hindi as Official Language etc. are being complied with.

Ninth five year plan outlay

Government of India have allocated Rs. 65 crores towards additional investment for the Yard during IX Plan Period. A provision of Rs. 10 crores has been made for the Annual Plan 1998-99.

ISO 9001

The Company has been accredited with certification under ISO 9001. The Yard is the first Indian Shipyard to secure ISO 9001 certification both for shipbuilding and shiprepair.

Hooghly dock & port engineers Ltd. Calcutta

Hooghly Dock & Port Engineers Ltd. (HDPEL), Calcutta is one of the oldest Shipyards in the country and is specialised in small/medium shipbuilding. There is hardly any Port in India for which it has not built and delivered a Tug for its operation. The Company was nationalised in June, 1984, and has two units, one at Salkia and another at Nazirgunge, Howrah. These are engaged in shipbuilding, ship-repairs, steel casting and general Engineering. The Authorised Capital of the Company has been enhanced from Rs. 20.00 Crores as on 31st March, 1998 to Rs. 25 Crores as on 31st March, 1999. The Paid-up Capital and Share Deposit are Rs. 17.20 Crores and Rs. 3.65 Crores respectively.

Performance

The Company has been incurring losses year after year due to :—

(a) Obsolete technology and lack of investment for modernisation;
(b) Cost price gap in Ship-building; Low
(c) Productivity;
(d) Heavy interest burden on Government loan;
(e) Liquidity crisis;
(f) Lack of orders; and
(g) Imbalance in manpower.

Since 1989-90, the networth of the Company has become negative. Due to continuous losses incurred by the Company, at one stage, the Government was considering to close down the Company. However, considering its potential, the Government decided to revive the Company. Revival Package was bifurcated in two parts, viz. (i) Short-term Revival Package as submitted by the Company; and (ii) Long-term Revival Plan. For Long term revival plan, M/s. Industrial Credit and Investment Corporation of India Limited (ICICI) was engaged who have since submitted its Report.

Revival plan for HDPEL

Government of India has already approved the short-term revival package and long term revival package is under its active consideration. It is expected that after full implementation of these two revival packages, the company would be able to turn the corner within next 2/3 years time. The company has also taken the following measures simultaneously to improve its performance : -

(i) Aggressive marketing for securing
(ii) Expediting the process of upgrading the facilities with the plan support given by Govt. of India;
(iii) Reduction of surplus manpower;
(iv) Computerisation;
(v) Implementing ISO-9000;
(vi) Improving industrial relations through involving employees in day-to-day functions of the Company;
(vii) Human Resources Development through training of Personnel.
(viii) Efforts to increase ship-building activity; and
(ix) Closing down non-remunerative production activities.

Order book position

The Order Book position of Hooghly Dock & Port Engineers Limited, as on 31st March, 1998, is as follows:-

(Rs. in lakhs)

Vessel	*Owner*	*value*
400-Passenger-cum 100 Ton Cargo Vessel	Andaman & Nicobar Islands Admn.	4995
Light house Tender Vessel	Director General of Lighthouses & Lightships, Govt. of India.	4963
Pontoons - 2 Nos. Authority of India.	Inland-Waterways	90
Survey Launch	-do-	133
Two Surface	-do-	1145
30 Ton Bollard Pull Tug	Calcutta Port Trust	618
Multipurpose Tug	DCI	1488

Financial performance for last three years

(Rs. in lakhs)

Year	*Production*	*Sales*	*Profit/Loss before Interest & Depreciation*	*Profit/ Loss*
1995-96	539	431	(-)673	(-)1576
1996-97	328	1065	(-)822	(-)1925
1997-98	799	333	(-)458	(-)1877

Ninth five year plan outlay

Govt. of India have allocated Rs. 17.60 crores towards additional investment for Yard during IX Plan Period. A provision of Rs. 7.30 Crores has been made for the Annual Plan 1998-99.

Future outlook

As a result of the implementation of the short-term revival plan which is to be followed up with a long term revival plan and various other steps taken, it is expected that the company would be able to make a turn around in coming years.

5

Light Houses

The Department of Lighthouses & Lightships provides all aids to marine navigation (visual and radio) in coastal and oceanic phase for mariners in Indian waters. In vast ocean, a mariner is not sure of his position, unless some sort of signal is received by him. The marine aids to navigation provides this much needed signalling, whereby the mariner is able to fix his position. The more accurate is the position, the better is to navigate.

The term 'Lighthouse' represents all aids to navigation, including light vessels, sound signals, buoys, beacons or any mark, sign or apparatus, radio aids such as Decca Navigator Chains, Loran 'C' , Radio Beacons, etc. There are two categories of aids to navigation, namely, "General" and "Local", as defined in the Lighthouse Act, 1927. The superintendence and management of 5.1.6 "General" aids to navigation is vested in the Department of Lighthouses & Lightships. The "Local" aids are the responsibility of the concerned State Governments, Port Trusts, etc.

Organisational structure:

The Department of Lighthouses & Lightships is headed by a Director General for the purpose of administration and management of various Lighthouses. The coastline is divided into 6 Districts/Regions with District/ Regional Headquarters at Jamnagar, Mumbai, Kochi, Chennai,

Calcutta and Port Blair. Each District is headed by a Director (Regional), who has under him Officers belonging to various engineering disciplines. **(See figure).**

Central advisory committee for lighthouses

A Statutory Body called the Central Advisory Committee for Lighthouses, consisting of representatives of Shipping, Sailing Vessels Associations, Chambers of Commerce, etc., advises the Government on matters relating to administration of Lighthouses. The Committee is constituted after every two years. The period of the present Committee will expire in February, 1999.

Internal resources:

The Department of Lighthouses & Lightships is a subordinate Organisation of the Ministry. Its revenue is derived from lightdues levied on ships entering or leaving Indian Ports. The rates of light due are :

a) Rs. 8.00 per ton for foreign going vessels.
b) Rs. 6.00 per ton for home trade vessels.
c) 50 paise per ton for sailing vessels.

The total lightdues collection is expected to be over Rs. 74.00 crores during the year 1998-99. On behalf of the Department, these lightdues are collected by the Customs Department. The Department is able to generate enough financial resources to meet its expenditure (both revenue and capital).

Navigational aids:

The Department of Lighthouses & Lightships is at present maintaining the following types of "General" aids to navigation

(a) Light houses	–	167	Nos.
(b) Light ships	–	1	No.
(c) Radio Beacons	–	20	Nos.

(d) Decca Navigator Chain Stations – 4 Nos.
(e) Loran 'C' Chain – 6 Nos.
(f) Racons – 23 Nos.
(g) Deep Sea Lighted – 12 Nos.

Lighthouse tenders:

To cater to the needs of Light Stations in the island and for maintaining the buoys, the Department is maintaining 3 launches, 1 mechanised boat and 2 large ocean-going vessels - M.V. Sagardeep & M.V. Pradeep. The above two vessels are run and maintained by Shipping Corporation of India on an agency basis on behalf of the Department.

R.T. Links:

To maintain communication with Lighthouses, Decca and Loran 'C' Stations, situated in remote and isolated places, the Department is maintaining 39 VHD/UHF Radio Telephone sets.

Staff:

The present staff composition is as under:

Group 'A'	–	51
Group 'B' (Gazetted)	–	52
Group 'B' (Non-Gazetted)	–	97
Group 'C'	–	711
Group 'D'	–	433

Achievements during 1998-99:

(a) A major Lighthouse at Kodikkarai along Tamil Nadu coast has been commissioned.

(b) The Revised Cost Estimate for the construction of new Lighthouse Tender Vessel, M.V. Sagardeep has been approved by the Government and a fresh Supplementary Agreement has been signed by the Department with M/s. HDPE. The work is expected to be completed by end of the year 1999.

(c) The Department has taken up the construction work of high range lighthouse at Daman on behalf of the Daman Administration. The work is nearing completion.

(d) The Department has constructed a 15m high new Lighthouse tower at Cavalerio (Diu) on behalf of Daman Administration at an estimated cost of Rs. 15.25 lacks.

(e) The Department has installed a new lighted beacon at Sutrapada for Gujarat Maritime Board at an estimated cost of Rs. 2 lacks.

(f) The Department has converted 3 Lighted buoys from DA Gas to Solar operated electronic light for Kandla Port Trust.

(g) The Department is also carrying out the improvement of local lights on agency basis for the State Government Organisations.

(h) The Office building at NOIDA has been completed except for electrical connection by CPWD. The new building is likely to be handed over to the Department by mid 1999 and thereafter the DGLL Office will shift to NOIDA.

(i) The 73rd Meeting of Central Advisory Committee for Lighthouses was held on 18th September, '98.

(j) Department has established statellite based 8 nos. Differential Global Positioning System (DGPS) along the coastline at Okha, Uttan, Aguada, Suratkal, Azhicode, Pondicherry, Dolphin's Nose and Saugar Island. Ninth and tenth stations at Minicoy in Lakshadweep and Keating Point in A&N Group of Island are in progress and are likely to be completed by early 1999. With the help of these light stations, mariners can fix their positions in the sea with an accuracy of 5 m.

(k) The Department proposes to introduce Vessel Traffic Service (VTS) in the Gulf of Kachchh

(GOK). The Advisory Committee on VTS has finalised a detailed report on introduction of VTS at an approximate cost of Rs. 165 crores. The project proposal is expected to be received from the department shortly.

(l) The work for the improvement of Puri Lighthouse started after taking necessary clearances from Konark Development Authority.

(m) A proposal has been submitted to the Government of India for introduction of Remote Control and Monitoring-Automation of Lighthouse in Saurashtra & Kachchh Lighthouse District at an estimated cost of Rs. 645 lacks. By this system, all the remote and isolated placed Lighthouses will be controlled from a conveniently placed Remote Control Centre.

Representation in international bodies:

India is represented through a delegation headed by Director General of Lighthouses & Lightships and continued to be elected for the Executive Council of International Association of Lighthouse Authorities, Paris, since 1982.

Energy conservation:

The Department has taken up at large scale conversion of lights from petroleum vapour/Dissolved Acetylene Gas/Kerosene to electric operation thereby conserving the conventional fossil fuel. The electric operation of the light is also achieved through solar energy. During day time, the solar energy is first converted into electric charge and stored in the storage batteries. During night time for the lighthouse operation, these storage batteries are being used to meet electric power requirement. In the past, the Department was using incandecent electric lamps of 3000 W and above. These have now been replaced with 400 W (metal halide)/100 W (halogen lamp) thereby saving considerable amount of electric energy.

Environmental protection:

The Department has minimised burning of fossil fuel for its lighthouse operation. Also, wherever possible, the running of Diesel Generator Sets has also been reduced by introducing solar power operation. There is less fuel burning, less smoke, no wastes, less noise and hence no pollution of the environment.

Department has also taken up afforestation of all the lighthouse premises to keep the environment clean.

The Department of Lighthouses & Lightships has been able to provide yeoman's service to the mariners sailing in our coastal water round the clock throughout the year, by keeping all the aids to navigation in perfect working condition, be it on mainland or in a remote island in Andamans or Lakshadweep.The Department endeavour is to keep abreast with latest technology for making the navigation safe for mariners navigating in the Indian coast or leaving a port or harbour.

6

Inland Water Transport

The Ministry is responsible for the coordinated development of Inland Water Transport in the country; and in particular, for the declaration and development of National Waterways (NW). Through Centrally Sponsored Schemes, the Central Government also makes available assistance to the States for developing Inland Waterways other than National Waterways.

Inland waterways authority of India

The Inland Waterways Authority of India was set up on 27th October, 1986 under the Inland Waterways Authority of India Act, 1985 for the regulation and development of Inland Waterways for purposes of shipping and navigation.

National waterways (NW)

The following waterways are declared through individual Acts of Parliament as National Waterways:-

(a) Allahabad - Haldia stretch (11620 kms) of the Ganga-Bhagirathi-Hooghly river system since October, 1986 as National Waterway No. 1 (NW-1).

(b) Sadiya - Dhubri stretch (891 kms) of the Brahmaputra river since September, 1988 as National Waterway No. 2 (NW-2).

National waterway no. 1

A navigational channel of minimum 2.Om depth and 45m width alongwith temporary navigational marks for day navigation is attempted to be maintained by taking up river conservancy works and regular hydrographic surveys in the Haldia-Allahabad stretch (1620 kms). River notices indicating depth are issued fortnightly to the IWT operators and also published in National Newspapers. Floating terminal facilities are provided and maintained at Haldia, Calcutta, Karagola, Bhagalpur and Monghyr. Fixed jetties are available at Calcutta (TT shed), Farakka and Pakur, the work of construction of permanent terminal at Gaighat, Patna was taken up through CPWD on deposit work basis. Land for permanent terminal at G.R. Jetty, Calcutta is being acquired from Calcutta Port Trust. River training works for stabilisation of river between Patna and Semaria is being taken up, In addition to execution of works of repair and maintenance of existing IWAI vessels, a major scheme for acquisition of hydraulic surface dredgers one each for NW-1 & NW-2 was sanctioned and construction is in progress. For providing floating jetties at Ballia and Karagola, two pontoons are under construction.

For providing 24 hrs navigational facilities in the Calcutta-Farakka Sector of NW-1, work has been awarded for supply of buoys and lights. Installation of the lighted buoys is scheduled to be completed during 1999-2000.

National waterway no. 2

A navigational channel of minimum 2.00m depth and 45m width alongwith temporary navigational marks for day navigation is provided by taking up river conservancy works and regular hyrographic surveys in the Dhubri-Dibrugarh Sector (768 kms.). River notices indicating depth are issued fortnightly to the IWT operators and waterway notices also published in National Newspapers. Floating terminal facilities have been provided and maintained at Dhubri, Jogighopa, Pandu, Tezpur & Neamati. A Scheme for providing floating terminals at Sadiya and Saikhowa is under implementation for which two pontoons are under construction. Works for renovation of on-shore facilities at Pandu terminal were completed. Preliminary design and estimate for construction of a permanent terminal at Pandu has been taken up through CPWID. For providing 24 hrs navigational facilities in Dhubri-Pandu (Guwahati) stretch (260 kms.) on NW-2, orders for supply of lights and buoys have been placed. Installation is scheduled to be completed during 19992000. The Central Inland Water Transport Corporation (CIWTC) have been operating cargo services between Calcutta-Pandu and Calcutta-Karimganj routes under the Protocol on Inland Water Transit & Trade between India and Bangladesh.

Procurement of one survey launch for NW-2 has been approved, work commenced and the same is scheduled to be completed during 1998-99.

National waterway no. 3

Project so far executed and those in progress include detailed hydrographic surveys, dredging in Champakara and Udyogmandal canals and at critical locations near Kayakla sea mouth and for land acquisition. Work of dismantling the Thottapally lock is in progress and modification of Thanneermukkam and Thrikkunnapuzha locks have been completed. Movement of POL by HPCL between Kochi and Kollarn continued during the year unhindered. Various studies on environmental planning, vessel design, bank protection etc. are in progress. The process of Land acquisition and capital dredging for widening of narrow sections of canal has been commenced. Scheme for land acquisition for terminals has also been approved and commenced through Government of Kerala.

For procuring one survey launch for NW-3, work was awarded and the launch is scheduled to be delivered during 1998-99.

Construction of office cum R & D complex of IWAI

The Inland Waterways Authority of India has its headquarters in a rented building at NOIDA at present. A scheme for its own office cum R & D complex, was sanctioned at an estimated cost of Rs. 4.57 crores with land taken on long term lease from NOIDA. The work of building is in advanced stage of completion and the H.O. of IWAI is expected to be shifted to new premises during 1998-99.

Training of IWT personnel

Regular training is being imparted to IWT personnel in various Indian Institutions. A scheme for setting up of a National Inland Navigation Institute (NINI) at Patna has been approved by the Government in February, 1998 and the work of construction of NINI has been initiated.

Status of other waterways

The sunderbans

The International Steamer Route in Sunderbans is extensively used by Cargo vessels which are plying between Calcutta and Assam/Bangladesh. A proposal to declare and develop this route as National Waterways had been formulated. Owing to the fragile nature of the eco-system in the region and the significant presence of wild life, biosphere reserve etc., environmental clearance of the proposed development has been delayed. Reconnaissance survey of alternate route along with the main International Steamer Route was completed and environmental clearance of the project are being taken up in co-ordination with various authorities at the Centre and State Governments. A scheme for conducting detailed Hydrographic Survey in this Waterway has been sanctioned.

Techno-economic studies on new waterways

Study on extension of NW 3 in north and south sides

A study for extension of NW-3 undertaken earlier in 1990 revealed that the extension was not techno economically viable. However, in view of changed economic and transport scenarios of the state consequent to the declaration of the NW-3 and other projects, a fresh study of potential of these stretches was completed and findings are under examination. A new study for extension of NW-3 from Kovalam to Kolachal has also been taken up during the year.

Feasibility study on canal system connecting Madras & Kakinada

Techno-Economic Feasibility Study on canal system connecting Madras & Kakinada (618 kms) consisting of North Buckingham Canal (316 kms), Commamur Canal (113 kms), Eluru Canal (139 kms) and Kakinada Canal (50 kms) was completed during the year. For creating a larger transport network, study has been further extended on Cooum River (71 kms) & South Buckingham Canal (102 kms) upto Mercaunum. The study has also completed.

Study on east coast canal

A feasibility study on the revival of East Coast Canal (ECC) to link Paradip Port and Calcutta including waterway link to Dhamara was taken up and has been completed. Based upon the findings of the study a scheme for preparation of a detailed project report of ECC integrated with Brahmani/ Mahanadi river system is on the anvil for which the tender process has been initiated.

Other studies

Study on semi-permanent river training works on N.W.-1, has been completed and DPR for improvement of existing terminals on N.W.1, also finalised. Studies for development of navigation on Karimganj-Lakhipur stretch of river Barak and studies alongwith Hydrographic surveys of Damodar Valley Corporation Canal were completed. In addition, the new Techno-Economic Feasibility Study (TEFS) for extension of NW-3, other studies namely TEFS on Visakhapatnam-Polavaram Canal System, TEFS on NW-2 for assessing IWT tourism potential, study on improvement of safety of life on river boats and a transport economic study of NW-1, 2 & 3 for attracting private participation in IWT movement has been taken up during 1998-99. Environmental Impact Assessment (EIA) study for proposed movement of POL/dangerous Cargo on NW1 is also completed and EIA reports submitted to Ministry of Environment and Forests for clearance.

Promotional schemes

In order to boost Inland Water Transport, IWAI operated a scheme of Interest Subsidy on Loans taken from Banks for the purpose of acquiring inland vessels. In this scheme, loans at 5-1/2% interest were made available for inland waterways vessel operators by subsidising the difference between 5-1/2% and interest charged by the banks.

To promote cargo movement on NW-1, trial commercial operation of departmental vessel M.V. Rajagopalchari (600T) is going on between Haldia/ Calcutta and Allahabad covering entire stretch of NW-1 successfully. The vessel and a convoy of the CIWTC Ltd. transported Cement, Urea, Silica Sand and China Clay amongst various destination along the river Ganga during the year.

Centrally sponsored scheme

Schemes with 50% assistance by the Central Government namely terminal facilities in river Hoogly in West Bengal, Capital dredging of rivers Mondovi, Zuari and Mapuca in Goa, Hydrographic Survey in rivers Gandak and Kosi in Bihar, Hy. Survey and TEFS and DPR on river Ghagra in U.P. and Terminal facilities for passenger ferry services in Kerala backwater are under progress. New proposals received from the State Governments of Kerala, Tamil Nadu, U.P. and West Bengal are under process for approval.

Private participation in IWT

As a part of privatisation policy of the Government, prospects of participation of private sector for cargo movement and infrastructure development are being explored. A National Conference cum exhibition for development of IWT was held at Calcutta on 14th November, 1998 jointly organised by IWAI and FICCI. Meetings with the representatives of the Industry were held and waterway information provided to the private operators.

Central inland water transport corporation limited
(A Government of India Undertaking)

Introduction

Central Inland Water Transport Corporation Limited was incorporated on 11th February, 1967 by taking over all the assets of the erstwhile River Steam Navigation Co. Ltd. (A Sterling Company) and liabilities to the State Bank of India and Govt. of India under a Scheme of Arrangement, approved by the Calcutta High Court on 3rd May, 1967.

Objectives & functions

The Principal objectives of Central Inland Water

Transport Corporation Ltd., is transportation of Cargo through Inland Waterways in the country. In line with the above objective, the company also performs the following functions :

1. Construction and repair of IWT Vessels at Rajabagan Dockyard, both for own use by River Services Division and for outsiders and General Engineering jobs.
2. Repair of Ocean-going vessels by the Deep-Sea Ship Repair Unit.

The following are the principal activities of the Company :

1. Transportation by Inland Waterways between Calcutta-Bangladesh-Assam, Farakka, Haldia, Budge-Budge.
2. Ship - Building and Repair as also General Engineering work in the Rajabagan Dockyard.
3. Repair of Ocean-going vessels.

The present authorised share capital of the company is Rs. 100 crore with a paid-up capital of Rs. 9761.23 lakh being contributed as follows:

i)	Government of India	:	Rs. 9,733.23 lakh
ii)	Government of West Bengal	:	Rs. 11.00 lakh
iii)	Government of Assam	:	Rs. 17.00 lakh

The Corporation, which is under the administrative control of the Ministry of Surface Transport, Govt. of India, has its Head Office at Calcutta. There are three main operational Divisions, viz. The River Services Division (RSD), The Rajabagan Dockyard (RBD) and the Deep Sea Ship Repair Division (DSSR).

Rajabagan Dockyard, the main factory establishment located in Calcutta, is engaged in Ship-building, Ship-repair and General Engineering activities. The River

Services Division has its main terminal at Calcutta and other terminals and branch offices at Haldia, Patna, Karimganj, Badarpur, Dhubri, Pandu and Guwahati. For running repair and maintenance of own crafts, the RSD has two workshops, one at Calcutta and other at Pandu, Assam. The DSSR, which undertakes repair of Ocean-going vessels for outside agencies, has one establishment at Calcutta. The Corporation maintains a Liaison Office at New Delhi.

The organisation

The Corporation which has about 2825 employees (as on 1st November, 1998) on its pay-roll, is headed by a full-time Chairman cum-Managing Director, appointed by the Govt. of India who is assisted by the Board of Directors.

Rajabagan Dockyard is headed by a General Manager, River Services Division and the Deep Sea Ship Repair Division are headed by General Manager & Chief Manager respectively. The Corporation, for the execution of its development plans, has a separate and independent Project Department.

The operating divisions

Renovation of Dry Dock No. 3 & 4 was undertaken with commissioning Level Luffing Crane under the 6th Five Year Plan.

The Original project for development of Rajabagan Dockyard's Ship-building and Ship-repair facilities was approved for implementation under the Indo-Dutch Bilateral Co-operation Programme in 1989. However, the Scheme was subsequently revised and the Ministry of Surface Transport has sanctioned revised cost estimate for modernising ship-repair facilities only for the time being in December, '92 at a cost of Rs. 71.34 crores. The Dutch Government further re-appraised the Scheme in

November, 93. According to the revised programme, a bilateral Project Document has been prepared to finalise the bilateral co-operation agreement for technical and financial assistance grant with a Minimum Investment Plan (MIP) of Rs. 20.00 crores. The draft Grant Agreement is still under consideration with Ministry of Finance.

River services division

As the mainstay of IWT operations in the Country, excepting in Goa and Kerala, the River Services Division has an existing fleet strength of 96 operating vessels and 21 support vessels.

Operations are generally being carried out on the following routes :-

Route	*Stop Over*	*Distance (k.m.)*
Calcutta-Bangladesh	Narayanganj	780
Calcutta-Guwahati	Dhubri, Jogighopa	1439
Calcutta-Karimganj		1218
Haldia-Patna	Beharampur, Dhulian, Farakka, Kahalgaon	935
Calcutta-Haldia		100
Calcutta-internal		10
Calcutta-Saugar		114
Haldia-Budge-Budge		80
Haldia-Nayachara		5
Haldia-Diamond harbour		**24**

With the acquisition of 55 (fifty five) new vessels (47 vessels already acquired) the corporation's carrying capacity will go upto 12.696 lakh M.T. per annum one way, which is further expected to reach 13.30 lakh M.T. per annum by the end of the 9th Plan Period, with the proposed new acquisition/ replacement of existing fleet.

Deep sea ship repair division

The principal function of this Division, operating from Calcutta, is to undertake all types of repair work for

Ocean Going Vessels. Besides, Private Operators, Public Sector Undertakings like Shipping Corporation of India, Dredging Corporation of India, various Port Authorities and other Government Departments are served by this Division. Maintenance and repair of Buoys for the Calcutta Port Trust are also undertaken by the Unit.

River services division

A review of the performance characteristics of this Division over the past 3 years is as follows :-

Year	*Cargo carried (M.Ton)*	*Freight earned (Rs. in Lakh)*
1996-97	1,88,444	718.42
1997-98(Un-audited)	2,43,106	802.35
1998-99	45,030	371.07

Deep sea ship repair division

A review of the performance characteristics of this Division over the past three years is as follows :-

Year	*Value of Production (Rs. in lakh)*
1996-97	101.00
1997-98 (Un-audited)	238.00
1998-99 (Upto Nov. '98)	57.50

Future prospects

The future of IWT movement and operators including CIWTC hold immense possibilities for establishing a well defined multi-modal transportation network in the country catering to a vast command area in the most economic manner from the stand point of operational economy.

Under the 9th Plan Scheme, various schemes have been proposed for acquisition of vessels, development of

RBD and modernisation of terminal facilities at a cost of Rs. 2.72 crore.

Through the introduction of Voluntary Retirement Scheme, the Corporation has been able to shed 799 employees (as on 1st November, 1998) reducing thereby the burden of cash out-go on account of salaries and wages.

Running hours of vessels are proposed to be improved with the installation in phases of night navigation facilities by IWAI. Mechanisation of river terminals, particularly on National Waterways, as the action plan of IWAI is expected to reduce the detention period of vessels for loading/unloading considerably.

The Corporation has also been engaging sub contractors for undertaking repair/ construction work wherever necessary. Moreover, charter hiring of Corporation's vessels has been introduced on experimental basis as per MOST's directive.

Other economic benefits to accrue from a well defined and improved IWT network would be by way of increased export trade between India and her neighbouring countries like Bangladesh & Nepal as also movement from/to under the multi modal transport arrangement. Besides, opportunities particularly for weaker/ backward sections of the society would open up with the planned development and growth of IWT movement in the country. Finally from the ecological viewpoint, IWT contributes the least to environmental pollution and provides opportunities for conservation of scarce resources like POL. Keeping abrest of time and technology, CIWTC contributes to the nation's progress by remaining the prime/sole inland water carrier on the national routes.

Development of hindi as an official language

In pursuance of the provisions contained in the Official Languages Act, 1963 read with Rules, 1976, due emphasis is given by the Company in implementation of its provisions. Activities in this regard are summarised as below: -

(a) Employees were regularly nominated for various Hindi Courses and Hindi Typing Training, incentives paid to the employees on passing these examinations, (b) Hindi newspapers, magazines and literary books were purchased for the employees of the Company, (c) 9 out of 12 Codes and Manuals of the Company were translated in Hindi and circulated amongst the employees and translation of the rest is in progress, (d) Forms and other stationery materials were printed bilingually, (e) Press advertisements issued were published trilingually, (f) Meeting of OLIC were held regularly, (g) Hindi day is regularly organised and (h) Employees, having working knowledge of the language are further trained through workshops on Hindi.

7

Ports

There are 11 Major Ports in the country viz., Calcutta (including Haldia), Paradip, Visakhapatnam, Chennai, Tuticorin on the East Coast and Cochin, New Mangalore, Mormugao, Jawaharlal Nehru, Mumbai and Kandla on the West Coast.

Cargo traffic handled at major ports:

The Major Ports handled a total traffic of 251.5 million tonne during the financial year 1997-98 and 184.3 million tonnes up-to December '98 in the financial year 1998-99. The Port-wise details are given below:

Traffic handled at major ports

(in Million Tonnes)

Port	*Target* *1998-99* *(April-Dec)*	*Actual* *1998-99* *(April-Dec)*	*1997-98* *(April-Dec)*
Calcutta	7.12	6.20	5.61
Haldia	15.36	14.45	14.54
Paradip	9.97	9.70	9.90
Visakhapatnam	27.07	26.89	27.08
Chennai	27.37	26.21	26.34
Tuticorin	7.65	7.47	7.50
Cochin	9.14	9.21	8.78
New Mangalore	11.17	10.62	11.23
Mormugao	13.13	12.03	13.66
J.L. Nehru	7.44	8.55	6.78
Mumbai	25.31	23.25	24.16
Kandla	29.34	29.70	28.74
All Major Ports	190.07	184.28	184.32

Cargo handled at major ports

Commodity	Percentage to Total (April - December)	
	1998-99	1997-98
POL	41.9	41.0
Iron Ore	12.5	14.8
Fertiliser & Raw Materials	4.0	4.3
Coal	16.2	15.5
Others	25.4	24.4
Total	100.0	100.0

Selected port performance indicators:

The details of major performance indicatiors of the Ports are given below:

Port	Average pre-berthing detention (on Port A/c) (April to November)		Average turn round time (April to November)	
	1998-99	1997-98	1998-99	1997-98
Calcutta	0.20	0.25	6.71	7.46
Haldia	0.44	1.06	4.33	6.03
Paradip	1.31	1.98	4.20	5.57
Visakhapatnam	0.91	1.74	5.92	6.13
Chennai	2.90	1.40	8.20	7.10
Tuticorin	1.05	1.33	4.85	5.01
Cochin	0.18	0.30	3.40	3.80
New Mangalore	0.47	0.71	4.17	4.41
Mormugao	0.43	0.53	5.26	6.01
J.L. Nehru	0.89	3.09	4.98	4.55
Mumbai	0.67	1.25	5.21	6.41
Kandla	1.77	3.82	4.83	7.45
All Major Ports	1.07	1.55	5.39	6.12

Financial results of the ports

State-wise and Port-wise Financial results achieved during 1996-97 and 1997-98. All Major Ports have shown operating surplus in both the years.

Major developments in port sector:

Privatisation of Port Facilities: The Government has laid down guidelines for private sector participation in the port sector Following areas have been identified : -

i) Leasing out assets of the Port,

ii) Construction and operation of container terminals, multipurpose cargo berths and specialised cargo berths, warehousing, storage facilities, tank farms, container freight stations, setting up of captive power plants, etc.

iii) Leasing of equipment for cargo handling and leasing of floating rafts from the private sector.

iv) Pilotage

v) Captive facilities for port based industries.

Government have also framed guidelines on joint venture formation in Major Port on 1st June, 1998.

List of approved private sector participation projects

List of approved private sector participation projects can be seen at Appendix-VI.

Higher powers delegated to port trusts

The powers of the Port Trust Boards have been increased to Rs. 50 crores in respect of additions/modifications/new investments and to Rs. 100 crores; in case of replacement/ renewal of assets.

Innovative proposals

There are cases where entrepreneurs come up with proposals for creation of facilities which have not been conceived by the port trust. Feasibility of such proposals would beevaluated by a Technical Committee set up under Development Adviser (Ports) which would act as a secretariat for receiving such proposals and submit their recommendations to an Empowered Committee under the Chairmanship of the Secretary (Surface Transport) with Secretaries of Expenditure, Commerce, Industrial Policy & Promotion and Environment and Forests as members. This Empowered Committee will decide whether the concerned Port should purchase the concept and the remuneration to be paid to the entrepreneur and whether the entrepreneur himself should be given the project on BOT basis.

Outlay proposed in the 9th Plan for port sector

An outlay of Rs. 8800 crores has been proposed in the 9th plan (1997-2002) for Port Sector for funding of various projects to be taken up by Port Trusts, in addition to the projects to be expected through privates e c t o r participation. The 9th plan proposals are expected to cater to a growth of traffic of 424 million tonnes per annum in 11 major ports as against 251.44 million tonnes per annum in 1997-98.

Some of the major ongoing and sanctioned new projects undertaken through public investment are indicated below:

Sl. No.	Name of the Schemes	9th plan outlay (1997-2002) proposed
1.	Mechanised Coal Handling Schemes in Paradip Port.	(Rs. 553.00 crores)
2.	Construction of new port at Ennore near Madras	(Rs. 600.00 crores)
3.	Replacement of Submarine Pipelines at Mumbai Port	(Rs. 165.00 crores)
4.	Modernisation of MOT Berths at Mumbai Port	(Rs. 137.00 crores)
5.	Capital Dredging at Tuticorin Port for deepening the Approach Channel	(Rs. 202.00 crores)
6.	Extension of Container handling facilities at Bharti Dock	(Rs. 52.70 crores)

In Private Sector, the most important schemes to be taken up at various Major Ports are as under : -

Sl. No.	*Name of the Project*	*Indicative Costs (in US $ Million)*
	Jawaharlal Nehru Port	
1.	Marine Chemical Terminal	44.5
2.	Liquid Cargo Berth	28.0
	Kandla Port Trust	
3.	Container Terminal	100.0
	New Managalore Port Trust	
4.	Port facilities for expansion of refinery	35.0
	Tuticorin Port Trust	
5.	Construction, Operation & Maintenance of Cargo Berth No. 8 on BOT basis (with container handling facilities)	40.0
6.	Construction of new outer Harbour Satellite Port.	1200.0
	Chennai port trust	
7.	Various captive facilities at Ennore Port	20.0
	Vishakhapatnam Port Trust	
8.	Construction of Multipurpose/ General Cargo Berths	20.0
	Cochin Port Trust	
9.	Expansion of modern container terminal	800.00
10.	Construction of LPG and LNG terminal at Puthuvypeen	100.0
	Calcutta Port Trust	
11.	Second Dock Arm at Haldia	245.0
	Mormugao Port Trust	
12.	Construction of outer harbour/West of Breakwater Berths	530.0
13.	Construction of FRH Master Plan Berths	60.0
14.	Construction of Floating Berths No. 6 & 8.	25.0
	Paradip Port Trust	
15.	Dry Dock Ship repair facilities	650.0
16.	Construction and Management of Cargo Berths on captive basis	8.3
17.	Management of Container Terminal & Container Freight Station	4.0
	Mumbai port Trust	
18.	Second Liquid Chemical Berth of New Pir Pau Pier	20.0

Port & Dock labour:

At the major ports of Mumbai, Calcutta, Visakhapatnam, Cochin, Chennai, Mormugao and Kandla, Dock Labour Boards (DLBs) were set up under the Dock Workers

(Regulation of Employment) Act, 1948. The function of DLBs is to provide regular employment to dock labour. The labour provided by the DLBs perform work on board vessels. On the other hand, the labour to be deployed on the shore are provided by the Port Trusts. It has been felt that to ensure optimum utilisation of labour, there should be complete interchangability of dock workers and port workers. The question of merger of dock labour with the port labour had been under consideration of Government of India, and the Dock Labour Boards at Mumbai and Cochin were superseded in 1994, and the supersession has been extended on yearly basis from time to time. Keeping in view the fact that the Dock Workers (Regulation of Employment) Act, 1948 does not contain any provision for merger of DLBs with Port Trusts, the Dock Workers (Regulation of Employment) (In-Applicability to Major Port Trust) Act, 1997 has been passed by the Parliament. Under the provision of this Act, the dock labour boards at Cochin and Mormugao have been merged with their respective Port Trusts. In other Dock Labour Boards, negotiations with the Labour Unions are under progress to effect merger at the earliest.

Check-off system

Strength of various unions operating in major port trusts was verified by the Ministry of Labour and the results of such verification were utilised for appointment of representative of labour unions/federations on the Board of Major Port Trusts/Dock Labour Boards, Bi-partite Wage Negotiations Committee and Dock Workers Advisory Committee etc. Keeping in view the demands raised by some of the major federations for replacing this system by Check-Off System, a scheme for Check-Off has been finalised and implemented in all the major port trusts from the year 1998 which is in replacement of verification system. However, in the Chennai Port Trust, the system could not be implemented because of stay obtained by one of the Unions from the High Court of Chennai.

A bi-partite wage negotiations committee

A Bi-partite Wage Negotiations Committee has been constituted which consists of the representatives of Port Management and the Federations of Port & Dock Workers.The Committee shall go into the wage structure of Class III & IV Port & Dock employees/workers and allied matters w.e.f. 1st January, 1998. The Committee has already initiated its proceedings.

Number of officers, employees and workers in port trusts/dock labour boards

Number of Officers, Employees and Workers in each of the Major Port Trust and Dock Labour Board as on 31st December, 1998 is at Appendix-VII.

Dredging corporation of India limited

The Dredging Corporation of India Ltd. (DCI)was incorporated in March, 1976 with an authorised capital of Rs. 30 crore and its paid up capital of Rs. 28 crore.

The main function of DCI is to help the Ports in capital dredging as well as maintenance dredging in order to ensure availability of adequate drought for ships.

The DCI own 2 Cutter Suction Dredgers, 7 Trailer Suction Hopper Dredgers, 1 Tug, 3 Inland Dredgers, 1 Desiltation Plant, 1 Work Boat and 2 'A' Frame Pontoons.

The dredging capacity available with DCI is 505.50 lakh cub. mtrs. During the period under review, a quantity of 494.42 lakhs cub.mtrs. was dredged as against the 497.41 lakh cub.mtrs. last year. The capacity utilisation was 97.81 %.

During the year 1997-98, the corporation achieved a record turnover of Rs. 238.14 crore, as against a target of Rs. 200 crore. The net profit before tax for the year 199798 was Rs. 72.28 crore.

Andaman lakshadweep harbour works

The Andaman Lakshadweep Harbour Works (ALHW) was set up in 1965 for planning, execution and maintenance of Port and harbour facilities in Andaman & Nicobar Islands and Lakshadweep. There is an outlay of Rs. 125 crore during 9th Five Year Plan for various schemes of ALHW.

Minor ports survey organisation

The Minor Ports Survey Organisation (MPSO) is entrusted with the task of conducting Hydrographic Surveys in the country required for various purposes such as Navigational Project-cum-Engineering for development of Ports, Dredging, River Surveys for Flood Control, Erosion and Siltation, Capacity Survey of Reservoirs and Navigational Survey of Port Approaches, Anchorages etc. Since its inception in the year 1962, MPSO has conducted Hydrographic Surveys for various purposes on east and west cost, inland waters and at Andaman, Nicobar and Lakshadweep Islands.

The Hydrographic Survey Committee is finalising the Annual programme of MPSO based on the Hydrographic Survey requirements of the coastal states, Government Agencies and other Maritime Organisations.

The MPSO is functioning on "No profit, no loss basis". The cost of surveys carried out is recovered from the requisitioning Authorities as per the hire charges of the Survey fixed by the Govt. every year.

There is an outlay of Rs. 15 crore for MPSO in the 9th Plan

Maritime states development council (MSDC)

With a view to have an integrated approach for the development of both Major & Minor Ports, a Maritime States Development Council was constituted under the Chairmanship of the Hon'ble Minister (Surface Transport). The Minister incharge of the Ports in all Maritime States, UT of Pondicherry, Lt.Governor, Andaman & Nicobar and the Administrator, Daman & Diu are its members.

Empowered committee on environment clearances (ECEC)

The authority for according Environment Clearance to the Port Projects within existing Port limits was delegated to the Ministry of Surface Transport. In order to process the environment clearances efficiently, transparent guidelines were issued. An Empowered Committee on Environment Clearances (ECEC) was constituted under the Chairmanship of the Secretary (Surface Transport) -

Tariff authority for major ports

The Major Port Trust Act, 1963 was amended by Port Laws (Amendment) Act, 1997 (15 of 1997) to provide for an independent Tariff Authority for Major Ports for fixing and revising the port tariff. An independent authority for the above purpose has been set up w.e.f. 10th April, 1997 with Headquarters at New Delhi.

Development wing

The technical support to Port Development is given by the Development Wing. The wing renders technical advice on matters relating to the development of Major Ports, Minor Ports, Andaman & Lakshadweep Harbour Works and Dredging Corporation of India. The Wing also monitors the implementation of important development works/projects with a view to identify bottlenecks and statutory remedial action.

8

Roads Development

The Ministry is primarily responsible for construction and maintenance of National Highways in the country. All roads other than National Highways in the State fall within the jurisdiction of respective State Governments. However, to assist the State Governments in their Road Development Programmes, Central Government also provides assistance in the form of loans for certain selected State Roads of Inter-State or Economic Importance. The Ministry is also responsible for evolving standard specifications for roads and bridges in the country besides acting as a respository Of technical information on roads and bridges.

National highways authority of India (NHAI)

The National Highways Authority of India which was constituted under the National Highways Authority of India Act, 1988, was made operational in February, 1995. It is intended to hand over to NHAI the execution of works of National Highways in the country in a phased manner. The Authority has been entrusted with the projects under National Highways Project (ADB Loan). Overseas Economic Co-operation Fund (OECF). In addition, NHAI will also be responsible for the maintenance and development of Golden Quadrilateral, North-South and East-West corridors, providing port connectivity, implementing the other externally aided projects, relating to way side amenities on selective basis and the projects to be taken up under BOT scheme as authorised by the Central Government.

National highway system

The length of National Highways for which the Government of India is constitutionally responsible is 38,517 km at the end of March 1998. During the current year, a further length of 11,068 km. has been added to NH network and at present it stands at 49,585 kilometer.

Development of national highways

Efforts are made not only to improve the existing National Highways by construction of missing road links, bridges, over unbridged crossings, improving low grade sections, widening including four laning and strengthening the existing pavement of Highways, improving geometrics etc., but also by modernisation the system through construction of some expressway links etc.

List of major projects completed/Likely to be completed during the year 1998-99

(1) Widening single lane to 2-lane without strengthening Km 256.71 to 263.40 Nagpur-Hyderabad Section costing Rs. 10.28 crore.

(2) Widening to 4-lane of existing 2-lane carriageway in Km 249/4 to 259/4 of NH-8 costing Rs. 14.35 crore.

(3) Widening the existing 2-lane carriageway to 4-lane divided carriageway in reach Km 229.0 to 233/700 & Km 239/1 to 246/1 including strengthening, costing Rs. 21.65 crore.

(4) Construction of Hassan Bypass in Bangalore-Manglore Section of HN-48 costing Rs. 10.00 crore.

(5) Strengthening Km 325-361 of NH-29 costing Rs. 8.23 crore.

(6) Construction of Phase-II bypass between Km 122.400 and 134.475 around the city of Faizabad-Ayodhya in Uttar Pradesh costing Rs. 18.19 crore.

(7) Construction of bypass from Km 324.160-330.160 and two major bridges on river Garrah and Khanaut in Km 337 of NH-24 around Shahjahanpur City costing Rs. 17.47 crore.

(8) Construction of 7 nos. of major bridges across river/streams on Ahmedabad-Vadodara Expressway Km 00 to 45.1 on NE 1 (Contract 1) costing Rs. 10.77 crore.

(9) Construction of 3 nos. of major bridges including earth work for 100 m on either side of bridge across river/stream on ABD-Vadodara Expressway Km 451-92.8 Contract-II costing Rs. 12.39 crore.

(10) Construction of 12 over bridges and 7 under bypasses between Km 0 to 45.1 on Ahmedabad-Vadodara Expressway Contract III costing Rs. 4.67 crore.

(11) Construction of 17 overbridges and 4 under passes between Km 45.1 to Km 92.8 on Ahmedabad-Vadodara 8.5 Expressway Contract-IV costing Rs. 5.18 crore.

(12) Widening to 4-lane construction of 4 major bridges of Bhubaneshwar-Cuttak-Jagatpur Section costing Rs. 43.88 crore.

(13) Widening to 4 lane construction of bridge over Mahanadi. Package 11 (Bhubaneswar-Cuttack-Jagatpur section costing Rs. 43.05 crore.

(14) Rehabilitation/strengthening old Sharavarthi Bridge on NH-17 costing Rs. 10.52 crore.

(15) Construction of link road NH-47A Phase-II connecting Willington Island and Cochin bypass costing Rs. 39.77 crore.

(16) Construction of 2 ROBs(i) Km. 8 section I and Km 21.5 Section III of Varanasi-Mughalsarai-Ramnagar bypass costing Rs. 11.81 crore.

(17) Construction of new Mandovi Bridge and its approaches at Panaji on NH-17 costing Rs. 18.18 crore.

(18) Construction of Banastarim Bridge (including approaches) costing Rs. 11.60 crore.

(19) Widening to four lanes including strengthening of existing two lanes of NH-7 between Km. 8 to 33 (Bangalore-Hosur Section) in Karnataka costing Rs. 48.11 crore (revised estimated cost Rs. 71.15 crore as approved by EFC) under Second ADB loan assistance.

(20) Widening to 4 lanes & strengthening of existing pavement of Alwaye to Vytilla and Aroor-Sherthalai Section and Strengthening of Vytilla-Arorr Section of NH-47 under second ADB loan assistance costing Rs. 93.97 crore.

(21) Construction of Second Nizamuddin Bridge across river Yamuna on NH-24 in Delhi with grant-in-aid of approximately Rs. 88.0 crore from Government of Japan.

Private sector participation

There is an urgent need to upgrade the road system in the country by widening and strengthening existing highways, reconstruction/widening bridges, and constructing expressways on a selective basis. While the Government is providing increasing budgetary allocation for projects in the highway sector and has undertaken major upgradation initiatives in high density corridors, it has not been possible to allocate sufficent funds matching the needs due to competing demand from other sectors, especially the social sectors. The present level of budget need for National Highways during 9th Five Year Plan is about Rs. 23000 crore. Besides, deficiencies of the order of Rs. 83,000 crore have to be removed in course of time. The physical programme of road development for removing the financial bottlenecks need concerted efforts in the form of mobilisation of funds from other sources as well as to meet the enormous requirement. In-flow of private sector funds thus, is expected to bridge the demand-supply mismatch to some extent.

Scope of private participation

Participation on Build, Operate and Transfer (BOT) basis is sought in projects of under mentioned categories :

1. Existing National Highways.
    - Bridges
    - Railway Over Bridges
    - Elevated Section through Urban areas
    - Interchanges
    - Widening of Roads
2. New Alignments
    - Bypasses
    - Super National Highways (expressways)

Legal framework

The Government has amended the National Highways Act, 1956 which provides the legal framework for private sector participation. Under the amended Act, it is possible to:-

(i) Assign to the private enterpreneur implementation and operation of the projects for specified period by an agreement with the Government.

(ii) Authorise the enterpreneur to collect and retain toll/fee charged from the users.

(iii) Authorise enterpreneur to regulate traffic on BOT road.

(iv) Any person encroaching and misusing the highway developed by the entrepreneur would be liable to punishment.

Selection of entrepreneur

Criteria for selection of an entrepreneur will be his financial strength and work experience as indicated in the technical bid. The financial bid will be evaluated on the basis of lowest cost to the user.

1. Project Development
   Government will carry out feasibility study which will form part of bid document.
2. For land acquisition and relocation of utility services, acquisition of land will be done by Government who will bear the cost of land acquisition and relocation of utilities.
3. Call of bids
   Bids will be called for BOT projects from prequalified bidders in two separate covers.

   -Technical Bid.
   -Financial Bid.

Financial bids will be considered only for those bidders who qualify on the basis of technical evaluation.

4. Project Implementation

Entrepreneurs will have full freedom in implementation, subject to design and performance satisfying the contract conditions. The projects will be overseen by a Steering Committee in which the entrepreneur will be represented.

5. Right and Liabilities of the entrepreneur

Entrepreneurs will be responsible for the construction of the project within the agreed time and cost, and consequences of time and cost overrun will be borne by him.

For resolution of disputes, he will have the option to take recourse to arbitration under Indian Arbitration Act, 1940 duly amended providing for arbitration procedure in accordance with United Nations Commission on International Trade Laws (UNCITRAL).

6. Policy Initiatives already taken to encourage private participation in the Road Sector

(1) Road sector has been declared as an industry, to facilitate commercial borrowings.

(2) Following tax and fiscal concessions have been given :

(i) Tax Holiday for Five years and 30 per cent deduction in the tax over the subsequent 5 years may be availed of in any period within 20 years of the commissioning of the projects.

(ii) Exemption of import duty on identified highway construction equipments.

(iii) Incentives to financial institutions to provide long term finance for highway through deduction upto 40 per cent of their taxable income from such investments.

(3) Where housing and other development activities are an integral part of the highway projects, land required for the same would be treated as land required for public purpose and profit from such activities to the extent they are ploughed back to highway project development will be eligible for tax concession as available to infrastructure sector.

(4) Creation of Infrastructure Development Finance Company (IDFC) with an authorised capital of Rs. 5000 crores to enable entrepreneurs to have access to cheaper funds for investments in the roads sector.

(5) Providing capital to NHAI to leverage its capital to

generate more private investments into the highway sector. It may however be stated that NHAI can provide upto 40 per cent of the project cost for the financial viability of the projects.

(6) NHAI is authorised to invest in the equity of a company promoted with public sector/private sector companies or State Governments upto 30 per cent of the total equity either directly or on deferred basis.

(7) For improved sections of NHs, bridges and Road Overbridge/Rail Overbridges, tolls can be levied in perpetuity and the funds so collected can be utilised for future development of NHs.

(8) Duty-free import of bitumen is permitted under OGL.

(9) Development of road through privatisation under MOU signed with other countries is permitted.

(10) Procedure for land acquisition/ environmental clearances simplified.

(11) Delegation of higher financial powers to Ministry of Surface Transport for approval of NH projects.

(12) Comprehensive guidelines for BOT projects issued.

(13) Treating the acquisition of the land for housing and other development activities forming integral part of highway project as for "public purposes".

(14) Maximum toll rates as under to be indexed to Wholesale Price index.

(15) External Commercial Borrowings upto 35% of project cost permitted.

(16) Foreign Direct Investment upto 100% have been allowed in the road sector (with total foreign equity up to Rs. 1500 crore).

As a result of the successful boost given to the privatisation in the Road Sector, the future scenario looks quite optimistic. In a short span of 3 years, several road projects have already been identified and taken up on BOT basis and are at various stages of implementation. Till date, 17 numbers of projects involving an investment of about Rs. 835 crore have already been taken up under BOT Scheme.

Upgradation of road user cost study

A study funded by the Asian Development Bank has been completed. The main objective of this study is to update the previous data developed in conjunction with World Bank for more optimum evaluation of highway projects and to prepare a manual along with computer software. Seminars/Workshops were held at number of places to disseminate the outcome of the study for highway engineers of the Central/State Governments.

Pavement maintenance system

Asian Development Bank has funded of Pavement Maintenance Management System on National Highways with the objective of scientific assessment of needs and optimisation of maintenance strategies in the face of financial constraints. Similar study has been approved for State Roads in the states of Bihar, Maharashtra, Rajasthan and Uttar Pradesh with World Bank Assistance. These studies have been conducted.

Development of highway management system

Ministry is seriously considering development of a total Highway Management System for National Highways in the country. It is proposed to collect the data on road inventory and road condition, use these data as input to planning and prioritization model like World Bank Model HDM.III, and develop an on-line Geopositioning Information System (GIS) so that the outputs can be obtained on network maps. The project is likely to cost about Rs. 100 crore and it is being processed for sanction.

Development and maintenance of national highways

Allocations of Rs. 497.50 crore and Rs. 496.00 crore have been made for the maintenance of National Highways during 1997-98 and 1998-99 respectively. Appendix-IX gives State-wise expenditure on the development and maintenance of National Highways.

Under the Government sector scheme for setting up passenger oriented wayside amenities along National Highways, development of such amenities have been taken up. These amenity complexes are now operational in Orissa and Tamil Nadu, while works are at different stages of progress at other locations in other states.

It was also decided by the Ministry to invite private entrepreneurs to finance and operate selected schemes of passenger-oriented wayside amenities along the National Highways. Under the private sector scheme, the Letters of Intent to 27 entrepreneurs were issued for setting up passenger oriented wayside amenities along the National Highways. Ministry of Petroleum had also agreed to allot a retail petrol/diesel outlet to these entrepreneurs. The Ministry of Petroleum had withdrawn from this scheme for the allocation of petrol retail outlets to the new cases in August, 1994. The facilities are now in operation at 14 locations. In 4 cases LOI's have been cancelled due to non-response of entrepreneurs. The remaining cases are in different stages of progress.

As a long term policy, Ministry has decided to provide Passenger Oriented Wayside Amenities at every 50 Km. of national Highways. All State PWDs have been requested to identify suitable sites for setting up of wayside amenities and initiate action for getting the land acquisition estimates sanctioned and necessary land acquired. Thereafter, this land could be offered on lease to entrepreneurs who agree to provide the stipulated wayside amenities as per drawings to be approved by the Ministry.

Under a World Bank loan assistance, Ministry has got prepared through M/s. Ross Silcock,UK. Transport Research Laboratory, UK, and Central Road Research Institute, New Delhi, a "Manual for Safety in Road Design".The manual will serve as a guide for adopting safety practices in planning, design, project preparation and traffic management during construction and maintenance of highways and bridges.

Augmentation of informatory signs on national highways

Private participation in provision of retro-reflective road signs on national highways.

Recognising the fact that due to lack of adequate resources, Government is not in a position to provide and augment road signs of retro-reflective sheeting to the desired extent, Ministry has formulated a policy for allowing privately sponsored signs at selected locations provided advertisement display is restricted to the name or logo of the firm without unduly attracting driver's attention.

Detailed guidelines and technical specification to be followed for such privately sponsored road signs to be introduced on trial basis have been circulated to all the States.

The State PWDs are required to invite proposals from private entrepreneurs through open advertisement indicating the likely locations or stretches of the road within their jurisdiction for such scheme. In exceptional cases, the entrepreneurs can also suggest locations and stretches under this scheme. The final selection will rest with the competent road authorities. The entrepreneurs will have to enter into an agreement with the State PWDs for provisions, installation, maintenance and up-keep of these road signs to the entire satisfaction of the road authorities. The initial contract period for the ,schemes shall be a maximum of 5 years. The agreement shall provide for removal of these signs, as and when required by the road authorities. A draft Model Agreement for this purpose has also been circulated to all States.

Mechanisation of road construction equipment in the road sector

The technology of Road construction and maintenance is changing very fast world wide and the road construction has become a totally mechanised activity with the use of many modern and sophisticated machines. Ministry has taken many steps for the introduction of modern and sophisticated machines for the road construction in the country. Following new techniques have been introduced recently by the Ministry :

i) Slurry sealing machine

i) The use of hot bitumen cause many environmental problem and hence with a view to have eco-friendly environment, the introduction of Slurry Sealing Machine for quick repairs of the cracks/ruts developed on the road have been introduced. The machine works on cold bitumen emulsion and is very fast in repair works.

ii) Mobile pot hole repair machine

For the maintenance of road surface especially for potholes as well as cracks, the sophisticated machines which also work on cold emulsion, have been introduced by the Ministry which carry out the repair work at a very fast rate without disrupting the traffic.

iii) Mobile bridge inspection unit

In order to study the condition of the bridges and to carry out timely repair and maintenance work under the bridges, Roads Wing has introduced the Mobile Bridge Inspection Units and supplied to the State Governments.

Introduction of latest technology equipment

iv) With a view to introducing most sophisticated machinery, Roads Wing has taken steps to allow import of duty free equipment required for the Highway Sector, which are not manufactured in India, at present. Custom Authorities have already issued the notification in this regard. Ministry has taken steps that the facility of duty free import to the contracting agency in the State Governments is also extended and Custom Authorities have agreed to the proposal. In addition to 13 categories of machinery for which duty free import facility is available, Ministry has also requested the Custom Authorities under Ministry of Finance to extend the facility of duty free import to 13 more machines as under : -

1. Hydraulically operated self propelled Piling rug with Accessories.
2. Hydraulically Operated Rough Terrain self propelled 100 Ton crane with Telescopic Boom.
3. Pneumatic Tyred Roller.
4. Hydraulically operated self propelled soil boring equipment with casing pipes for deep earth anchor.
5. Mobile concrete pump placed 90/120 Cu.m/hr. Capacity.
6. Automatic Asphalt Extraction equipment.
7. Fully automatic, hydraulically operated, pre cast segment moulds.
8. Hydraulic Gantry crane of 100 Ton capacity for Launching truss.
9. Skid Steer Loaders.
10. Vibratory Rollers.
    A. Vibratory soil compactors.
    B. Vibratory Tandem Roller.

11. Combination Rollers.
12. Reversible Plate Compactor.
13. Stone (Aggregate) Crushing Plants.

v. Apart from the above, Roads Wing has taken initiatives for providing better riding surface, better quality control at site and for ascertaining the traffic volume and load capacity and for monitoring these parameters, following equipments have been imported for use in the Highway Sector.

   a) Nuclear Density Meter.
   b) Falling Weight Deflectometer.
   c) Asphalt contents gauge.
   d) Bump Integrators for measuring serviceability of the road.
   e) Weigh-in-Motion equipment.
   f) Automatic Traffic Counter cum Classifier.
   g) Automatic Road Analyser (ARAN).

Computerisation activities

As decided in the CEs meeting, Roads Wing has provided necessary funds to IRC to conduct 5 Training Workshop on "Computerised MIS on Road Sector using NICNET". NIC jointly with IRC has already conducted three such programmes covering Western, Southern and Eastern Regions of the county. The participants were from State PWDs and ROs of MOST of these regions. During these programmes, the software packages developed by Transport & Highways Informatics Division of NIC for Roads Wing on project monitoring, NH Inventory, Traffic Inventory etc. as well as the methodology for data transfer through NICNET were demonstrated. It is expected that remaining two Training Workshops for Northern and North-Eastern regions will also be held during this financial year.

Decision Support System (DSS) for status of on-going schemes has been implemented for monitoring zone.

Computerised system for generation of sanction letters has been implemented.

NIC has provided leased data circuit in Roads Wing for exclusive use of NICNET/E-MAIL.

Training of highway engineers

The cadre training plan of the Roads Wing envisages foundational training at entry, structured refresher courses including management development programmes and specialised courses for in-service technical officers.

National Institute for the Training of Highway Engineers (NITHE), a collaborative body of the Central and State Governments, was set up in 1983 with the primary objective to fill the long standing need for training of highway engineers in the country both at the entry level and during the service.

NITHE since its inception has trained 6500 highway and bridge engineers from India and abroad through its 260 training programs organised at Regional, National and International levels. Participants are drawn from Ministry of Surface Transport, various State Public Works Departments, Public &Private Sector Organisations involved in the field of highway engineering. Besides, Engineers from India, considerable number of overseas engineers from foreign Government Departments have participated in NITHE's International and SAARC level programs. NITHE has developed a handful of Computer Softwares and compilation of manuals useful for engineers and their organisations.

Documentation cell

The Ministry has set up a Documentation Cell to obtain

and preserve coloured slides, photos (both coloured and black & white) and other audio-visual materials pertaining to Road Development activities and proper source of materials for reference, etc.

Roads of inter state economic importance

Initiated in May, 1954, the scheme seeks to promote Inter-State facilities and to also assist the State Governments in their economic development through construction of roads/bridges of Inter-State Economic Importance. Keeping in view the financial constraints, only modest programmes of works with Central loan assistance of about Rs. 20.28 crore could be approved during the 8th Plan. An amount of Rs. 19.00 crore has been released during the year 1997-98 under the E&I Scheme.

A provision of Rs. 20.00 crore exists in the budget for 1998-99 for the scheme. A statement indicating the funds released during 1997-98 is at Appendix X.

Central road fund

Central Road Fund (CRF) which is a non-lapsing fund has been in existence since 1929. It derives its revenue at the rate of not less than 3.5 paise per litre out of the customs and excise duties levied on same, (motor-spirit) and the proceeds thereof are to be utilised for purpose of road development in the States. A revised resolution has been adopted by the two Houses of Parliament in May, 1988. According to the revised resolution, an amount not less than 5% of the basic price out of the duty of Custom & Excise Levied on motor spirit and diesel will accrue to the fund. Implementation of this resolution has all along been under consideration. It has now been accepted by the Government to implement it, in principle, and a case for working out the modalities is under consultation with Ministry of Finance. Statement indicating the total cost of schemes approved upto 31st December, 1998 and the total funds allotted state-wise upto 31st March, 1998 under CRF is at Appendix XI.

Second hooghly bridge

The Second Hooghly Bridge is a State Project of Government of West Bengal and has been declared a project of national importance. The bridge costing Rs. 388.34 crore has been opened to traffic on 12th October, 1992. Out of the Central non-plan loan assistance of Rs. 340.00 crore, an amount of Rs. 330.6361 crore has been released to the State Government upto December 1998. Supplementary roadworks under this project are under progress.

Border roads development board

The Border Road Development Board (BRDB) was set up in March, 1960 for accelerating the economic development of the North and North East region, and for strengthening defence preparedness through rapid and coordinated development of road communications. Its important functions are as follows :

(a) To formulate policy in respect of border communications, prescribe priorities and specifications;

(b) To lay down the responsibility of various agencies (e.g., State and Central) PWDs, Boarder Roads Organisation, etc.) as may be employed for the construction of road works out of BRDB Budget to ensure implementation of projects by them and to co-ordinate their work.

The Board is headed by the Raksha Mantri and the Raksha Rajya Mantri is the Vice Chairman. Minister of State for Surface Transport, Cabinet Secretary, the Chief of Army Staff and Chief of Air Staff are its Members. The

Secretaries of the Department of Defence, Home, Surface Transport, External Affairs and Planning Commission are also its members. The Board exercises financial and other powers of a Department of Govt. of India.

The Border Roads Organisation (BRO) is its field agency. It is a self contained Organisation with dedicated work force, plant equipment, repair facilities and medical cover for its personnel. The Organisation has adopted the latest techniques of road construction.

The Ministry of Surface Transport provides funds for the establishments of the BRDB Secretariat, DGBR Headquarters, Integrated Financial Adviser and the Headquarters of 13 Projects. The funds are also provided for the maintenance/construction of certain National Highways and other roads of operational significance. These are called the "General Staff Roads". The budgetary allocation for the purpose in 1998-99 (BE) is Rs. 516.34 crore. The pay and allowances of 29 Task Forces, (i.e. the basic field units) are charged to different works. The Works which are not included in the BRDB budget are called the "Agency Works". In the year 1998-99, the Agency Works to the tune of Rs. 410.04 crore are being taken up.

The Ministry of Surface Transport have also assigned some other works to the BRO. For example, the BRO is participating in the construction of Varanasi Bye-pass (NH-2) and the Panvel-Nhava Sheva Port road (NH4B). Similarly, the Ministry of External Affairs have utilized the BRO for executing infrastructure developmental works in Bhutan and Myanmar. So far, a total of 27,000 Kms of roads have either been constructed or upgraded by the BRO.

The BRO is manned by personnel of General Reserve Engineer Force and the Army. Out of the total strength of 39,000 officers, 1 179 officers and other ranks are from the Army. On 14th August, 1985, the GREF was declared to be an integral part of the Armed Forces of India, Some important provisions of the Army Act and Rule have been made applicable to the BRO personnel.

Although the BRDB's Budget flows out of the Ministry of Surface Transport, from the inception of BRDB, the administrative control of the Board has been vested in the Ministry of Defence. This arrangement has ensured cohesion in planning for roads in border areas. It has also facilitated effective coordination at the field level.

The BRO has undertaken successfully many tasks allotted to it by the Government. It is a vibrant leading construction organisation in the country. The devotion to duty and gallantary of the employees of BRO have been recognised by awarding Medals and Commendation Cards given to 88 Officers and other ranks during 1998 as follows : -

(a) Shaurya Chakra	1
(b) Vishisht Sewa Medal	2
(c) Uttam Jeevan Raksha Padak	1
(d) Jeevan Raksha Padak	1
(e) Govt. Commendation Card	20
(f) DGBR Commendation Card	62
(g) Sarvottam Jeevan Raksha Padak	1
Total	88

Achievements of the BRO

Important ongoing works:

(a) *General staff works* : The BRO is constructing developing and maintaining roads for the General Staff of the Army Headquarters.

(b) Major highways :

(i) NH-2A (Varanasi Byepass) - This 28.67 Km long byepass is being constructed to NH Double Lane Specification.

(ii) NH-16 - This is a very long highway from Nizambad in Andhra Pradesh to Jagdalpur in Madhya Pradesh. 255 Km long stretch from Andhra Pradesh/MP Border to Jagdalpur.

(iii) NH-17B - The task of development/ improvement of 18 Kms long stretch of NH 17B from Varna to Sada in Goa, have been entrusted in 1998-99.

(iv) NH-53 - It is being developed to NH Double Lane Specifications.

(v) NH-54 - This road is being developed to NH Double Lane Specifications from Silchar to Aizwal.

(vi) Improvement and maintenance are in progress on other NHs under BRO viz. NH-1A, NH-22, NH-31A, NH-44, NH-52 and NH-52A. The BRO is making concerted efforts to improve the trafficability of NH-1A Road Jammu-Srinagar, which is the life line of the Kashmir Valley.

(c) Agency Works

(i) North Eastern Council (NEC) Roads - BRO has been constructing roads for NEC since 1980-81. The Annual budget for NEC roads with BRO is approximately Rs. 75 crore.

(ii) Indo-Bangladesh Border Roads - These roads are being constructed by BRO on behalf of the Ministry of Home Affairs. The total length of roads entrusted to BRO as per revised content is 863.79 Km equivalent Cl-9, out of which 711 Km have been completed so far.

(iii) Maharashtra Govt. Works -The BRO is constructing approximately 2400 Km of roads for Govt. of

Maharashtra in two phases, in the districts of Gadchiroli and Bhandara.

(iv) Goa Port Trust Works - Mormugao Port Trust Goa has entrusted work for development of approach road (Length 15 Kms) to NH-4 lane costing approximately Rs. 30 crore and Permanent Works worth Rs. 3 crore. Work has been planned for execution during 1998-99.

(v) IGNP Works - IGNP authorities have entrusted the task of construction of 114 Krn long Gadra sub-branch canal road, for which works are in progress and likely to be completed by March, 1999.

(vi) MEA Works in Bhutan - The BRO is carrying out a large number of works for MEA in Bhutan, including terminal works for Paro airfield.

(vii) MEA Works in Myanmar - The Construction of road Tamu-KalemyoKalewa in Myanmar has also been undertaken for MEA. Resources were inducted from April 1997 onwards and the actual work convened in October, 1997. These works are likely to be completed by December, 2000.

(d) Airfields:

(i) Kargil Airfield - The task of construction of Kargil airfield has been taken up on behalf of AAI and works are in full swing.

(ii) Srinagar and Pune Airfields - BRO has successfully completed the works pertaining to Srinagar Airfield in September 1998. It was inaugurated on 25th November 1998. Works on Pune Airfield for IAF are in progress.

(iii) Goa Airfield -Work for strengthening of Goa Airfield has recently been entrusted by Navy costing approximately Rs. 6 crore. Works have been planned for execution during 1998-99.

(e) Bridges -

10 bridges have been completed during the current financial year and put into service of the Nation.

(f) Snow clearance

It would not be out of place to record, the commendable work being done every year in the field of snow clearance. The Snow Clearance is carried out by BRO on a number of roads in high altitude areas, both during summers and winters. However, the real test lies in speedy opening of road Srinagar-Leh, across the Zozilla Pass and Road Manali-Sarchu, across the Rohtang Pass.

Conferences and seminars

(a) FIP Symposium - Lt. Gen. R.J. Mordecai, AVSM, Director General Boarder Roads and Shri B.K. Basu, SC, Chief Engineer Project Pushpak attended the 13th FIP Symposium and Exhibition from 23rd May, 1998 to 29th May, 1998 at Amasterdam (Netherlands).

(b) International Congress on Road Maintenance and Uses - Lt. General R.J. Mordecai, AVSM, Director General Border Roads and Shri B.L. Tikoo, DDG (D&S) attended the 4th Congress on Road Maintenance and Uses, organised by Directorate of Roads, Ministry of Public Works, Transport and Housing, France, in Grenoble, France from 29th September, 1998 to 1st October, 1998.

(c) Chief Engineers Conference - A Conference of all Chief Engineers of BRO was held from 9th to 14th November, 1998 in New Delhi.

Publications

During 1998-99 BRO brought out the following publications :-

(a) Reflections - On 7th May, 1998 on the occasion of the 38th Raising Day of Boarder Roads Organisation, this publication was brought out. This is an annual publication giving the resume of BRO works under various projects.

(b) Oonchi Sadaken -Published on 10th November, 1998, this is an annual publication in which topical articles and technical papers by BRO are published.

Use of hindi as an official language :

BRO continues to make good progress in the use of Hindi as an official language. Adequate impetus is provided not only in the HO DGBR in this direction but also in all the Projects and functional units. Hindi fortnight was organised from 1st to 15th September, 1998, jointly by BRDB Sectt., office of the Controller of Defence Accounts (Border Roads) and the Directorate General Border Roads. Various competitions were organised during that period. 20 personnel were awarded prizes on 29th October, 1998. Cash awards of rs. 500, 300 and 200 were given to the participants who stood first, second and third respectively.

Exploitation of BRO's potential

The BRO is a dynamic, result-oriented, successful and highly popular construction organisation. It has transformed the frontiers of our Nation into an integrated network of roads. The BRO has tremendous potential, which can be tapped gainfully for the further development of the Nation. The motto of the BRO is "Speed, Economy and Quality". That is why the BRO is a sought after construction organisation.

9

Road Transport

To keep pace with the economic development in the country and consequent surge in demand for transport services -both passenger and freight, various modes of transport have experienced substantial growth over the years. Road Transport, however, is the most dominant mode of transport both for movement of passengers and goods and is likely to continue to enjoy this status increasingly in the coming years. The users preference towards the road transport is on account of its inherent advantages viz. easy availability, adaptability to individual needs, door to door service, and reliability. At present, 80% of passengers and over 60% of freight is estimated to move by roads. It also acts as a feeder service to Railways, Ports and Air Traffic.

This Ministry is concerned with the formulation of broad policies relating to road transport, besides making arrangements for movement of vehicular traffic with the neighbouring countries. The following Acts/ Rules are being administered in Road Transport Sector which embody the policy relating to Motor Vehicles & State Road Transport Corporations in the Country :

i) Motor Vehicles Act, 1988.

ii) Central Motor Vehicles Rules, 1989.

iii) Road Transport Corporations Act, 1950.

In its tasks for development of roads and road transport in the country, the Ministry is assisted by Transport Development Council. It is an apex advisory body on roads, road transport and inland water transport. Minister of Surface Transport is its Chairman; concerned Central Ministers namely Industry/ Railways/ Urban Development/Tourism/Rural Development/ Planning Commission and Minister-in-charge of Roads/ Road Transport, Inland Water Transport in States/UTs and Lt. Governors/Administrators of UTs without legislature are its members.

The 28th meeting of the Council was held on 10th October, 1998 and the following important items including others were discussed in the meeting : -

a) Composite Fee and Authorisation Fee on National Permit.
b) Collection of Road Accident Data.
c) Amendment of Motor Vehicles Act, 1988.
d) Hike in freight by transport operators.
f) Expanding role of private finance in passenger transport.
e) Scheme to provide central assistance for purchase of pollution testing equipment.
g) National Highway Patrolling Scheme.
h) Popularising the use of multi axle vehicles.
i) Problem of overloading of two axle vehicles on National Highways.
j) Creation of a dedicated fund for development of Highways.
k) Enactment of legislation for control of Ribbon Development along National Highways.
l) Need for setting up of Inland Water Transport Organisation in various States and framing of rules under Inland Vessels Act, 1917.

This Ministry is contemplating to enter into bilateral agreement regarding regulation of movement of vehicular traffic with neighbouring countries viz. Bhutan, Bangladesh, Nepal and Pakistan. This Ministry is considering to enter into an agreement with the Government of Bhutan, for the movement of both passenger & goods through road transport. In case of Government of Nepal and Bangladesh, this Ministry is considering an agreement for the movement of passenger traffic with these countries. Discussion with Government of Nepal and Bangladesh on the draft agreement is in progress. Recently, this Ministry has initiated dialogue with Government of Pakistan for entering into an agreement for Delhi-Lahore Bus Service and vice versa. In this connection, a high level delegation visited Islamabad from 1st to 4th December, 1998. After detailed discussion, a draft agreement for the operation of the above bus service was initiated by the competent authorities of the two Countries. Approval at the Government's level is under process.

It is also contemplated to make certain important amendments regarding Road Safety, Pollution etc. in the Motor Vehicles Act, 1988 and Central Motor Vehicle Rules, 1989.

In order to curb the menace of vehicular pollution, this Ministry has taken several steps in this direction. Four Workshop-cum-training programmes were organised, two each at Automotive Research Association of India, Pune and Indian Institute of Petroleum, Dehradun. In these workshops, officials of the State Transport Departments were given training regarding checking of vehicular pollution more scientifically and effectively.

Further, this Ministry has also made budget provision for the reimbursement of the cost of Pollution

Testing Equipment to be purchased by the States/UTs for the checking of vehicular pollution. In this regard, the proposal of reimbursement received from the Government of Goa and Kerala for the release of an amount of Rs. 1,54,983 and Rs. 34,34,250 respectively has been agreed to in principle by this Ministry.

State road transport undertaking

There are 71 State Road Transport Undertakings having a fleet of nearly 1,05,201 vehicles providing passenger transport in various parts of the country. These Public Sector Organisations, put together carried nearly 6.40 crore passengers approximately, per day during the year 1997-98.

Most of the Road Transport Undertakings are incurring losses. Low fare structure, absence of automatic fare revision, congestion on roads, operation on uneconomic routes, concession in fares to students and weaker sections of the society etc., along with rising cost of operation due to older buses, are responsible for their poor financial health. In the context of boosting sales in commercial vehicles industry, the Finance Ministry has asked the State Governments and STU's to place purchase orders for passenger buses for replacement of old age fleets.

This Ministry in consultation with Planning Commission is actively considering revival of the scheme of granting capital contribution to SRTCs. This will give an opportunity to SRTCs to replace old aged vehicles and expansion or augmentation of Road Transport Services in the country. The Ministry is also considering amendments required in RTC Act, 1950 to enable SRTCs to operate in competitive environment.

Road safety

A Road Safety Cell was set up in the Ministry of Surface

Transport in September, 1986 to formulate policies for road safety so as to minimise road accidents in the Country. The Road Safety Cell compiles road accidents data and prepares schemes and programmes envisaging road safety. The important schemes include publicity programmes, Grants-in-aid to voluntary organisations for organising Road Safety Programmes, National Highway Patrolling Scheme, Refresher Training to Drivers in unorganised sector etc. During the year 1998-99, the following activities were undertaken:-

i) A massive public awareness campaign was carried out through Directorate of Advertising and Visual Publicity (DAVP) viz. Printing of calender depicting road safety messages, display of cinema slides, broadcasting of radio jingles, computerised animation display, display on colour railings, closed circuit T.V. System for screening of Video spots etc.

ii) Grants-in-aid were provided to various voluntary organisations for undertaking Road Safety Programmes.

iii) The 10th Road Safety Week, with the theme of 'Safe Transportation of School Going Children' was observed from 4th to 10th January, 1999 throughout the country with the involvement of state Governments, voluntary organisations, vehicle manufacturers, State Road Transport Undertakings etc. All the above agencies have been asked to carry out a number of measures on Road Safety during the 'Week'. A list of such suggested measures is given at Appendix-VIII.

iv) Refresher training to heavy motor vehicle driver in the un-organised sector was arranged through the Automobile Association of Upper India, New Delhi (AAUI) and Krishna District Lorry Owner Association, Vijayawada, Andhra Pradesh

v) Financial Assistance to the tune of Rs. 25 lakhs each was provided to 8 State Governments under National Highway Patrolling Scheme for purchase of Crane and Ambulance.

10

Research and Development Studies-Road Research

The R&D efforts in the road sector mainly consist of improvement in design and construction techniques, evolving specifications, circulation of guidelines, encouraging use of new technologies and compilation of state-of-the-art reports. In recent years, considerable stress has been laid on the development of computer software for design etc. Research schemes are generally of applied nature in the fields of roads, bridges, traffic and transportation. The schemes are sponsored by the Ministry and executed by various research agencies and academic institutions and, in a few cases, by consultants.

During 1997-98, an amount of Rs. 414.00 lakh was released for Research and development. During 1998-99 an outlay of Rs. 450.00 lakh has been provided.

Research and Development schemes completed during the year 1999-99 are given below: -

Roads

1. R-16 : Studies for flexible pavement under different traffic and climate Conditions.
2. R-56: To develop computer programmes and design charts for analytical design of flexible pavements.
3. R-65 : Improvement of computer aided system for high embankment.

4. R-66 : Automation of Benkelman Beam.
5. R-71 : Upgrading the State of Art Report-line soil stabilization.
6. R-74 : Development of road condition evaluation equipment.

Traffic & Transportation

7. R- 47 : Estimate for short hand urban an and sub-urban freight traffic.
8. R-64 : Establishment of system for identification and rectification of accident black spots.

Notable Research and Development schemes nearing completion are as follows :-

Roads

1. R-41 : Use of geogrids in improving performance of pavement overlays.
2. R-42 : Use of additives in bitumen to improve durability and strength of bituminous courses.

Traffic & Transportation

3. R-3, Ph.III : Establishment of Permanent Traffic Count stations in Andhra Pradesh.
4. R-35 : Development and application Traffic Simulation Model.
5. R-44 : Pattern of Traffic on Secondary Road System.
6. R-62 : Evolving guidelines on infrastructural facilities for freight traffic movement of multi-axle vehicles along National Highways.
7. R-69 : Preparation of Guidelines for Geometric Design Standards for Expressways in India.
8. R-73 : Evaluation of Capacity Augmentation options of National Highways & State Highways.
9. R-79 : Evaluation of Road Accident costs.

Performance study is under process for the test sections constructed in respect of following schemes : -

i) Use of additives in bitumen to improve durability and strength of bituminous mixes.

ii) Use of Rubber/Polymer modified bitumen binders for road pavements on National Highway No. 2 near Allahabad.

iii) Use of geo-synthetic pavement reinforcing fabric as inter-layer to control reflective cracking in bituminous overlays on Kanpur-Varanasi section of NH-2 near Allahabad.

Some important ongoing Road Research Schemes in different stages of progress, are as under :

Roads

1. R-19 : (NPS) Highway Design study; Pavement performance study for new pavement sections.
2. R-42 : Use of additives in bitumen to improve durability and strength of bituminous courses.
3. R-54 : Use of Rubber/Polymer modified bitumen binders for road pavements on NH-2 near Allahabad.
4. R-59 : Development of Computer Programme for analysing Box Cell Culverts.
5. R-63 : Use of geo-synthetic pavement reinforcing fabric as interlays to control reflective cracking in bituminous overlays-construction of test section in km. 239.5 to 240.5 and 261.0 to 262.0 of Kanpur-Varanasi Section of NH-2 near Allahabad.
6. R-67 : Third revision of Pocket Book of Highway Engineers and Bridge Engineers.
7. R-70 : Updating the state-of-the-art report on lime-soil stabilisation.

Traffic & transportation

8. R-68 : Development of Aesthetic Designs of Roadside Furniture.

9. R-72 : Development of Automatic Counting and classification system for Highway vehicles.

Bridges

10. B-21 : Preparation of SOAR on Under Water Scanning (implementing agency-IRC & SERC).
11. B-22 : Preparation of SOAR on development of Bridges bearings (implementing agency-IRC & CRRI).
12. B-23 : To evaluate live load characterisation for evolving partial safety factor for live loads on concrete bridges (Phase-1) (implementing agency-SERC).
13. B-24 : Updation of Standard Data Book of Analysis (1995) (implementing agency - IRC).
14. B-26 : Use of fiber reinforced concrete in repair and rehabilitation of bridges (implementing agency - CRRI).

During the year, works on the following R&D Schemes have been initiated :

1. R-80 : Updation of Road User Cost Study.
2. R-81 : Structural Evaluation of pavements in Eastern India using falling weight deflectometer.

Research applications

i) As part of Ministry's Research Scheme No. R-56, computer programmes and design charts for analytical design of flexible pavements have been developed.

ii) Computer aided system for design of high embankments has been developed under Ministry Research Scheme No. R-56.

iii) Working of Benkelman Beam for determining thickness of strengthening.

iv) A State-of-the-Art report for earthwork and subgrade has been prepared for use of professional engineers.

Transport research

The Transport Research Wing (TRW) continued to render necessary data support to various Wings of the Ministry for policy planning, transport coordination, economic and statistical analysis on various modes of transport with which the Ministry of Surface Transport is concerned.

This Wing regularly collects, analyses and disseminates statistics on roads, road transport, ports, shipping, ship-building, ship-repairing and inland water transport. This Wing also brings out annual statistical publications in booklet form on the above aspects. It also brings out "Pocket Book on Transport Statistics in India" bi-annually covering data on all modes of transport including Railways and Civil Aviation.

During 1998-99, the following publications have been brought out : -

1) Pocket Book on Transport Statistics of India - 1997
2) Statistics of Inland Water Transport -1997-98.
3) Basic Road Statistics of India - 1995-96.
4) Motor Transport Statistics of India, 1997.

The following publications are in the final stages of completion and are likely to be brought out shortly : -

1) Basic Port Statistics of India, 1997-98.
2) Statistics of India's Ship-building and Ship-repairing Industry, 1997-98.
3) Indian Shipping Statistics, 1998.

This Wing reviews the progress of implementation of port projects costing more than Rs. 100 crores on monthly basis and the projects costing Rs. 20 crores and above on quarterly basis with a view to identify the critical areas requiring urgent attention of the Ministry for their timely completion. Besides, it is also monitoring the work relating to the major port projects identified for creation of additional capacity in the 9th Plan. In addition, TR Wing brings out a note on "Performance Indicators of Major Ports" every month highlighting achievements, slippages vis-a-vis targets across 4 indicators viz. traffic handled, average pre-berthing detention, average turn round time and average output per ship berthday.

Transport Research Wing also brings out Occasional Research Papers on important topics concerning Transport Sector. One such paper entitled "Problems and Prospects of Minor Ports in India" was brought out during 1997-98. Another Occasional Research Paper on "Recommended Actions to Reduce Vehicular Pollution in Delhi by 50% by 2005 and Policy options for Improvement of Urban Transport" was also brought out during 1998-99. It is proposed to bring out one more Occasional Research Paper on "Integrated Approach for Development of Road Transport Infrastructure in India" during 1998-99.

In the Road Transport Sector, the Wing continued to undertake review of the performance relating to passenger services run by State Road Transport Undertakings (SRTUs) on quarterly basis. At present, there are 71 SRTUs constituting 21 Corporations, 31 Companies, 8 Government Undertakings and 11 Municipal Undertakings which include certain freight carriers as well. For the purpose of review, this Wing liaises with the SRTUs for statistics on major physical and financial parameters.

The Transport Research Wing organises training programmes and workshops covering Management

Information System on certain specialised topics from time to time. The main objective of these programmes is to streamline the flow of information from the various agencies to create a data bank for the researchers, scholars and planners at the Centre and State levels. During the year one such Workshop on "MIS in Major Ports" was organised at Visakhapatnam in the port sector.

Transport Research Wing is the nodal agency of the Government of India to collect and disseminate information on the length of various categories of roads in the country. It has been experienced by TRW that collection of data on roads has been a complex task since multiple agencies are engaged in the construction and maintenance of roads in the country. In order to have first hand understanding of the situation and to evolve a system of smooth collection of data in this regard, TRW organised three Regional Workshops on Road & Road Transport Sector in the country during 1998-99. These Workshops have been conducted at Pune, Calcutta and Chennai.

Transport studies

i) Study on traffic flows

Over the years, roads have become the most dominant mode of transport. While the precise data on traffic movement by railways is being collected by the Ministry of Railways, similar information for roads is not available. Maximum cargo movement by roads are controlled by a large number of truck operators; most of these operators are single truck owners and there is no institutional arrangement both at Central and State levels for collection of data on road traffic flows. Similarly, authentic and reliable data on passenger traffic by various modes of road transport except for passengers carried by State Road Transport Undertakings, are not available. Considering the importance of the data for further planning and development of the sector, M/s RITES was awarded an All-India study for estimation of passenger and goods movement by roads. M/s. RITES has submitted its Draft Final Report on the Road Traffic flows in the country. The report has been examined. The RITES would be submitting the final report after incorporating the suggestions/ observations made by the Review Committee.

ii) Other proposed studies

In order to undertake systematic research on various issues in the transport sector, guidelines have been formulated for identifying, awarding and monitoring of research proposals. A Standing Committee with Joint Secretary (Transport) as Chairman has been in existence for awarding studies. A Review Committee with Adviser (TR) as Chairman has also been functioning to process the proposals, monitor the programmes and distil out the findings of the studies. In a recent meeting of the Standing Committee, it was decided to undertake a research study on "Rationalisation of Motor Vehicle Taxation" in the country.

11

Administration

Administration Wing of the Ministry consists of three Establishment Sections, three General Administration Sections and two Cash Sections. The Administration Wing is entrusted with the service and administrative matters of 1251 employees (Gr. A, B, C & D) of the Ministry and Regional Offices of the Roads Wing of the Ministry, house keeping jobs of the Ministry and the drawing and disbursing of salaries and other expenditure. Efforts are being made to manage the various cadres as per the instructions and guidelines issued by DOPT, UPSC and Department of Administrative Reforms etc. The implementation of the reservation for OBC has also been started in the Ministry as per the Government Policy in this regard. Efforts are also being made for the automation of office as far as possible.

Special efforts are being made by the Ministry to ensure compliance of the orders issued from time to time regarding reservation for SC/ST/OBCs and to fill up vacant posts. Information with regard to the total number of Government Servants separately for Secretariat, Technical sides in the Ministry.

Finance wing

The Finance Wing is headed by Additional Secretary and

Financial Adviser. He is assisted by a Deputy Financial Adviser and two Assistant Financial Advisers.

As per the Scheme of Integrated Financial Advisers, the Financial Adviser is associated with the administrative Ministry to assist the Secretary of the administrative Ministry and other senior officials in the planning, programming, budgeting, monitoring and evaluation functions of the Ministry. The Additional Secretary and Financial Adviser is required to advise the administrative Ministry in all matters falling within the field of delegated powers. The duties of Financial Adviser include the following :

(i) to furnish material to Parliamentary Standing Committee on Transport and Tourism in connection with Plan/Budget etc. of this Ministry and to furnish clarificatory information in connection with points raised by the Parliamentary Committee;

(ii) to scrutinise all proposals to be placed before Expenditure Finance Committee/ Public Investment Board/Cabinet Committee on Economic Affairs/ Cabinet and act as a Secretariat for EFC/PIB, BOT proposals and their scrutiny;

(iii) to render financial advice/concurrence to the proposals and schemes emanating from different administrative wings of the Ministry;

(iv) to assist the administrative wings in the preparation of Five Year Plans and Annual Plans;

(v) to assess the internal resources of the Public Sector Undertakings and Autonomous Bodies under the administrative control of the Ministry.

(vi) to scrutinise and vet the budget proposals received from the various Autonomous Bodies and PSUs;

(vii) to evaluate the progress/performance of the projects and other continuing schemes

(viii) to ensure observance of financial discipline, enforcement of the economy measures and to assess financial viability of the proposals;

(ix) to watch the settlement of Audit objections, inspection reports/reviews, draft Audit paras etc.;

(x) to ensure prompt action on Audit Reports and Appropriation Accounts, Reports on Public Accounts Committee, Estimates Committee and Committee on Public 11.3.2 Sector Undertakings;

In addition to rendering financial advice, the Financial Adviser is also in overall charge of Budget and Accounts. It is his duty to:

(a) ensure that the schedule for preparation of Budget is adhered to by the Ministry and the Budget is drawn up according to the instructions issued by Finance Ministry from time to time;

(b) scrutinise budget proposals thoroughly, before sending them to Ministry of Finance;

(c) see that complete departmental accounts are maintained in accordance with the requirements under General Financial Rules;

(d) watch and review the progress of expenditure against sanctioned grants.

Recently, a Project Monitoring Cell (PMC) has been set up as per the directions of Ministry of Finance. The main function of PMC is to monitor all projects including Externally Aided Projects. The Cell functions under the charge of Additional Secretary & Financial Adviser.

Departmental accounting organisation (accounting set up)

The accounting division under the Chief Controller of Accounts is inter-alia responsible for accounting, payment, budget, internal-audit and cash management. The organisation comprises of Chief Controller of

Accounts, two Deputy Controller of Accounts, two Assistant Controller of Accounts, eighteen Pay & Accounts Officers/ Regional Pay & Accounts Officers and other staff at Delhi, Calcutta, Mumbai, Chandigarh, Jaipur, Bangalore, Lucknow and Guwahati. Both the Cash Branches of the Sectt. are also working under the over all supervision of Chief Controller of Accounts.

The annual accounts of the Ministry such as Statement of Central Transactions, Appropriation Accounts in respect of Grant Nos. 78, 79 & 80 and Finance Account for the year are compiled and rendered to the Controller General of Accounts, Dept.. of Expenditure, Ministry of Finance. Computer generated monthly expenditure figures are also furnished to all divisions of the Ministry to facilitate monitoring of programmes and schemes. The monthly compilation of accounts has already been computerised in a phased manner, other items of works are also being computerised.

The budget of Ministry of Surface Transport is presented to the Parliament in the form of following Demands for Grants :

(i) Grant No. 78 - Ministry of Surface Transport.

(ii) Grant No. 79 - Roads

(iii) Grant No. 80 - Ports, Lighthouses and Shipping.

Position of saving/excess in respect of above mentioned grants for the year 1997-98 has been reflected in Appendix XVI. Source and Uses (Application) of fund for the year 1997-98 has been reflected in Appendix XVII.

Through an effective network of PAOs, the personal claims of the Government employees i.e. Pension, Family Pension, Gratuity, Provident Fund, CGEGIS and Leave Encashment etc. are being settled promptly.

The Internal Audit of the expenditure incurred by the Ministry and its subordinate formations were also conducted during the year by this Organisation. Headquarters and Regional Pay & Accounts Officers (NH) also conducted Internal Test Check of Public Works Division of the State PWDs which incur expenditure on National Highways on behalf of Ministry of Surface Transport. In addition, special audits were also conducted which yielded significant results.

Reserve funds of ministry of surface transport

The Ministry of Surface Transport is maintaining several funds for providing certain services which are required to develop transportation facilities in the country. Four funds namely Depreciation Reserve Fund, General Reserve Fund, National Highways Permanent Bridges Fee Fund and Central Road Fund are being maintained by the Ministry. The balances under these funds are shown in Appendix XVIII.

O & M unit

Government have laid emphasis on providing an effective and responsive administration so as to cause minimum irritation to the citizens when they deal with the Govt. and the need to create awareness and to give information to citizens. On the directions of Dept. of Administrative Reforms & Public Grievances, an Information and Facilitation Counter in the Ministry was set up and made operational on trial basis w.e.f. 31st August, 1998.

The Induction Material indicating the details of list of subjects allotted to each Section/ Desk, Telephone Nos., Organisational Charts etc., was reviewed and updated in June, 1998.

Due attention was paid towards records management. Annual Inspection of Departmental Record

Room (D.R.R.) was conducted on 27th November, 1998 by the National Archives of India who have recorded that there was a phenomenal improvement in the maintenance of the D.R.R. and it is in a very good condition. Half-yearly Special Drives were launched to record, review and weed-out old records and about 5,500 files were weeded out. 718 files of non-current nature over 25 years old have been transferred to NAI during December, 1998.

Necessary data relating to disposal of work was collected from various units of the Ministry and analysed. O&M meetings were organised with a view to monitor the performance of various sections and on this basis, senior officers were kept informed about the trend of disposal of paper work in the Ministry. In this direction, a random checking of a few sections/desks were carried out to ascertain as to whether all the cases that are pending have been included in the pendency list and correct position reflected. 38 Sections/Desks were got inspected during the year.

The Grievance Cell in the Ministry, headed by the Joint Secretary (Admn.) as the Director of Grievances, received approximately 70 grievances and took action for their prompt redressal by the concerned Administrative Units, Port Trusts, Public Sector Undertakings, etc.

Internal work study unit (IWSU)

The role of this Unit is to ensure implementation of the instructions of the Government for effecting economy in relation to the manpower requirement of the Ministry and its subordinate formations.

During the year, the following studies were undertaken :

(i) Work Measurement Study of Tuticorin Port Trust for creation of posts for revamping of the Port's Fire Service.

(ii) Work Measurement Study of New Mangalore Port Trust for creation of posts to set up a legal cell.

(iii) Work Measurement Study of Directorate General of Shipping, Mumbai, for creation of Group 'C' posts in its Official Language Wing.

The IWSU also co-ordinated with SIU (Ministry of Finance) in respect of the following activities:

(i) Work Measurement Study of various organisations under the Ministry to be undertaken by the SIU.

(ii) Watching the progress of implementation and furnishing progress reports in respect of various studies carried out by SIU earlier.

(iii) Obtaining information required by SIU, for the studies proposed to be undertaken by it, from the concerned organisations and forwarding it to SIU expeditiously.

Vigilance

The Vigilance Wing of the Ministry is a nodal point for coordinating and supervising the activities relating to Vigilance work in the Ministry and in the Organisations under the administrative control of the Ministry. The Wing is headed by a Chief Vigilance Officer of the rank of Joint Secretary, who is appointed with the approval of the CVC. Each organisation under the Ministry has a CVO to look after the vigilance functions pertaining to that organisation. Some organisations have part-time CVOs while some organisations have full-time posts of CVOs. The part-time CVOs are appointed from amongst the officers of the concerned organisation with the approval of the CVC. The full-time post of CVOs are filled-up from officers of organised services in consultation with DOP&T.

During the year under report, the Vigilance Wing had processed a large number of complaints and other on-going vigilance cases of officers of the Ministry/Port Trusts/ PSUs and subordinate organisations under the control of the Ministry. A large number of CBI cases have been handled during this year. In the continuous endeavour to make vigilance more effective and also to discuss the problems being faced by the Vigilance Departments/functionaries of different organisations, Regional Conferences of CVOs were organised at Cochin on 16th & 17th April, 1998, at Mormugao on 7th & 8th August, 1998 and at Paradip on 5th & 6th November, 1998. In these conferences, the role of preventive vigilance has been paid special attention and organisations have been impressed upon to make special efforts in making preventive vigilance more effective. Punitive action, wherever necessary, has been taken in consultation with the CVC.

Integrated facilitation counter (IFC)

The IFC in the Ministry was made operational during August, 1998 in line with the directive of the Department of Administrative Reforms and Public Grievances.

Project monitoring cell (PMC)

PMC of the Ministry has been set up this year for monitoring External Aided Projects (EAMIS). NIC has also developed software for PMC activities.

Other computerisation activities

(i) Establishment of Local Area Network (LAN): A LAN comprising of seven nodes was set up in the Finance Wing of the Ministry to facilitate development and implementation of software such as OPA, Monitoring of Plan Expenditure etc.

Other computerisation activities

(i) Setting up of RF link: RF Link was set up to facilitate the Internet access for the users of the

Ministry. Following this a mail server 'transport' has been set up to enable the users to access E-mail from their terminals/PCs.

(ii) Implementation of OPA system: In the first phase of implementation of OPA, Labour Division has been selected and implementation work has started there. It is proposed to implement the system in selected sections initially in a non-networked environment. On completion of LAN, the same could be implemented in a network environment to facilitate monitoring movement of files etc.

12

Service Directory under Telecom Commission

Provision of new telephone connection

During the year 1997-98, a record number of 32.59 lacs new telephone connections were provided. This achievement was 22.40% more than the achievement of 25.64 lacs new connections provided during the preceding year.

Village telephone

Telephone facilities in villages is an essential prerequisite for the development of rural sector. As against the target of 83,000 villages, 42855 villages have been covered with telephone facility during the year, bringing the total number of villages provided with telephone facilities to 310687. This represents a growth of 16 per cent over the previous year.

STD stations

The direct dialing facility is very useful for accessing distant stations instantly. The Department has, therefore, been constantly increasing the number of STD stations in the country.

It was decided to increase the number of NSD/STD stations at a faster rate and, accordingly, 2799 new stations were added during 1997-98. There were 16019 NSD/STD Stations in the country as on 31.3.1998.

Accessibility

Since there is a long waiting list for telephone connections and also considering the fact that telephone facility is needed by general public who cannot afford to have a telephone of their own, it was decided that the accessibility should be improved by providing a large number of PCOs for general public.

Rural communication

Improvement in rural communications is evident from the following facts

Type of rural exchanges commissioned during the year 1996-97

Sl. No.	Type of Equipment	No. of gross lines
1.	64 Port MILT	23494
2.	128P C-DOT RAX	113718
3.	256P C-DOT RAX	664304
4.	200L E PAM	1148
5.	512Port C-DOT SBM	121808
6.	1000L C-DOT SBM	406288
7.	1200/1400L C-DOT SBM	49396
8.	512P ILT/2048 Port ILT	38305
9.	200L E-PAM	1148
10.	Upgradation Kits(128P-256P)	81974
11.	NEAX 61/S	1524
12.	Other Exch	28822
13.	Line Module-I	101551
14.	Line Module-II	91926
	Total	1724258

Telephone metered call units

The number of metered call units (accounting for local and STD/ISD calls) increased to 11770.9 crores during the year compared to 9329.6 crores during 1996-97 representing an increase of 26.18%. The number of Telex metered call units declined to 9.12 crores in 1997-98 from 12.86 crores in 1996-97, representing a decrease of 29.08 %.

Mission better communication

An intensive drive was launched under "Mission Better Communications" to enhance subscribers satisfaction by improving quality of existing services, accessibility to Telecom services in rural and urban areas, specially in hilly and backward areas through replacement of fault prone and worn-out equipments, computerisation of services, upgradation and modernisation of technology and motivational training of staff.

Steps taken under "Mission Better Communications" brought fruitful results which are evident from the following:

	Target 1997-98	Achievements 1997-98
(i) Faults/100stns/month Telephones	12.0	16.8
(ii) Trunk efficiency (%)	87.7	81.5
(iii) Call completion rate (%) (Live)		
a) Local	60.0	57.4
b) Junction	50.0	45.2
c) STD	43.0	40.5

Telecom Directorate Observation Team carried out 16 observations of telephone systems during the year.

Factors which adversely affected the performance of telephone systems were analysed and brought to the notice of the concerned field units and remedial action taken.

Participation of private sector in basic telephone service and the licencing process

Policy provisions

In accordance with National Telecom Policy, 1994, the private operators are permitted to operate Basic Telephone Services in addition to the Department of Telecom (DOT). The monopoly position of DOT is, thus, changing to duopoly where one private operator will provide Basic Telephone Services in each circle alongwith DOT/MTNL.

Only Indian registered companies are permitted to operate Basic Telephone Services.

Foreign equity in these companies is permitted only upto 49%.

The prospective operators need to have an experience of providing 5 lakh lines of Basic Telephone Service. The new National Telecom Policy is presently under consideration of the Government.

Achievements

Three rounds of tenders have been invited since Jan' 1995 in respect of 21 Telecom Circles in the country.

Based on these biddings 9 companies were issued Letters Of Intent (LOI) for 13 Telecom Circles.

Six companies have signed the Licence and Interconnect Agreements for six circles.

Out of four companies which had filed Civil Suits in High Court of Delhi, two private companies have entered into an out of court settlement with the Government.

Based on this M/s Essar Commission has already signed the Licence Agreement for Basic Telephone Service in Punjab Circle. M/s Techno Telecom, the second company, have also agreed to pay the licence fee and other required guarantees and sign the Licence Agreement.

The Court cases of two companies which were given Letters of Intent for 5 circles are still pending in the High Court of Delhi.

M/s Huges Ispat Ltd. which was issued LOIs for Maharashtra and Karnataka circles have signed the Licence for Maharashtra circle and have applied for creation of a separate legal entity for Karnataka Circle. The case is under consideration of the Government and likely to be finalised soon.

M/s Bharati Telenet Ltd., the Licensee for Basic Telephone Services in Madhya Pradesh Circle have started service in the city of Indore on 4.6.98 and in Bhopal on 9.10.98. M/s. Hughes Ispat Ltd., the Licensee for Basic Telephone Service in Maharashtra Circle has started service in Navi Mumbai on 30.10.98.

Issues raised by private operators

The Basic Service Licensees have raised various issues like deferment of IInd year Licence Fee, increasing the licence period from 15 to 25 years, relaxation of licence condition in respect of use of copper cable etc.

All these issues are under consideration of a recently constituted Group on Telecommunications. These have been, resolved with the approval of the Government.

Incentives announced by the government

Telecom Sector has been declared as "Infrastructure" with all the attendant benefits like five year Tax Holiday and after five years from the start of operations, the projects would get exemption for the balance number of years within a twelve year period.

Telecom Sector would be exempt from the Minimum Alternate Tax (MAT).

The limits on External Commercial Borrowings for the Telecom projects have been made flexible, raising the ECB limits from the level of twice the equity to 50% of the Project Cost. Moreover, rupee expenditure, including the Licence Fee, has been permitted to be met from the External Commercial Borrowings.

Amortisation of Licence Fee has been permitted from the Accounting Year 1996-97.

The investments made in debentures and equity shares of a public company providing telecommunication services are made eligible for tax rebate under section 88 of the Income Tax Act.

Participation of private sector in value added telecommunication services

Telecommunication has been identified the world over as a basic infrastructure essential for socioeconomic development. Modernisation and expansion of existing telecom services and introduction of new services is of utmost importance for further growth of telecommunication services in the country.

Franchise for certain value added services is being given on a nonexclusive basis. Proposals for permission/ operation of these services on a licence basis is considered by DOT for following Value Added Services:

(i) Electronic Mail Service.

(ii) Voice Mail/Audiotex Service.

(iii) Closed User Group Domestic 64 kbps Data Network Service via INSAT.

(iv) Videotex Service.

(v) Video Conferencing Service.

(vi) Credit Card Authorisation Service.

(vii) Internet.

Following services are franchised on a tender basis:

(i) Radio Paging Service.

(ii) Cellular Mobile Telephone Service.

Proposals were also invited at one time in January, 1995 for the operation of "Public Mobile Radio Trunked Service" on nonexclusive basis due to limitation in frequency spectrum in discrete service areas of 300 KMs. radius without connectivity to PSTN.

Proposals for grant of licenses for other Value Added Services may also be considered on nonexclusive basis on submission of detailed technical and commercial proposal.

Status

(i) Electronic Mail: The licences for this service have been issued on all-India basis to 15 companies. All companies have started the operation of the service in the country.

(ii) Voice Mail/Audiotex Service:- The licence for this service is issued on a city-wise basis. Licences have been issued to 14 companies for operation of this service in 40 cities. The service has been started in 11 cities.

(iii) Closed User Group Domestic 64 kbps Data Network via INSAT The licence for the service is issued on all-India basis. 12 companies have been granted licence to operate this service. Ten companies have started operation of this service in the country.

(iv) No licence has been awarded for operation of Videotex Service, Video-conferencing and Credit Card Authorisation.

(v) Public Mobile Radio Trunked Service:- 139 License Agreements signed with 25 companies for operation of PMRTS in 54 cities are current. The service has already started in 21 cities by 17 companies.

(vi) INTERNET:- Policy for privation of INTERNET Services alongwith Guidelines and Terms and Conditions of the Licenses was announced in January, 1998. TRAI in its order dated 17.2.1998 has held that the INTERNET Policy formulated and announced by the Government without obtaining TRAI's recommendation regarding terms and conditions of the licenses to such service provider cannot be held valid. This has delayed the entry of private sector in the field of INTERNET Services.

(vii) Cellular Mobile Service:- The service is available in four metro cities of the country by two operators in each city. 33 Licences have been issued to 13 Indian companies for the franchise of the service in 18 Territorial Telecom Circles. The service has already started in selected cities of 17 Telecom Circles. The total number of Cellular customers in the Country are approximately 8.5 lakhs.

Telecom regulatory authority of India

The Telecom Regulatory Authority of India (TRAI) was established through an Act of Parliament in early 1997, inter alia, to regulate the Telecom Services in the country and for matters connected therewith. As per the Act, the Authority shall consist of a Chairperson and not less than two but not exceeding six members to be appointed by the Central Government. At present, the Authority has a Chairperson and 5 members. The Head Office of the Authority is at New Delhi.

The powers and functions of the TRAI include recommending the need and timing for introduction of new service provider, the terms and conditions of licence to a service provider, ensuring technical compatibility and effective interconnection between different service providers, ensure compliance of terms and conditions of licence, and revocation of licence for noncompliance of terms and conditions of licence. It is also required to facilitate competition and promote efficiency in the operation of telecommunications services, protect the interest of consumers of telecom services, monitoring the quality of service provided by service providers, conduct periodical survey of such services, settle disputes between service providers and ensure effective compliance of universal service obligations. Another important function which has been entrusted to the Authority is to notify the rates at which the telecommunications services shall be provided both within and outside India.

Telephone demand

A record number of 32.59 lakhs additional new telephone connections were provided during the year 1997-98.

Quality of service

Telecom Directorate Observation Team carried out 16 observations of Telephone systems during the year. Factors which adversely affected the performance of Telephone system were analysed and brought to the notice of the concerned field units.

Public grievances

There are several means for redressing public grievances, including Customers Service Centers, Public Grievances Cells, Telephone Adalats, Open House Sessions. During 1.4.97 to 31.3.98, 8940 complaints were received by PG Cell of Headquarters; 8518 complaints were disposed off.

Long distance services

Subscriber trunk dialing:- There has been an addition of 32 Nos. Trunk Automatic Exchanges during the year bringing the total to 379 TAXs in the country. The equipped capacity increased by 314300 lines bringing the total to 1261500 lines. The number of stations connected to the National Subscriber Dialing Network through these TAXs increased by 2799 bringing the total to 16019.

There is an increase of 26.18% in the number of telephone metered call units, the figures for the year under review being 11770.9 crores as against 9329.6 for the previous year.

Trunk services

Trunk Circuits were added in the Telecom Network during the year 1997-98, bringing the total number of trunk circuits to 326851 as on 31.3.98. The percentage increase in the trunk circuits during the year was 40.54%.

The number of trunk calls booked touched a total of 7.18 crores of which 5.62 crores were effective.

Computerisation of trunk manual exchanges

As on 31.3.97,17 ITI make SFK Digital systems (also called CTMX) were operational at various stations in the country. With further commissioning of one system each at Jodhpur, Guwahati and Agra, during the year, the figure has now gone to 20.

Implementation of food dialing scheme

As on 31.3.97, Group Dialling scheme was fully available in 1893 SDCAs in the Country. With the implementation of the scheme in another 92 SDCAs during the year, the figure has gone to 1985.

Home country direct service

In the year 1991, in association with Videsh Sanchar

Nigam Ltd. (VSNL), Home Country Direct Service was first introduced to eight countries. As on 31.3.97, this service was available for 31 countries. With the introduction of this service to Bahrain, Norway and Poland during the year, the figure has gone to 31.

"90" Service

To enable the STD barred subscribers to have an access to their District as well as Tehsil headquarters within a Long Distance Charging Area (LDCA), the Direct Dialling facility with Dynamic control and Detailed Billing using "90" as dialling code has been introduced during the year. All the Telecom Circles and Districts are making their best efforts to introduce the service in all the exchanges wherever it is technically feasible.

National sanchar doot awards

National Sanchar Doot Awards for the year 1995-96 and 1996-97 were given away to the meritorious employees of Department of Telecommunication by the Hon'ble Minister for Communication on 17.05.97, on the World Telecommunication Day. The amount of Cash Award for Sanchar Doot was also enhanced from Rs. 10,000/- to Rs.51,000/- for each of the categories.

Transmission system

17995 RKMs of Microwave system were added with 8250 number of channels during the year. The total RKMs and total number of channels working on microwave media are 72592 RKMs and 129322 respectively at the end of the year.

23822 RKMs of optical fibre systems with 277110 channels were commissioned during the year bringing the total to 76261 RKMs and 576465 channels as on 31.3.1998.

8009 Speech channels on Open Wire Carrier Systems were commissioned during the year raising the total number of channels to 90928 as on 31.3.98. 36388 channels have been added on PCM systems raising the number of channels to 560716 as on 31.3.1998.

Wireless links

During the period 1.4.97 to 31.3.98 DOT commissioned 4 Nos. of low power point to point single channel H.F. Wireless Stations on Rent and Guarantee with a route kilometer of 506 KMs. At the end of March, 98, the total number of point to point single channel H.F. Wireless Stations were 446 with a route length of 64,000 KMs.

Telex service

Due to introduction of FAX, better STD facilities and other new technologies, telex demand is being reduced continuously. At all the stations sufficient capacities are available to meet telex on demand. The demand of telex connections is reducing day by day so much that at some places working exchanges are being closed due to withdrawl/surrendering of telex connections. In fact telex has become an obsolete technology now.

Equipped Capacity of the network has reduced from 60376 lines to 60026 lines.

The number of telex working connections were 25188 as on 31st March,1998.

The number of Telex metered calls decreased to 9.12 crores during 1997-98 compared to 12.86 crores in. 1996-97 representing a decrease of 29.08%.

Public telegraph services

Access to public telegraph services

All the cities (300) and towns (4689) as per 1991 census and a large number of villages have access to Public Telegraph Services through Telegraph Offices.

There were 957 Departmental Telegraph Offices, 44622 Combined Offices and 981 Telecom Centres as on 31.3.1998.

Telegraph traffic

A total of 512.18 lakhs inland telegrams were booked during the year compared to 538.8 lakhs during the previous year which represents a fall of 4.94%. Of the total telegrams booked, 9.73% were on state business and 0.60% on press business. 4.09 lakhs international telegrams were booked during the period as against 5.72 lakhs in the previous year showing a decrease of 28.49% over the previous year.

Modernisation of telegraph network

SFMS-32 lines systems was commissioned at Bhubaneswar (Orissa) on 18.5.97

32L SFMS at Shillong installed & kept on traffic trials.

Five FTCS have been commissioned at Bareilly, Moradabad, Meerut, Delhi and Kanpur. Sixteen FTs in Delhi and 10 FTs in U.P.(W) have been installed.

Quality of service

95.8% of telegrams were delivered within 12 day light hours during the period 1997-98 against the yearly target of 94%.

Developmental activities

Six Telegraph Offices and seventeen Telecom Centres were opened during the period 1997-98 and status of T.Os/T.Cs. on 31.3.98 was 957/981.

Customer's facilities

Express Money Transfer Service is working well in Andhra Pradesh and Tamil Nadu and now introduced in Maharashtra and Kerala circles with limited transactions within state.

Particulars of EMTs (1997-98)

i)No. of EMTs booked

a)	A.P	1,67,049
b)	Tamilnadu	58,872

ii) EMT Transactions

a)	A.P	14,76,38,069
b)	Tamilnadu	4,85,71,091

iii) EMT Revenue (Commission)

a)	A.P	40,14,175
b)	Tamilnadu	13,96,891

Total No. of bureaufax centres on 31.12.97 was 1,283.

Total no. of fax messages booked. upto 31.3.98 was 32,34,466.

No. of fax messages delivered (incoming fax message) upto 31.3.98 was 5,29,591.

Total revenue earned from booked fax messages upto 31.3.1998 is Rs. 13,19,39,662.

Total revenue earned from incoming fax messages upto 31.3.1998 Rs.52,35,187.

Policy matters

Decision has been taken for decentralisation of equipments used in Telegraph network and power delegated thereto.

New technologies and projects of special significance

Installation of Multichannel per Carrier (MCPC-VSATs)

Number of MCPC-VSATs were made operational from 1.4.97 to 31.3.1998 at various places in country. Under this scheme, the stations which cannot be provided long distance media through terrestrial system, are provided STD facility through INSAT system. Such stations are mostly located at remote, hilly and inaccessible places including Islands having small telephone exchanges with low traffic areas.

Installation of Remote Area Business Message Network (RABMN)-VSATs

Only 2 number of RABMN-VSATS were commissioned during the period 1.4.97 to 31.3.1998. These VSATs are low speed terminals and entry of private sector with High Speed Terminals have badly affected the commissioning of RABMN-VSATS. RABMN-VSATs are directly purchased by the customers from suppliers. These terminals are also able to switch on to the Telex network of the country, I-NET (i.e. terrestrial packet switched public data network) and to GPSS (i.e. Gateway Packet Switching System) for international connectivity.

Installation of High Speed VSAT Network (HVNET)

A satellite based network using Very Small Aperture Terminals (VSATs) to provide high speed 64 Kbps switched data service known as HVNET was made operational by 31.3.1998 alongwith 14 nos of VSATs provided temporarily for Amarnath Yatra. This network also has been badly affected by the entry of private sector in this field. The network has access to DOT's Packet Switched Public Data Networks (INET/RABMN) and International data 'networks through the Gateway Packet Switching System of VSNL. The Network envisages voice facility amongst VSATs including connectivity to Public Switched Telephone Network (PSTN).

New works

Digital satellite facility

Purchase Order was issued for supply of IDR (Intermediate Data Rate) equipment for providing digital facility at 14 stations in different parts of the country. Supply of equipment was not received during 97-98.

INSAT Mobile Satellite Services (INSAT-MSS)

Installation of INSAT-MSS equipment had been completed at Jayanagar Earth Station (Bangalore), but service could not be commissioned due to level variation in INSAT-MSS transponder observed during Nov., 1997 which is still continuing. This system shall provide encoded voice service between land portable, maritime users & fixed users on public switched telephone network (PSTN). This shall also support data, fax, massaging & reporting services. The project is being executed by CDOT on behalf of Deptt. of Telecom. Mobile Terminals shall be purchased by the customers directly from the identified indigenous manufacturers.

Digital Circuit Multiplying Equipment (DCME)

Field trial for DCME facility to be provided at 4 stations namely Delhi, Mumbai, Calcutta and Chennai had been started at Delhi and Mumbai.

Ku-Band Facility 6.1.7.1 Ku-Band digital facility was to be provided at 3 places namely Delhi, Bangalore and NOCC at Sikandrabad in U.P. The equipment had been procured from Ms ISL.Antennae had been installed and alignment completed. DOT/QA testing had been completed and installation of equipments had been started at respective sites.

Data communications services

Inet Phase-II network was planned to provide data services in 89 cities, including 8 cities of Inet Phase-I. The target was extended to 102 cities. These cities have been categorised in 3 groups on the basis of business activity and demand for different types of connections and facilities. This network will have a capacity of high speed data transmission at maximum speed of upto 64 KBPs between computers as well as interactive access from public switched telephone network (PSTN).

The following were the activities for the period

(i) Type I location at Mumbai-II was commissioned.

(ii) 14 locations have been upgraded (earlier covered by ACX-40 concentrators) to type-II nodes with PSX. These are Belgaum, Chandigarh, Jabalpur, Ludhiana, Madurai, Mangalore, Mysore, Panjim, Trivandrum, Vijayawada, Bhopal, Guwahati, Patna and Vizag.

(iii) Following type-III locations were commissioned:- Ahmadnagar, Ajmer, Bikaner, Durgapur, Fariclabad, Gandhinagar, Gorakhpur, Haldia, Jodhpur, Kakinada, Kalyan, Karnal, Kota, Mathura, Moraclabad, Muzzafarpur, Ooty, Pathankot, Quilon, Raipur, Rohtak, Rourkela, Sambalpur, Shillong, Sholapur, Siliguri, Tirupur and Trinelvelly.

Integrated Services Digital Network (ISDN)

The ISDN services have been introduced in six more cities during this year and now the facilities are available at seventeen towns viz Hyderabad, Ranchi, Ahmedabad, Rajkot, Bangalore, Indore, Jabalpur, Pune, Nagpur, Jaipur, Tuticorin, Kanpur, Lucknow, Delhi, Mumbai, Chennai and Calcutta. The total number of ISDN subscribers at the end of March 98 is 1211.

Introduction of internet in rural area - "Tele-villages"

To commemorate the 50th Anniversary of India's Independence and to popularise and create awareness amongst the rural populace, Internet demonstration services were inaugurated in 15 rural centres, named "Tele-Villages", spread over 14 Telecom Circles on the birthday of the Father of the Nation, i.e. 2nd October, 97.

These free of cost demonstrations were initially introduced for a period of three months. It was further extended by another three months. These demonstrations of Internet have been received well by the rural masses.

Achievements in Computerisation

Customer related activity

350 (Three Hundred Fifty) more towns have been computerised for Directory Enquiry (DO). 276 (Two Hundred Seventy Six) more towns have been computerised for Fault Repair Service (FRS). 24 (Twenty Four) more towns have been computerised for Commercial Service (CS).

Standardisation of software packages

Fault Repair Service (FRS) and Directory Enquiry (DO):-COMMANDI R Package for Fault Repair Service (FRS) & Directory Enquiry Services (DQ), standardised by DOT, has been implemented in 222 SSAs for Directory Enquiry and in 219 SSAs for Fault Repair Service.

The COMMANDIR Package for DQ services has been tested for ten lacs lines with 150 operators under simulation conditions.

The Package has also been modified and its upgraded version 1.3.1 has been released by TEC, which contains number of new features like import of data from Commercial Service etc.

Nation wide Directory Enquiry Services (NDQ): As decided in 1995 to implement ONLINE Nation Wide Directory Enquiry Service using X.25 and X-28 INET connections. 127 SSAs have been provided Host connectivity with data of whole SSAs.

Computerised Commercial Service System (CSS): Commercial Service System (CSS) Package developed at Chandigarh by M/s dde-ORG have been modified to incorporate additional features and ver. 1.2 has been validated.

The Package has been made over to C-DOT for maintenance, upgradation, integration with other Packages and for distribution to field units.

The instruction Manual for installation & operation of CSS Package was prepared and circulated to the field units.

The guidelines for Acceptance Testing (A/T) of the CSS package by T&D circle were prepared & circulated to the field units.

Regular Training is being imparted in this package. During this period, six training courses have been organised at BRBRAITT Jabalpur. Training in SCO UNIX and ORACLE is also being imparted.

Computerisation of TR Billing and Accounting (TRBA): Trichur package for TR Billing and Accounting (Trichur), Standardised in DOT, has been made over to C-DOT alongwith source code and documentation for further maintenance, development and integration of this package with other customer related packages.

Inventory management: Inventory Management Package for use in CTS and CSD has been tested and Version 1.1 has been standardised for implementation in CTSs/CSD. A Steering Committee constituted under the Chairmanship of Advisor (production), Telecom Commission completed its work and submitted its report. The package (IMTC) has already been implemented in 7 CTSs/CSDs and it is under implementation at other places.

The Draft specifications for procurement module for CGMTS, Calcutta and MM Cell of DOT has been finalised for making over to C-DOT for the development of software package.

Software for project management: MS Software package for Project Management has been standardised for use in

DOT 40 copies of the software have been purchased and distributed one copy each to all field units. Training to field staff has been imparted for its use.

Computerised facilitation counters: As a measure of responsive and effective administration, it has been decided by the Cabinet Secretary to set up Computerised Facilitation Counters (CFC) at the Reception of all the Ministries/Departments of the Government of India for disseminating information to the citizen/user regarding schemes/procedures of the organisation, forms and applications, and about individual applications.

CFC at the Reception of Sanchar Bhawan has been made operational. All the Telecom Circles and PSUs of DOT have been asked to setup similar CFC at their Headquarters, in response of which CFC has already been made operational at the HQ of Maharashtra Telecom Circle and Kerala Telecom Circle and at other places action is being taken to set up such Facilitation Counters.

Interactive Voice Response System (IVRS): Rajasthan Telecom Circle, who had been nominated for the development of Software for Integrated Interactive Voice Response System (IVRS), has awarded the tender for development & implementation of Software at Alwar, as a pilot project. The Company has developed the software and TEC/C-DOT has been asked to validate the software.

Integrated customer management software package: TEC/C-DOT has recently tested an Integrated Software Package "AP-SOFT' for DQ, TRB&A and Commercial Service System. This package is being developed indigenously by AP Telecom Circle.

Zonal meeting in computerisation: Four Zonal Meetings were organised under the Chairmanship of Adv(T) in New Delhi, Mumbai, Chennai and Calcutta during the year, in which all the field units participated, for reviewing the progress in computerisation and to discuss various problems being faced both in the computer Hardware and software front.

Workshop in computerisation: Two workshops were organised during the year by Information Technology Cell, one for TRA Billing at C-DOT Bangalore and another on Computerisation at ALTTC, Ghaziabad to discuss computerisation in DOT

Activities in Sanchar Bhavan

(i) LAN Server working in Sanchar Bhawan and Dak Bhawan have been upgraded to Pentium Pro. Connectivity between Sanchar Bhavan and Dak Bhavan Server has been established.

(ii) During the period 39 more Pentium PCs, printers & 5 servers have been added and another 53 Pentium PCs with latest MS Office'97 software is being procured.

(iii) Computerisation Gate Pass has been introduced at the Reception of Sanchar Bhawan to issue gate pass to visitors since Dec. 97.

(iv) DOT-MAIL facility has been made operational in the Sanchar Bhawan through which data and file can be transferred. E-mail facility is also available through Internet on DOT-MAIL.

(v) Admn. IV section has been selected as one of the sections in TCHQ for full computerisation working. For this a private vendor "Prodata" has completed the system study, the report of which is under approval.

(vi) Microsoft Corporation of India Ltd. has been associated for system study of TCHQ working with an objective of bringing Office Automation and modernising the way of working in Telecom Directorate.

(vii) A Quarterly News Letter on Information Technology has been started from the IT Cell to dissiminate the information on Information Technology. First issue of this News Letter has been published and distributed in Feb. 98.

(viii) Additional Books on computer and IT has been added in the computer library for use of the Officers of DOT A list of computer books available in the Computer Library is made available on LAN for accessing by the users.

(ix) The report of the Committee set up for scrapping, the old version computers of the type PC XT286/PCAT-286 working in Telecom Directorate has been finalised. Case is being processed to replace the old Computers of configuration - PC AT/286 and its earlier versions.

(x) Internet Connections are being provided to all senior officers, of the level of IDDG & above of Telecom Directorate.

(xi) LAP-TOP Computers are being procured for providing to Senior officers of Telecom Commission.

Future plan

(i) Standardisation of Integrated Package for Customer related service like Commercial Service, TRBA, DO FRS etc.

(ii) Establishment of Call Centre.

(iii) Upgradation of LAN at TCHQ, New Delhi.

(iv) Creation of DOT web site and Wide Area Network.

(v) Creation of Multimedia Centre.

(vi) Computerisation of Material Management System of DOT by development of a Software package for Procurement Module of Accounting modules of M.M.System.

(vii) Replacement of old Computers and Printer Working in Telecom Directorate and providing state of art Pentium Computers, Printer, UPS and latest Software for office working.

C-DOT

Projects in the field

MAX-XL:- The infrastructure assessment for M/s ITI was completed by QA and the type approval was given to M/s. ITI. After commissioning of Indira Nagar exchange, the MAX-XL switches are now being installed at more sites namely, Bihar (Madhubani), Karnataka (Chikmaglur, Yelahanka, Gadag, Mandya)), Tamil Nadu (Dindigal, Namakkal, Kumbakonam, Nagercoil), Kerala(Affingal), Punjab (Abhor). TOT training program was completed for nine more manufacturers namely, BEL, BHEL Crompton Greaves, Keltron, IL-Kota, Hindustan Teleprinters, Punjab Communication, United Telecom and ECIL. Order for two lakh lines of MAX-XL exchanges (including 40K lines for Jayanagar, field trial site with ISDN and 800 K BHCA capability) was placed with the M/s Indian Telephone Industries (ITI). So far, 10 exchanges (One lakh lines) were commissioned in the field.

Technology for C-DOT SBM-RAX based on "XL" hardware and MAX-XL has also been offered to the C-DOT switching products manufacturers.

ISDN CPEs: Functional evaluation of ISDN customer premises equipment, namely, Network Termination (NT310) and Terminal Adapter (TA210) by TEC was completed successfully and TEC approval has been accorded. The interworking of these equipment with all the new technology exchanges has been satisfactorily proven Technology transfer for NT310 and TA210 to M/s ITI model plant was completed.

TAX-XL: The TAX-XL at Ratfam was commissioned with CCS # 7 signaling towards OCB TA) at Bhopal and Siemens EWSD TAX at Indore. Bhopal TAX was synchronized with national clock and the field trial was completed successfully.

CCS # 7 signalling system: CCS #7 (SS7) field trial for MAX-L was completed at Kharagpur. Environmental tests of Signalling Unit Module (SUM) were also carried out at Bangalore C-DOT SBM RAX MAX-L and MAX-XL exchanges have become capable of supporting IN and ISDN services.

Non A/C RSU: The development of non-A/C RSU (Remote Switching Unit) capable for QM333 category B operation was completed. After the successful field trials at Ratnagiri (Maharashtra and Vapi (Gujarat), TEC clearance was obtained.

Detailed billing and bulk billing: The detailed billing and bulk billing facilities on junctions for C-DOT exchanges were tested satisfactorily. The bill monitoring software package was developed, tested and TEC clearance was obtained after successful field trials.

Network Synchronization Equipment (NSE): The Network Synchronization Equipment (NSE) developed for level 2 operation in the synchronization network was successfully tested for clock stability and jetters transfer function by TEC. This equipment fully satisfies ITU-T standards and can be used for network synchronization of E-10B and C-DOT SBM RAX, as well as MAX-L exchanges. The equipment was offered to TEC and after field trial with E-10B exchanges clearance for production has been obtained Transfer of Technology is in progress to M/s ITI, Mankapur.

Regional access barring ('90') facility: Testing of regional access barring '90' facility in C-DOT exchanges (256P RAX/SBM/RAX/MAX-L/MAX-XL) was completed by TEC. C-DOT organized 30 workshops in different telecorn circles and about 900 DOT officials were trained on retrofitting the facility The new versions of the software are being ported on all the existing exchanges in the field.

SBM RAX: With the commissioning of 317 exchanges (4.68 lakh lines) during the year, the total number of the same commissioned in the field so far has gone up to 2300 exchanges (21.64 lakh lines).

MAX-L: With the commissioning of 47 exchanges (2.97 lakh lines) during the year, the total number of the same commissioned in the field so far has gone up to 310 exchanges (12.53 lakh lines).

256P RAX:

— Country adaptations for Ethiopia, Colombia, Gambia, Bangladesh were completed. RAX software version (DOT version) 2-1 -1 was released with following enhancements

— Dynamic O/G restriction matrix.

— Regional STD (90) facility

— STD/ISD restrictions on CCB subscribers.

— Total number of RAXs (256P & 128P RAX) operational in the network is 19,000.

TDMA PMP: The validation of the equipment including environmental testing was completed by TEC. The field trial of the equipment was successfully completed with Mysore as a base station and remotes; at Harohalli, Doora and Varuna. After the formal technology approval the equipment would be ready for bulk production.

MCPC VSAT: The MCPC VSAT equipment in C-Band was evaluated by TEC. The equipment was installed for a field trial with hub at Jaynagar and remote at Maralwadi (Bangalore).

INSAT Mobile Satellite System (INSAT MSS): This project was undertaken for providing mobile satellite services through indigenous satellite INSAT-2C. Hub equipment, portable and maritime terminals were developed jointly to meet these requirements by C-DOT and COMSAT laboratories of USA.

The installation and testing of the system was completed at Jayanagar, Bangalore with satellite simulator and INSAT-2C satellite during its availability. The system supports voice, data and fax communication between the mobile terminals and also between mobile and PSTN subscribers with hub as gateway. The transfer of technology (TOT) process for these terminals to the indigenous manufacturers is proposed after commissioning.

Progress in the development of key projects

Integrated Services Digital Network (ISDN): C-DOT has developed Integrated Services Digital Network (ISDN) capability for its exchanges. The ISDN interfaces, bearer services and supplementary services have been developed according to ITU-T and national standards. The basic functions of ISDN interfaces, supplementary services, fax, and video calls were demonstrated to the Telecom Commission during August, 1997. The ISDN capability can be retrofitted on existing exchanges by deploying the ISDN Terminal Unit (ISTU) in addition to SS7 Signalling Unit Module (SUM).

Intelligent Network (IN) Services: Service logic was develop for Service Control Point (SCP) for creation of a number of services using SSP on C-DOT switches. IN services hold immense value-addition and revenue earning potential for the service providers. Besides, the subscribers would be able to get improved service flexibly and economically.

The trial for SSP (SSP functionality implemented in C-DOT SBM Exchange) with Toll - Free Phone Service was launched in MTNL (Delhi) network at Karol Bagh on the occasion of the 50th Anniversary of India's Independence and subsequently in Calcutta Network. The toll-free phone service aims at providing the subscribers charge-free access to MTNL officers. IN services based on C-DOT technology are now proposed to be provided at Ahmedabad, Chennai, Bangalore, Hyderabad, Jaipur, Lucknow, Patna and Pune.

V 5.1/5.2 interface for C-DOT switches: C-DOT worked on V5.2 interface which is an emerging concept for connecting Access Network Product (ANP) to the main exchange. This interface can serve different type of interfaces including radio system of the "Wireless In Local Loop (WILL)".

C-DOT is implementing the standardized protocols related to V 5. 1 /V 5.2 to interface access network with C-DOT switches. This will help in interconnecting various access technologies to C-DOT exchanges. Currently, the product is under system validation and its interface with C-DOTs composite MUX to provide remoting features for POTs and ISDN (basic rate) subscribers has been established in the lab.

Composite MUX (remote line concentrator): A 120 line unit is under development which will serve both analog and ISDN subscribers. This remote line concentrator has connection to the C-DOT main exchange or remote BM

(Base Module) using V 5.2 interface. Another version of the unit with V 5.1 interface can function as a multiplexer.

The equipment will be available in two versions-Wall mounted and Desktop.

Asynchronous Transfer Mode (ATM) System: The Asynchronous Transfer Mode (ATM) is an emerging technology for meeting broadband transmission and switching requirements. The first prototype ATM cross-connect switch has been designed.

Fibre Access System (FAS): Lab realization work progressed further. The equipment would provide Fibre To The Curb (FTTC) and Fibre To The Home (FTTH) solutions in the access part of the telecom network. Some hardware sub modules were tested and other modules are in various stages of design. Software sub-systems are under development.

Synchronous Digital Hierarchy (SDH) system: These projects constitute a series of products namely, STM-1, STM-4, Digital Access Cross-connect (DACCS) and Network Management System. The development of these products are in different stages of product cycle. While, the STM is in the internal validation stage, the STM-4 and DACCS are in the lab realization stage.

Digital Enhanced Cordless Technology (DECT) system: This system provides Wireless In the Local Loop (WILL) solutions both in the urban and in the rural scenarios. While on solution uses Base Station Controller (BSC), Base Station Units (BSU) and remote radio units, the other uses an interface card in the remote line of the TDMA system the later can serve wireless subscribers instead or wired subscribers usually supported by TDMA. Both the systems are in the final stages of lab integration.

Field and manufacturing support

To reassure its manufacturers on C-DOT support, many workshops and discussions were held with the manufacturers.

C-DOT continued to provide product support to 21,000 switches with 5.8 million lines of C-DOT technology in the network in terms of upgradation, retrofitting and training to field staff. C-DOT continued its interaction with the manufacturers and field installations for providing all types of maintenance support.

TEC clearance received

Bulk production clearance was received for ASIC Based SignaiProcessing (ISP - Integrated Signal Processing) card after field trial at Ambala and other sites in Haryana. This card will replace the existing Signalling Processor Card (SPC) being used in 256P RAX, SBM RRAX, MAX-L and MAX-XL.

Bulk production clearance was received for high performance version of existing IOP (after field trials at Haldwani MAX-L) used with SBM RAX, MAX-L and MAX-XL exchanges (IOP-VII) developed with the entire control circuitry implemented on a single PCB and more powerful CPU. This will make the equipment more reliable and easy to maintain.

Clearance for the S/W link 1-4-5.43-3 was received after successful field trials at Hoshiarpur (MAXQ, Dasua (MAX-M) and Indira Nagar (MAX-XL). Some of the features supported in the link are:

— Regional ('90' level) barring.

— 16 PCM connectivity between RSU and the main exchange.

— IOP booting from the unix cartridge.

Clearance for the S/W link 1- 4-2.25- 4 was received after successful field trials at Sonepat (Haryana). Some of the features supported in the link are:

— Metering and detailed billing, on junctions.

— Call saving on bus failure.

— Calling line identification.

— Centralised Automated Message Accounting (CAMA).

Clearance for the S/W link 1- 4- 8.1- 3 was received after successful field trials at Ratlam (M.P.) and Kharagpur (West Bengal).

Standards and specification

General requirements

GRs finalised

PTC Thermistor for use on MDF; Digital Loop Carrier System (DLC) on SDH; Bill Processing system for INET Phase II; Frame Relay switch; Router; Internet Service Provider; Frame Relay Access Device; Smart Card Payphones; Smart Card Pay Phone Control Unit; Smart Card Pay Phone Management System; Boss-Secretary Telephone System; Pocket sized Card Reader for Smart card Payphone systems; Key Telephone System; Intelligent Network Application Part-National standard; NT1 for interface approval; C-DOT Trunk Automatic Exchange-XL; Noise Figure Meter; Digital Radio Measurement System; Stand Alone Synchronisation Equipment; Electromagnetic Compatibility Standard; Multi Protocol Frame Relay Concentrator; Managed Leased Line Network; 2048 KBPS Line Driver; ATM/ Frame Relay Protocol Analyser; Aerial Optical Fibre; National Internet Backbone; Store and Forward Fax

Service; Line Jack Unit; Indian Script Code for Language Paging; Indian Script Code for Language Paging Devanagri/Marathi; Indian Script Code for Language Paging Gujarati; Subscriber Service Unit for calling Line Identification Purpose.

GRs revised/amended/errata

Saddles for fitting Cl brackets and struts of tublars poles; Angle Iron Ties; Caps for tublar poles; Mole Skin; Iron line stores; Bracket and Plastic insulated telephone stalk; HDPE pipes; Brace Angle Iron; Saddle for fitting Angle Iron Guard Bracket on Hamilton Tubes A & B; Coupling of different types of Clamp for couplings; 10/20 pair DP with 10 pair Quick connection (IDC) Drop wire module and casing; GD Tubes for Internal/External use; FRP Moulded DP Box 10 & 20 pairs with moulded tag block; Discrete Connectors; Intelligent Network Services; TR Billing Hardware; VSAT based distance Education system; V.32 bis modem card; Voice band data modem (V.29); ISP equipment dimensioning/configuration; Amendment No.1 to Single pair/1 0 pair Screened PCM Cable for Inter bay digital equipment wiring; Additional climatic and environmental tests for Electronic Push Button Telephone for 98-99 procurement; ISDN Customer Premises Equipment; Large size local cum Tandem Digital Switching system; National routing, switching and numbering plan; Wireless local loop System; PCM MUX equipment; 2/ 8 Mb/s Direct Digital MUX; Third Order Digital MUX. equipment; Fourth Order Digital MUX. equipment: 2/34 Mb/s Direct Digital MUX; MDF for 512 lines and above; Commercial System; TR Billing and Accounting System.

GRs withdrawn

Cable paper core unit twin lead sheathed armoured; Cable paper core star quad trunk armoured; Cable paper core star quad local armoured; Cable paper insulated PE sheathed Al moisture barrier with steel tape armouring and PE jacket; Cable lead sheathed PCUT PE protected un-armoured; Copper wire for UG cable 1955 spec.; Insulating or wrapping paper used in telephone cables; Lead sheath for UG telephone cables; Steel tapes used in UG telephone cables; Jute (hessian cloth) used in dry Core telephone cables; Bitumen base filling compound; Copper strips for wires, copper and copper weld; House Bracket; Compression sleeve for making crimped joint for 2.12 mm GI wire and drop wire; RCC sockets forming the bottom sockets - section of hamilton poles; CT Box Intl 6 pairs; Cable Terminal Box 20 pairs External; Asbestos cement ducts; Self supporting PVC Drop Wire with integral barrier; PE insulated and sheath with GI wire as integral barrier; Voice band data modem (V.29); 2400/ 1200/300 bps voice band data modem cards with addendum; Videotex terminal; Add-on unit to Coin box Telephone (CBT-80); Single Channel VHF system; 2/15 Shared Radio System (Issue-02); 2/15 Shared Radio System (Issue-04); 4/36 Analogue MARR; Development spec. for PCM cable for 2 Mb/s digital line; Development spec. for PCM cable for 2 MB/s digital system; Programming Loading Coil; General specification for all testing instruments; Digital Multimeter; Base Band Data Modem; STD Coin Collection Box; Line Jack Unit for Termination Telephone Line amendment; Quarter Modular Line Cord; Electronic Telephone Instrument; Add on Unit to Coin Box Telephone; Card Vending Machine; Disposable Smart Card; Monitoring and Control System for Direct Exchange Line.

Engineering guidelines

Frame Relay Service through Inet Phase II; Integration of INET Phase-I equipment into INET Phase II network; For X.75 gateway for connecting other Data network" to Inet: PSTN Access Procedure in Inet Phase II; Digital Satellite Phone Terminal (DSPT); CCS-7 implementation; Internet connectivity for DOT, Space/power requirements for ATM equipment; 18 GHz Digital M/W system; "90" dialling scheme within LDCA; INMARSAT-VPT numbering, routing plan; Switching and Routing Plan for Cellular Mobile Telephone Services.

Test schedule prepare

SDH Analyser 1/4/16; NT interface approval; SSU (Subscriber Service Unit); CLIP (Calling Line Identification Presentation); ISDN Customer Premises Equipment; PTC Thermistor; FRP DP Box 10/20 pairs with moulded tag block; ISDN Protocol tester; 16 KHz Metering PUlseAnalyser; Key Telephone System; CMTS Monitoring for circles; Point of interconnection test; Public Mobile Radio Trunking Service; Cellular Mobile Telephone Services; Network Termination Equipment; Installation of Accessory and Fixure for installation of self Supporting Metal Free Aerial Optical Fibre Cable; Terminal Adapter; Multipath Fade Simulator; IR between PSTN and Network of licensed service providers interface at 2048 kbps.

Validation of new technology system

Barring and detailed billing for 90/98 level in C-DOT SBM, RAX and MAX - L exchange and for level 90 in new technology exchanges; Software link 1-4-5,43-3 supporting dynamic barring and detailed billing over level 90 for C-DOT, SBM, MAX-L, MAX-XL exchange; C-DOT MAX-XL software with link 1-4-8.1-3 with dynamic barring and detailed billing for level 90; C-DOT ISP and IOP card; Synchronisation of C-DOT MAX-XL exch. to increase the modem Data rate of Subs; C-DOT exch. for bill monitoring functionality (BMON), C-DOT NSE 2.0 (Network Synchronisation Equipment); Non-A/C RSU of CDOT, CLI P facility in C-DOT MAX-L at Sonepat with software Link 1-4-2.25-4; 16 PCM RSU connectivity for C-DOT MAX-L; Environmental testing of

C-DOT Network Synchronisation Equipment (NSE); Environmental testing on CCS-7 unit of C-DOT, Technology approval for C-DOT-NSC (Networking Synchronisation Controller) in MAX-XL exchanges; 10 digit CLI in FETEX 100L switching system; Software patch for 1/3 tariff for FETEX 150; Pending points of validation in 5ESS Exchange; Tandem working for 5ESS system; PRI interface in 5ESS; Software patch in EWSD switching systems; Software version 9 in EWSD local exchange; ISDN PC card of M/s CMC; Line parameter measurements on ISDN lines; CCS7 and ISDN interworking of NEAX-61E; International ISDN; national and International roaming for Mobile Services; IIT developed WLL system based on DECT Technology; Field trial of DECT WLL system of M/s Ericsson at New Delhi; VSAT services; Ku band Hub Station Equipment except HPA in association with QA at ISL, Bangalore tested; STM-4 in ring Configuration and Point to Point of M/sAlcatel at Hyderabad;ADM-1 of M/s Fibcom. completed; ADM-4 of M/s Fibcom. Gurgaon; Field trial of STM-16 of M/s Fibcom at Bombay; Optical fibre Splicing machine of M/s Seven Hills Optic Communication, Calcutta; Pending points of CDTMX at Chennai; New features of CTMX system of ITI; Testing of AMS (Alarm Management System), DEL (Digital Error Logger) and DPM (Digital Performance Monitoring) in the Telestra NMS system at Chennai; Voice Mail/ Audiotex services of M/s Sawarkar Telecom Pvt. Ltd.; Video conferencing over ISDN at 128 Kbps between TEC, N.D. and BRBBRAITT, Jabalpur; Video Conferencing at 364 Kbps; CSMS (Customer Services Management System) offered by MTNL at Bhikaji Cama Place for commercial and billing modules; Credit Card Authorisation service; 20 GHz Signal Generator and VSWR test set of M/s Meera Agencies; Frame Relay Access Device (FRAD) of M/s PCL, New Delhi; 2.7 GHz synthesized Signal Generator of M/s HP India; ISDN feature Phone in OCB-283 and F-1 50 exchanges; New features for EWSD technology against 1.3 m tender; Validation of NEAX-61 E exchange at Modinagar; Validation of FETEX-1 50 exchange Version 4.0 for CCS7, Supplementary Services, Charge Band and ILT features; STM-1 6 of M/s Fibcom; Chandigarh Commercial System; Commercial modules and TRA modules of APSOFT of A.P Telecom Circle at Hyderabad; Digital Line Concentrator of M/s MIC; C-DOT SBM RAX based on XL hardware with software 1-4-5.43-3 with IOP-VH; Validation software developed by Indore Telecom District for recording of traffic measurements in EWSD TAX on hourly basis for CCR study; DCME equipment installed between Delhi and Mumbai; C-DOT, TDMA-PMP system; WLL, CDMA technology field trial; Validation of 11 GHz, 140 Mbps Microwave equipment of M/s NATELCO Nasik.

Network planning/engineering

Planning of PON network based on optical fibre technology in rural communication; Proposal identified to provide reliable Telecom Services to the rural sector with high demand and potential growth at Ludhiana Telecom Distt.; Memorandum to Telecom Commission in respect of pilot project on "Distance Learning and Remote Library access" as Asia Pacific Telecommunity Bangkok Project prepared; Engineering guidelines for C-DOT TDMA PMP System; Data Analysis for the Propagation Measurement at Mumbai; New Humidity and Temp. Sensor procured from USA tested at Chingelputte; Data Analysis for the Propagation Measurement at Mumbai.

Field support

Distributed COMMANDIR package to various places and provided support for installation; Enquiry Module of Commandir (2 Exch. Ver.) modified as per the requirements given by Bhavnagar Telecom Distt.;

Synchronisation of OCB Jullandhar with OCB TAX Karol Bagh, N.Delhi; Synchronisation of Bhopal OCBTAX with Bombay EWSDTAX and OCI3 TAX Karolbagh, N.Delhi; Supplied IMA Ves. MS software of E-10B exchange to different places; Distributed E-10B maintenance Advisor package to various field units; Developed and tested and provided assistances for implementing E-10B software for 8 digit depth analysis; Provided technical support in E-10B upgradation of 2L version software; Supplied Exec., Real data and SDF tapes to Chirala, Okhla and Pathankot E-10B exchanges; Provided technical assistance in upgradation of local EWSD exch. at CUFF Prade to patch status 17V; Implemented upgraded software in EWSDTAX at Raipur and Ahemdabad; Modified FOCIN command for Network Management System implemented at Delhi Gate exch. for field trial; CCS7 introduced between Ratlam, Bhopal and More; Instructions on ISDN testing.

Field problems solved

International ISDN access from Kanpur; Call failure on C7-R2 interworking at Bhopal OCB-283 DTAX; Analysis of nature of Address indicator in OCB Tandem Exchange; CCS7 internet working between EWSD MSG and OCIB -Tandem; Creating CCS-7 signalling link over satellite media in OCB TAX Calcutta; CCS7 interworking between C-DOT, SEIM and OCB 283 exchanges at Shimla; Signalling Transfer Point (STP) function introduced in MTNL Delhi Network for CCs-7 working in AXE-1 0 exch. at Nehru Place; in EWSD TAX at Ahemdabad; Disconnection of Dial tone at Delhi Gate E-10B exch.; False alarm from BT rack at Nehru Place El 08 exch.; Non-functioning of status for dynamic STD at Jammu E-10B exch.; For OCHALA printout at E-10B exchange Bhatinda; Creation of new file by data correction in MTR file at E-10B Guwahati exchange; Corruption in ADB in

E-10B exchange Dehradun by data correction in TR files; Restored DI Nehru Place exchange OMC by using OMC backup; File creation at Dilshad Garden E-10B exchange Delhi by data correction in catalogue file; Prepared Exec. tape for Hoshiarpur E-10B exchange; Unstable link between E-10B exchange and OMC at Gorakhpur; Non-suppression of Directory nos. and wrong announcement on incoming calls at Karolbagh E-10B exch.; Initialisation of TR due to corruption in Catalogue file solved by disk data correction in E-10B Kanpur; Creation of SR5 subscriber due to corruption in TMNE file solved by OMC data modification in E-10B Kotakapura.

Tender evaluation

Procurement of solid state disk drive/Winchester drive for the replacement of UD50 disk drive at E-1 OB software centre; Procurement of PCM analyser; Procurement of software for TEC LAN; Assisted Telecom Commission in evaluation of the tender 6 GHz and 11 GHz SDH Microwave equipment; ADB tender for Rural communication for Eastern U.P; For procurement of Line Drivers and stand alone enclosure; Procurement of UPS system and laser printer; Assisted MTNL Delhi in evaluation of the tender for Managed Leased Data Network (MLDN); Router; 1.69 million line tender for local exchange.

Other activities

13 GHz 34 Mbps digital radio system installed at MTNL Mumbai; Impact of Y2 K problem in DOT reviewed; Technical paper prepared on "Spectrum issues for Radio based PCS"; Test report for Roaming in CMTS using STP sent to VAS cell; Seminar on ISDN, OCB 283, ATM, INET and SDH Network on Video Conferencing between BRBRAITT Jabalpur and New Delhi as part of distance learning; List of specifications and equipments finalised

for Multimedia Project; Multimedia Kit installation completed; Presentation on TEC LAN on UTP demonstrating access to TEC Web pages on Intranetware, Unix Server and Internet was given at TEC computer Lab. to ADET Trainees of ALTTC Ghaziabad; Multiparity Video Conferencing demonstration among TEC Delhi, MTNL Bombay, TTC Jabalpur and Bangalore Telephone District; Updated the Internet TEC Web Pages; Analysis of Ku band propagation data for calculation of Annual exceedance and worst month statistics completed; Seminar on ATM was organised at Bombay, in co-ordination with MTNL, Bombay; Specifications for Pentium PCs, Laserjet, Printers, Modems and UPS System; The PSX loaded with new software release supporting Frame Relay and their configuration updated at ALTTC; Modified guidelines for Inet Ph I and Ph II connctivity and sent for field trial.

Comments provided on

National Preparatory Committee (NPC) to the World Radio Communication Conference; Final report of the working group on fixed services for allocation of exclusive bandwidth for higher density fixed services in 40 GHz and 50 GHz band.

Management information system (MIS)

MIS Cell helps in monitoring the performance of Telecom Circles, Metro Districts, MTNL & Mtce. Regions through various MIS Reports.

The following Monthly statements are submitted to the Telecom Commission.

— Top Management Report.

— Status Report of Equipped Capacity, DELs and Waiting List of Telecom Circles/Metro Disfts./MTNL in respect of Telephones.

— Achievement Report in respect of net increase in Telephone Equipped Capacity and DELs against the target fixed in respect of Telecom Circles/Metro Distts./MTNL.

— Special Monthly MIS Report.

(a) Service performance of Telecom Circles/Metro Distts./MTNL.

(b) Development activities on all-India basis.

(c) Financial Performance of Department on all-India basis alongwith Collection Efficiency circle-wise.

(d) Position of supplies from suppliers in respect of equipments for Department against the target of supplies for the month.

MIS publication on Telecom Network, Telecom Development & Financial Performance and other statistical information for each financial year is published every year. It contains information about performance of all the Telecom Circles, Metro Districts, MTNL and Telecom Maintenance Regions alongwith the information about Volume & Growth of various services provided by Department. The data compilation work for the publication of MIS book for the year 1997-98 is in final stage.

Economic research unit (ERU) and statistics (STT) section

The following studies/exercises were completed during 1997-98:

(i) Call Slab Wise Distribution Pattern of Subscribe rs/ Calls - A case study of 8/28 Telecom Districts : 1993-94 and 1994-95.

(ii) Impact of Tariff revision effective from 1.5.93 on subscribers calling pattern and revenue.

(iii) Telephone Demand Projections - Towns having exchanges with 200 lines and above 1997-2007.

(iv) Telephone Revenue - An analysis of Trends and An Examination of Determinants for 1993-94 and 1994-95.

(v) Examination of "Federal Communications Commission (FCC)" Document - Notice of Proposed Rule making (NPRM) - from economic angle.

(vi) Two Decades of studies in Telecom Economics.

(vii) Committee on "Metered Calls and Revenue per DEL per day"

International co-operations/seminars\meetings

International co-operation

Bilateral co-operation meetings

i) Joint Working Group/Joint Working Commission & Inter-Ministerial meetings.

ii) 26 Bilateral Co-operation meetings held in various Ministries from 1st April,97 to 31st March,98. 12.9.1.2. Delegation (Dignitories from Foreign Countries)

(A) 9 delegations have visited DOT, as mentioned below:

i) H.E.Mr.Mimoun Aoujil, Secretary General of the Ministry of Posts & Telecom, Morocco.

ii) Mr. Pitak Intrawideyanunt, Dy. Foreign Minister of Thailand.

iii) H.E. Mr.Wolfgang Boetsch, Minister of Posts and Telecommunications, Federal Republic of Germany alongwith a large German Government business delegation.

iv) H.E.Mr.Alyaksandr Lukashenka, President of Belarus.

v) Mr. V.Goncharenko, Minister of Communication of Belarus.

vi) Mr. Reed Hunt, Chairman, US Federal Communications Commission (FCC) and Chief Regulator of the Telecom Industry in the United States, alongwith his delegation team, has called on the Hon'ble Minister of Communications on 26th June 1997 & Chairman TC on 27th June'97 in Sanchar Bhawan, New Delhi.

vii) Mr.Vonya Mccann US Co-ordinator for International Communication& Information policy, alongwith a large American delegation of FCC officials and businessmen.

viii) Mr. William Daley, United States Commerce Secretary alongwith a large delegation of American businessmen.

ix) H.E.Dr.Peter Medgyessy, Finance Minister of the Republic of Hungary.

x) Ms. Rita Murrell, and Mr. Ashok Pasricha, Engineer from the U.S. Export-import Bank (EXIM) called on DDG (IR) to meet with EXIM Borrowers, guarantors and appropriate Government entities in India to discuss pending and potential business.

xi) Mr. David Brar of Agriteam Canada and Mr. Shabir Ahmad of JPs Associates called on DDG(IR) to discuss CIDA's project, (a) establishment of radio advisory council and (b) Consumer watchdog facility regarding telecom services.

(B) MOU Signed:-

i) A Memorandum of Understanding was signed between Government of India & Germany in the field of Posts & Telecommunications in DOT Sanchar Bhawan at Ministerial level on 2.9.97.

ii) An agreement was signed between Government of India & Belarus in the field of Posts & Telecommunications in Vigyan Bhawan at Ministerial level on 27.9.97.

iii) A Memorandum of Understanding on Mutual Cooperation on Telecommunications between Deptt. of Telecom India and the Ministry of Industry, France was signed at Secretary level on 21.1.98 in Paris.

Seminars/workshops/meetings/training -national level

i) 35 DOT Officers participated in Seminar/Meetings etc. held in India organised by various International Organisations.

ii) Procured cases regarding grant of permission to foreign Telecom Companies for establishing their branch offices in India.

Exhibitions (international & national):-

(A) International:-

i) "Asia Telecom'97" in Singapore from 9-14 June,1997. Department of Telecommunications participated alongwith its associated Public Sector Undertakings and private companies.

ii) Industrial and Technological Exhibition of India at Beijing (China), from 7-11 July'1997. C-DOT & TCIL participated in the exhibition. A delegation led by Chairman (TC) also visited the exhibition.

iii) "Telecom Expo'90" at Hanoi (Vietnam) from 2-6 December'1997: Department of Telecommunications participated alongwith Public Sector Undertakings such as C-DOT, ITI, and TCIL.

iv) "The Pride of India" Exhibition from 14-17 January,1998 in Hanoi (Vietnam): Public Sector

Undertakings of the Department of Telecommunications, ITI, HTL and C-DOT participated. The event was to commemorate 50 years of India's Independence.

v) An "Indian Trade Exhibition" was organised at World Trade Centre, Mexico City (Mexico), from 3-9 March'98.

vi) "Cebit'98" at Hanover (Germany) from 9-25 March, 1998.

(B) National/regional:-

i) Gateway'97 at Science City Calcutta, from 5-9 November'l 997.

ii) Sishu Utsav'97 at Durgapur, West Bengal from 11 -25 November'l 997.

iii) India International Trade Fair'97 was held at Pragati Maidan, New Delhi from 14-27 November' 1997. DOT pavilion was inaugurated by Hon'ble Minister of Communications.

iv) COMMS India'97 from 9-11 December' 1997 at Pragati Maidan, New Delhi.

v) 11th Industrial India Trade Fair at Calcutta 19-31 December' 1 997.

vi) All India Agriculture, Science and Industrial Trade Fair'98 at Kalyani, Nadia (West Bengal) from 1 st to 15th January, 1998. It was organised by Jai Prakash Narayan Janmotsav Committee.

vii) "Sunderban Mela'98" at Canning Town, West Bengal, from 3rd to 12th January, 1998. It was organised by Bandhu Mahal.

Deputation of officers to foreign countries from !st April'97 to 31st March,1998 is as follows:-

i) Deputation of 31 officers to Geneva, Singapore Cascais (Portugal), Manila, Tornoto & Seoul for different study groups of ITU-T/ITU-R/ITU-D.

ii) Deputation of 16 officers to Shanghai (China), Kathmandu, Tokyo, Bangkok, & Chaingmai (Thailand) for attending APT Meetings/Seminars.

iii) Deputation of 18 officers to Phuket (Thailand), Bangkok, Singapore, Geneva and Kathmandu for attending Meetings/Workshop/TCDC, Consultancies with UNDP/ITU Project.

iv) Deputation of 36 officers for attending miscellaneous International Meetings/Seminars/Conferences to Germany, USA, Seoul, London, Chicago, Copen hengon (Denmark) and Auckland.

v) A high level business delegation led by Sh. R.N.Bhardwaj, DDG(IR), accompanied by Sr. officers of the level of Executive Directors from I.T.I., C-DOT, & TCIL visited Hanoi (Vietnam) from 28-31 st July, 1997, to explore the possibilities of business in Telecommunications.

vi) Indian delegation participated in Asia Pacific Telecommunity (APT) Regional meeting for WRC-97 organised by APT from 28th July to 1 st August'97 at Seoul, Republic of Korea.

vii) Hon'ble MOC inaugurated the Conference of India Industry in association with US Trade and Development Agency & U.S. Department of Commerce.

viii) A four member DoT delegation headed by the Chairman, Telecom Commission visited France from 19th to 21 st January 1998 to participate in the meeting of Indo-French Joint Committee on Posts and Telecommunications.

ix) A three member DoT Delegation headed by the Chairman, Telecom Commission visited Canada from 2nd to 6th February, 1998 in connection with CIDA proposals in the session of Telecommunications.

x) A satellite Coordination meeting was held between Administrations of USA and India, during 9-13 February, 1998 for Coordination of PANAMSAT and INSAT Satellite networks.

xi) Indo-Ethiopia Joint Trade Committee meeting was held on 25-26th February, 1998 in Addis Ababa. Sr. representatives from C-DoT, HTL and R&D attended the meeting.

About 55 foreign delegates and 200 officers from DOT & other PSU's (TCHQ, C-DOT MTNL, TCIL, ITI, HTL, & TEC etc.) participated in "Asia-Pacific Telecom Trade & Finance Colloquium" held in Vigyan Bhawan, New Delhi from 3-5 Nov. 1997. Hon'ble MOS (C) has inaugurated this event on 3.11.97.

"A National Telecom Seminar' was held on 14th Jan'98 in Hotel Ashok, Chanakya Puri, New Delhi to celebrate "50th year of our Independence." The seminar was inaugurated by Chairman Telecom Commission. Dy. Secretary General (ITU)), Geneva, Mr. Henry Chasia delivered a keynote address on the occasion.

Network division

(i) DSLCC: meeting was held with the representatives of Defence authorities and Deptt. of Telecom on 4-4-97 at Sena Bhawan, New Delhi.

(ii) Joint Study group meeting with officers of Defence authorities and Deptt. of Telecom were held on 23-9-97 and 10-11 -97 in Sena Bhawan.

(iii) Steering Committee meeting between representatives of Defence and Dir (NW), DOT was held on 19-8-97 in South Block, New Delhi.

Miscellaneous activities

ATNs & audit paras

(i) 17 ATNs have been vetted and cleared by Audit.

(ii) For one ATN of 95-96, the cell is vigorously taking up the case with CGMT(MHR) for want of detailed particulars of dues.

Territorial army cases

(i) Additional benefits viz Best training Award among TA Trainees and introduction of TA medals among TA Personnel are under process of sanction. The case has not yet been finalised by Finance.

(ii) Case of splitting of Annual Trg. Camp for TA personnel is under process.

(iii) Out of 14 proposed TA personnel, 7 have been trained in Satellite communication through NW cell. For the remaining personnel Trg. programme has been scheduled in this year.

(c) War contingent circuit

Feasibility reports of War contingent circuits from pending units are being updated. Some more information has been received from different units.

(d) Army HQRS

Sanction of 13 STD, PCOs for the Border area of J&K has been obtained from MOD upto 28th Feb'98. The case for extension upto 28-2-99 has already been processed.

Civil wing

The Civil Wing in the Department of Telecom came into existence in the year 1963. It is responsible for executing and maintaining the Buildings and services infrastructure for the Department. Its activities include planning and execution of:-

i) Technical Buildings for housing Telecom Equipment.

ii) Administrative Offices.

iii) Staff Quarters.

iv) Cable Ducts.

v) Civil Works for Transmission Towers.

vi) Air Conditioning.

vii) Substations Engine Alternator.

viii) Services such as Fire Fighting and Environmental Works.

It is also responsible for maintenance, rehabilitation and retrofitting of Building assets.

Work load

The activities of the Civil Wing have increased many folds over the years. The workload of the Civil Wing has progressively increased from a mere Rs.4 crores in the year 1963 to Rs.1,000 crores in the current financial year. In order to cater for the stringent requirement of high technology telecom equipment, the Civil wing is constantly upgrading the technology of designs, construction, air conditioning and other systems installed in the Buildings. Microprocessor Control Systems have been introduced for regulating Air-conditioning Systems. Recently Civil Wing has taken up a pilot project of construction of a 100 metre high RCC Transmission Tower at Machilipatnam. Civil Wing has also progressively computerised various activities of designs, estimation, tender evaluation etc. Special thrust on Construction of Staff quarters for achieving the target of 20% satisfaction ratio by the end of 9th Plan.

Organisational set-up

The Civil Wing has three disciplines viz. Civil, Electrical

and Architecture. All these three disciplines provide inputs for planning and construction of a Building Project. Each discipline is headed by a Sr.DDG in the headquarter reporting to Member (Production). The field set up is headed by Chief Engineers/Chief Architects located at various places.

Achievements

The physical achievements of the Civil Wing during the period 1997-98 are as follows:-

SI.No.	Type of Bldg.	No. of Building Completed During 1997-98
i)	MAX-I	62
ii)	MAX-II	500
iii)	CTO/DTO	10
iv)	Transmission Buildings	78
v)	Towers Foundation	257
vi)	Admn. Buildings	16
vii)	Staff Quarters	2486
viii)	Other Buildings	212
ix)	Cable duct (in route Kms.)	124.94